Lecture Notes in Computer Scier

Commenced Publication in 1973
Founding and Former Series Editors:
Gerhard Goos, Juris Hartmanis, and Jan van Leeuwen

T0238085

Willem Jonker   Milan Petković (Eds.)

Secure Data Management

Second VLDB Workshop, SDM 2005
Trondheim, Norway, September 2-3, 2005
Proceedings

 Springer

Volume Editors

Willem Jonker
Milan Petković
Philips Research Eindhoven
Information and System Security
Prof. Holstlaan 4, 5656 AA Eindhoven, The Netherlands
E-mail:{Willem.Jonker,Milan.Petkovic}@philips.com

Library of Congress Control Number: 200593521

CR Subject Classification (1998): H.2.0, H.2, C.2.0, H.3, E.3, D.4.6, K.6.5

ISSN   0302-9743
ISBN-10   3-540-28798-1 Springer Berlin Heidelberg New York
ISBN-13   978-3-540-28798-8 Springer Berlin Heidelberg New York

Springer is a part of Springer Science+Business Media

springeronline.com

© Springer-Verlag Berlin Heidelberg 2005
Printed in Germany

Typesetting: Camera-ready by author, data conversion by Scientific Publishing Services, Chennai, India
Printed on acid-free paper   SPIN: 11552338   06/3142   5 4 3 2 1 0

Preface

Although cryptography and security techniques have been around for quite some time, emerging technologies such as ubiquitous computing and ambient intelligence that exploit increasingly interconnected networks, mobility and personalization put new requirements on security with respect to data management. As data is accessible anytime anywhere, according to these new concepts, it becomes much easier to get unauthorized data access. Furthermore, it becomes simpler to collect, store, and search personal information and endanger people's privacy. Therefore, research in the area of secure data management is of growing importance, attracting the attention of both the data management and security research communities. The interesting problems range from traditional ones, such as access control (with all variations, like dynamic, context-aware, role-based), database security (e.g., efficient database encryption schemes, search over encrypted data, etc.), and privacy-preserving data mining to controlled sharing of data.

In addition to the aforementioned subject, this year we also called for papers devoted to secure data management in healthcare as a domain where data security and privacy issues are traditionally important. The call for papers attracted 38 papers both from universities and industry. The Program Committee selected 16 research papers for presentation at the workshop. These papers are also collected in this volume which we hope will serve you as a useful research and reference material.

The volume is divided roughly into four major sections. The first section focuses on encrypted databases addressing the topics of key and metadata management, as well as searching in the encrypted domain. The second section changes slightly the focal point to access control, which remains an important area of interest. The papers in this section deal with this topic from a different point of view and in a different context: two papers in the medical domain, one in the area of the Semantic Web and one in XML databases. The third section focuses on disclosure detection, control and prevention, again in a database environment. The last paper in this section addresses in particular the topics of inference control and anonymization in medical databases. Finally, the fourth section addresses privacy and security technologies which are required in a modern world to support concepts like ubiquitous computing or location-based services.

July 2005   Willem Jonker and Milan Petković

Organization

Workshop Organizers

Willem Jonker (Philips Research/University of Twente, The Netherlands)
Milan Petković (Philips Research, The Netherlands)

Program Committee

Peter Apers, Twente University, The Netherlands
Gerrit Bleumer, Francotyp-Postalia, Germany
Ljiljana Branković, University of Newcastle, Australia
Sabrina De Capitani di Vimercati, University of Milan, Italy
Ernesto Damiani, University of Milan, Italy
Eric Diehl, Thomson Research, France
Csilla Farkas, University of South Carolina, USA
Eduardo Fernández-Medina, University of Castilla-La Mancha, Spain
Simone Fischer-Hübner, Karlstad University, Sweden
Tyrone Grandison, IBM Almaden Research Center, USA
Ehud Gudes, Ben-Gurion University, Israel
Marit Hansen, Independent Centre for Privacy Protection, Germany
Pieter Hartel, Twente University, The Netherlands
Sushil Jajodia, George Mason University, USA
Ton Kalker, HP Research, USA
Marc Langheinrich, Institute for Pervasive Computing, ETH Zurich, Switzerland
Nick Mankovich, Philips Medical Systems, USA
Stig Frode Mjlsnes, Norwegian University of Science and Technology, Norway
Eiji Okamoto, University of Tsukuba, Japan
Sylvia Osborn, University of Western Ontario, Canada
Günther Pernul, University of Regensburg, Germany
Birgit Pfitzmann, IBM Zurich Research Lab, Switzerland
Bart Preneel, KULeuven, Belgium
Jean-Jacques Quisquater, Universit Catholique de Louvain, Belgium
Kai Rannenberg, Goethe University, Frankfurt, Germany
Morton Swimmer, IBM Zurich Research Lab, Switzerland
Sheng Zhong, Stevens Institute of Technology, USA
Josip Zorić, Norwegian Telecom, Norway

Additional Referees

Maarten Fokkinga, University of Twente, The Netherlands
Ling Feng, University of Twente, The Netherlands

Table of Contents

Encrypted Data Access

Efficient Key Updates in Encrypted Database Systems
  Hakan Hacıgümüş, Sharad Mehrotra 1

Metadata Management in Outsourced Encrypted Databases
  *E. Damiani, S. De Capitani di Vimercati, S. Foresti, S. Jajodia,
  S. Paraboschi, P. Samarati* 16

Experiments with Queries over Encrypted Data Using Secret Sharing
  *Richard Brinkman, Berry Schoenmakers, Jeroen Doumen,
  Willem Jonker* 33

Access Control

An Authorization Framework for Sharing Data in Web Service
Federations
  Martin Wimmer, Alfons Kemper 47

User-Managed Access Control for Health Care Systems
  Amir H. Chinaei, Frank Wm. Tompa 63

Specifying an Access Control Model for Ontologies for the Semantic Web
  Cecilia M. Ionita, Sylvia L. Osborn 73

A Formal Access Control Model for XML Databases
  Alban Gabillon 86

Information Disclosure Control in Databases

Can Attackers Learn from Samples?
  Ganesh Ramesh 104

Dynamic Disclosure Monitor (D^2Mon): An Improved Query Processing
Solution
  Tyrone S. Toland, Csilla Farkas, Caroline M. Eastman 124

Detecting Privacy Violations in Sensitive XML Databases
  Stefan Böttcher, Rita Steinmetz 143

Suppressing Microdata to Prevent Probabilistic Classification Based
Inference
  Ayça Azgın Hintoğlu, Yücel Saygın 155

On Deducibility and Anonymisation in Medical Databases
  David Power, Mark Slaymaker, Andrew Simpson 170

Privacy and Security Support for Distributed Applications

Protecting Privacy Against Location-Based Personal Identification
  Claudio Bettini, X. Sean Wang, Sushil Jajodia 185

Information SeeSaw: Availability vs. Security Management in the
UbiComp World
  Boris Dragovic, Calicrates Policroniades 200

XML Security in the Next Generation Optical Disc Context
  Gopakumar G. Nair, Ajeesh Gopalakrishnan, Sjouke Mauw,
  Erik Moll 217

Improvement of Hsu-Wu-He's Proxy Multi-signature Schemes
  Yumin Yuan 234

Author Index 241

Efficient Key Updates in Encrypted Database Systems

Hakan Hacıgümüş[1] and Sharad Mehrotra[2]

[1] IBM Almaden Research Center, USA
hakanh@acm.org
[2] University of California, Irvine, USA
sharad@ics.uci.edu

Abstract. In this paper, we investigate efficient key updates in encrypted database environments. We study the issues in the context of database-as-a-service (DAS) model that allows organizations to outsource their data management infrastructures to a database service provider. In the DAS model, a service provider employs data encryption techniques to ensure the privacy of hosted data. The security of encryption techniques relies on the confidentiality of the encryption keys. The dynamic nature of the encrypted database in the DAS model adds complexity and raises specific requirements on the key management techniques. Key updates are particularly critical because of their potential impact on overall system performance and resources usage. In this paper, we propose specialized techniques and data structures to efficiently implement the key updates along with the other key management functions to improve the systems' concurrency performance in the DAS model.

1 Introduction

The commodity pricing of processors, storage, network bandwidth, and basic software is continuously reducing the relative contribution of these elements to the total lifecycle cost of computing solutions. Operating and integration costs are increasing, in comparison. The research community has responded by working on approaches to automated system administration as in [2]. Increasingly, large companies are consolidating data operations into extremely efficiently administered data centers, sometimes even outsourcing them [4].

The *Database-as-a-Service* (DAS) model [8] is one manifestation of this trend. In the DAS model, the client's database is stored at the service provider. The provider is responsible for provisioning adequate CPU, storage, and networking resources required to run database operations, in addition to the system administration tasks such as backup, recovery, reorganization etc.

A fundamental challenge posed by the DAS model is that of database privacy and security [8]. In the DAS model, the user data resides on the premises of the database service provider. Most companies and individuals view their data as an asset. The theft of intellectual property already costs organizations great amount of money every year [3]. The increasing importance of security in databases is discussed in [6][13][12][1][8][7][5][9][10]. Therefore, first, the owner of the data

W. Jonker and M. Petković (Eds.): SDM 2005, LNCS 3674, pp. 1–15, 2005.

needs to be assured that the data is protected against malicious attacks from the outside of the service provider. In addition to this, recent studies indicate that 40% of those attacks are perpetrated by the insiders [3]. Hence, the second and more challenging problem is the privacy of the data when even the service provider itself is not trusted by the owner of the data. Data encryption is proposed as a solution to ensure the privacy of the users' data. The first problem is examined in [8] and the second one is studied in [7], which explores how SQL queries can be executed over encrypted data.

The security of any encryption technique relies on the confidentiality of the encryption keys. Hence, key management plays an essential role in a system, which employs encryption techniques. In this paper, we mainly focus on the key management issues in the context of the database-as-a-service model, where the clients' databases are stored at the service provider site in the encrypted form. We argue that the key management in the hosted databases requires special consideration especially due to the dynamic nature of the database systems.

The update transactions are an essential part of the database systems and applications. Each update transaction requires at least one invocation of the encryption function to encrypt the data in the system.[1] It is known that encryption is a CPU intensive process [8]. Therefore the update transactions may hold locks on the certain set of database records for an extended period of time causing a decline in the system performance. Besides the database update transactions, re-keying is another process, which requires the invocation of the encryption function in the system. As we discuss in Section 3, re-keying is recommended and sometimes required for the systems that employ encryption. Re-keying large amounts of data entails significant encryption costs and interferes with the other transactions thereby causing performance degradation in the system. In this study, we address these issues by proposing a specialized key management architecture in Section 3. Our main focus is the key updates. We propose new lock modes, key update locks, which are leveraged by the database lock manager to efficiently handle the key updates along with the other database update transactions. We present the necessary lock management protocols based on the key management architecture we explain in the paper. We also introduce a system architecture taxonomy in Section 2.3, which is coupled with the key management architecture to enable the performance-conscious encryption key management in dynamic database environments.

2   System Architectures

2.1   Overall DAS Architecture

The system we use in this study is based on the architecture proposed and described in [7]. The basic architecture and the control flow of the system are

---

[1] The actual number of invocations depends on various factors such as the data unit subject to the encryption, i.e., the granularity of the encryption, specifics of the transaction, e.g., an insert only transaction, a transaction on a number of data objects, etc.

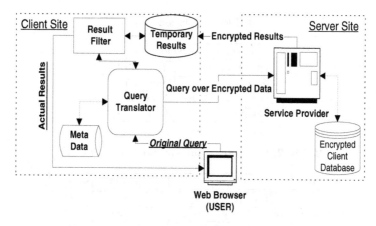

Fig. 1. Database-as-a-Service architecture

shown in Figure 1. It is comprised of three fundamental entities. A *user* poses the query to the client. A *server* is hosted by the service provider that stores the encrypted database. The encrypted database is augmented with additional information (which we call the index) that allows the certain amount of query processing to occur at the server without jeopardizing the data privacy. A *client* stores the data at the server. Client[2] also maintains the *metadata* for translating the user queries to the appropriate representation on the server, and performs post-processing on server query results. From the privacy perspective, the most important feature is, the client's data is always stored in the encrypted form at the server site. The server never sees the unencrypted form of the data, and executes the queries directly over the encrypted data without decrypting it.

2.2 Storing Encrypted Data in the Database

We briefly summarize how the client's data stored at the server in an encrypted fashion in the DAS model.[3]

For each relation $R(A_1, A_2, \ldots, A_n)$, we store, on the server, an encrypted relation: $R^S(RID, KID, etuple, P_1^{id}, P_2^{id}, \ldots, P_i^{id})$, where $1 \leq i \leq n$. Here, an *etuple* stores an encrypted string that corresponds to a tuple in a relation R. Each attribute P_i^{id} stores the partition index for the corresponding attribute A_i that will be used for query processing at the server.

For example, consider the relation *emp* given in Table 1 that stores information about employees. The *emp* table is mapped to a corresponding table, shown in Table 2, at the server: $emp^S(RID, KID, etuple, eid^{id}, ename^{id}, salary^{id})$.

The RID represents the *record identifier*, which is a unique number created by the client for each tuple. Here, the RIDs are not the same as unique identi-

---

[2] Often the client and the user might be the same entity.

[3] We will not repeat all of the details of the storage model here, since it is thoroughly discussed in [7]. Rather, we only provide the necessary notations to explain the constructs we develop in this work.

Table 1. Relation *emp*

eid	ename	salary	addr	did
23	Tom	70K	Maple	40
860	Mary	60K	Main	80
320	John	23K	River	35
200	Sarah	55K	River	10

Table 2. Encrypted representation emp^S of *emp*

RID	KID	etuple	eid^{id}	$ename^{id}$	$salary^{id}$
1	45	=*?Ew@R*((¡¡=+,-...	2	19	81
2	78	b*((¡¡(*?Ew@=l,r...	4	31	59
3	65	w@=W*((¡¡(*?E:,j...	7	59	22
4	52	ffΓi* @=U(¡?G+,a...	8	49	59

fiers, which are used as references to the records and assigned by the database manager, as it is done in most of the commercial database products. Instead, these RIDs also uniquely identify the records, however, they are created and assigned by the client to facilitate the schemes we present in the study.

The KID represents the *key identifier*, which is also created and assigned by the client. The KID indicates which key is used to encrypt the *etuple* of the corresponding tuple. We elaborate on the use of KIDs in Section 3.5.

The column *etuple* contains the string corresponding to the encrypted tuples in *emp*. For instance, the first tuple is encrypted to "=*?Ew@R*((¡¡=+,-..." that is equal to $\mathcal{E}_k(1, 23, Tom, 70K, Maple, 40)$, where $\mathcal{E}$ is a deterministic encryption algorithm with key k. Any deterministic encryption technique such as AES, DES etc., can be used to encrypt the tuples. The column eid^{id} corresponds to the index on the employee ids.[4]

2.3   Classification of the System Architectures

In this section, we propose different instantiations for the overall system architecture presented above. Our classification of the system architecture alternatives is *client-oriented*. In other words, we identify the architecture model based on how the clients interact with the service provider. We classify the system architecture models under three categories; *standalone clients*, *group of clients*, and *client networks*. Each model has implications on the characteristics of the system including the control flow, index management, key management, and query processing. We first present the details of each architecture below.

Standalone clients: In the standalone clients model, shown in Figure 2(a), each client is a single node connecting to the service provider individually. The client does not directly share the data with the other clients. Possible example

---

[4] The details of creation of those index values can be found in [7].

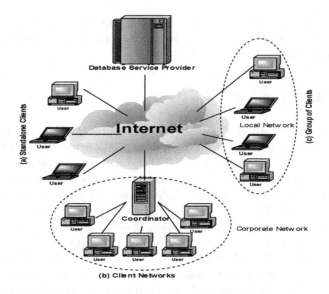

Fig. 2. Architectural model alternatives for database service

for the clients of this architecture is personal users accessing to the services, such as e-mail, rent-a-spreadsheet etc., via a web browser or a lightweight application interfaces.

Client networks: In this architecture, shown in Figure 2(b), the client of the service is a network rather than the individual nodes. A characteristic example for this architecture is larger corporations, which maintain their own network infrastructure as corporate networks and outsource some or all of their IT operations. In this model, the nodes inside the network utilize a connection point (or multiple points) to communicate with the service provider. We call this distinguished node as *coordinator node*. The coordinator node is responsible for set of operational tasks, such as maintaining metadata information required to execute queries directly over encrypted data (as described in Section 2.1), executing transactional semantics in the multi-tier client/server architecture, and the key management tasks as we describe in Section 3.

Group of clients: In this case, as shown in Figure 2(c), multiple clients access to the same service individually. Those clients are somehow related to each other. The relationship can be organizational, i.e., the group of clients belonging to an organization, or data sharing or both. A typical example for this model is small companies, which have multiple but limited number of users. They do not want to (or need to) maintain an integrated network infrastructure containing the coordinator nodes as in client networks case. Nonetheless, they need to enable collaboration among the user nodes in the organization as the users (or employees) of them would be sharing the data in terms of querying and updating and are related by business means. Therefore the user nodes are connected to each other to share local information, such as the metadata. Inherently this information is managed in a distributed fashion. We will not further discuss the distributed data management techniques in this context since it would cause us to diverge from the main content of the paper.

3 Key Management

Key management is a group of policies and procedures that regulate the maintenance of the encryption keys within the system. The key management techniques have been extensively studied in the applied cryptography literature [14]. We discussed the relevant aspects of the key management techniques to database-as-a-service model by considering their implications on the system implementation issues elsewhere [11]. Therefore, here, we only provide necessary background on the specific key management functions. We consider the following components of the key management architecture: *key generation, key installation, key distribution*, and *key update*. We will discuss each of these functionalities in the context of the DAS model and indicate where the each of the tasks are identified in the respective subsections. Key updates are discussed separately as they are the main focus of the paper. We also define the key assignment granularity, which affects the discussion of the techniques presented in the paper. In addition, we introduce a data structure, called *key registry*. The key registry is used to store the encryption key in the system.

3.1 Key Assignment Granularity

A key can be used to encrypt different database objects in the database, such as a table or a row. We call this as the assignment granularity of the key. The selection of granularity would have its own pros and cons, depending on the system setup, limitations on computing and storage of the client etc., and the security requirements. Discussion on these alternatives can be found in [11]. In this paper, we assume that the key assignment granularity is vertical-partitions-level.

In *vertical-partitions-level* key assignment granularity case, a group of database rows are encrypted with the same key. In the most extreme case, a different key is used for each row. Alternatively, the rows can be grouped. In our system we define the groups as the non-overlapping intervals on the RIDs. All rows in a value interval are encrypted with the same key. For example, the key k_1 can be used to encrypt the rows of *emp* table, whose *mgr.RID* values fall in $[1, 10]$ and the key k_2 can be used for the rows, whose *mgr.RID* values fall in $[11, 25]$.

3.2 Key Generation

Key generation involves the creation of the encryption keys that meet the specifications of the underlying encryption techniques. These specifications define the properties, such as size, randomness, that the keys should have. The medium in which keys are generated is of particular interest for the DAS model since the decision has both security and performance implications [11].

In the DAS model there are two places where the key generation may take place. The first option is the client itself and the second option is a third party trusted server, which provides the key generation (and possibly additional key management functions) as a service. Note that, we do not consider the server as an option since the server is considered as an untrusted party in the model. In this paper, we assume that the client generates the keys.

3.3   Key Installation

Once the keys are generated, they need to be operational and accessible for the authorized users. The key installation defines how and where the key are stored during the regular use. We propose a specialized data structure, *key registry*, that is responsible for storing the key material information. We present the details of the key registry in Section 3.5.

3.4   Key Distribution

After a key is generated, a corresponding entry is created in the key registry. Upon request, the keys should be provided to the authorized users. This process is called *key distribution*. Similar to the case for the key generation function there are different alternatives where the key distribution can be handled, the client site, a trusted third party service provider, and the server site.

For the standalone clients model, the client either stores the key registry on its machine or utilizes a trusted third party server for this purpose. Yet another possibility is to store the key registry at the server site unlike key generation function. The key registry can be encrypted by using a *master key* and stored at the server securely. When the client needs to use key material, it can be downloaded from the server and be decrypted with the master key. These alternatives are also valid for the client networks and the group of clients models. For the former, coordinator node can act as a medium for storage and communication with the other users.

If the server or a third party server is chosen for the key distribution, the user authentication is an issue to address. This can be solved by using public key infrastructure (PKI). After the key generation, the key registry can be locked with the public key. This way anyone can request the encrypted key registry but only the authorized users can decrypt using their private key.

3.5   Key Registry

The *key registry* is the data structure that stores all the required information to manage the keys. It has a tabular structure, shown in Figure 3, which consists of five columns corresponding to *Key ID (KID) List, Correspondence, Expiration, Cardinality, Key,* and an indefinite number of rows, each corresponding to a different key that is used in the system.

KID	Correspondence	Expiration	Cardinality	Key
45	mgr.RID:[1,200]	06/12/05	120	*the key*
92	mgr.RID:[1,200]	06/12/05	30	*the key*
52	proj.RID:[1,500]	06/09/05	275	*the key*
77	emp.RID:[1,300]	07/01/05	130	*the key*
23	mgr.RID:[201,500]	06/08/05	40	*the key*

Fig. 3. Key Registry

•*Key ID (KID)* provides key identifier, which is a numerical value, that is used to identify the corresponding key. To obfuscate the correspondence between the records and the encryption, we can assign different KIDs to the same encryption key, i.e., a key does not need to have a unique identifier. These numbers are just used to make the associations between the records read from the encrypted database tables and the key registry entries. When an encrypted tuple is read from the database (or a tuple is to be inserted into the database) the system should know which key had been used to encrypt the record. The KID column in the encrypted storage model (Section 2.2) provides that information. Maintaining multiple identification numbers for the keys increases the security afforded by the system, especially against certain types of attacks, such as, known-ciphertext attacks, related-key attacks [14]. An adversary cannot directly recognize the *etuples*, which are encrypted with the same key.

• *Correspondence* indicates the records to which the key is assigned. In the correspondence column of the key registry, we use a special notation to indicate the correspondence to the database objects. The notation is:

$$table\_name.RID : [RID_1, RID_2]$$

Here we describe the conceptual implementation of the key registry. An actual implementation of this framework could be done in different ways to achieve a better performance.) The *table_name* specifies the name of the table to which the RIDs belong. *RID* indicates a set of record identifiers. An *RID* is associated with a closed interval. For example, [20,50] indicates the continuous interval of values, i.e., RIDs, between 20 and 50.

As an example, in Figure 3, the first entry defines the with KID=45. That key is assigned to the records of *mgr* table whose RIDs are between 1 and 200. The second record in the registry defines another key, KID=92. This key is also used for the same set of records in *mgr* table. The client will know which key had actually been used when a specific record is fetched from the server along with the KID information.

• *Expiration* specifies expiration date of the key. It also possible to use finer granularity in time, such as hours, minutes etc. Using expiration date limits the lifetime of a key in the system. This is useful for many reasons in key management and facilitates the creation of key management policies.

• *Cardinality* is essentially the counter for the number of records that have been encrypted with the key. The RID interval defined in the *Correspondence*

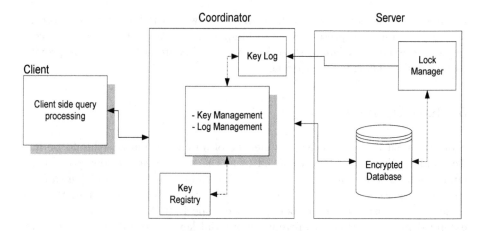

Fig. 4. System architecture for key management

column does not give that number but just defines a partition over the RID values domain. The cardinality information can also be used in creation and management of the key management policies like the *Expiration* information. The system could be designed in a way that it eliminates the keys that are used for very few records for a long period of time or splits the RID intervals that are exceedingly populated constantly.

- The *Key* field contains the actual encryption key.

4   System Architecture for Key Management

In this section we present the detailed system architecture that is used for key management. Overall key management system architecture is shown in Figure 4. This is a detailed view of the clients network system architecture in Figure 2(b) in Section 2.3. The client submits the queries and perform the client side query processing as it is described in Section 2.1 and in [7].

For the coordinator, we show two specific functions, key management and log management, and respective data structures for those function, key log and key registry. The coordinator initiates the key update processes based on the system key update policies. Those policies are reflected on the *expiration* and the *cardinality* fields of the key registry. The key registry is explained in Section 3.5. *Key log* is another tabular structure that is maintained by the coordinator for efficient concurrency control.

The key log consists of three columns: $<RID, current\_key, new\_key>$. RID is the record identifier for a record as described earlier. *Current_key* is the encryption key that was used to encrypt the record and *new_key* is the key that will be used as the encryption key for re-keying. We will make use of this structure to keep track of conflicts between the update operations and the key updates in Section 5.

The server runs a *lock manager* that implements the procedures we illustrate in Section 5. Essentially, the lock manager implements a new lock mode,

key update locks, and resolves the conflicts between the lock modes according
to the techniques we present. Our techniques always aim at reducing the con-
tention between the client transactions and the key updates thereby improving
the system's concurrency performance.

5   Key Updates

From the security perspective the lifetime of an encryption key should be limited and the key should be removed from the active usage under certain cir-
cumstances. The lifetime of a key can be determined by the *Expiration* value in
the Key Registry. Re-keying is recommended and sometimes required. Periodic
re-keying is considered as a good practice, especially, for data stored over an
extended period of time to prevent a potential key compromise. If a key compromise is suspected or expected, an emergency re-keying has to be performed.
In those cases, all affected keys should be changed.

The key update has significant implications on the DAS model in which
large amount of data is divided into the parts and encrypted with different keys.
Therefore we particularly emphasize the need for the efficient mechanisms to
handle the key updates. Above, we presented how the encryption keys can be
applied at different granularity levels by defining the RID intervals accordingly
in the key registry. Choosing a finer level granularity would increase the security,
at the increased cost of key management since larger number of data items would
be encrypted with different keys.

From a database system point of view, the interference between the key
update procedure and regular database queries, being executed by the users,
should be minimized. This relates to the concurrency performance of the system.
Generally, the key update procedure consists of five main steps:

1) Generation and installation of a new key
2) Fetching the *etuple*s that are subject to key change
3) Decryption of the *etuple*s
4) Re-encryption of the *etuple*s with the new key
5) Replacement of the *etuple*s, re-encrypted with the new key

In this procedure, the records, which are subject to the key change are re-
encrypted with the new keys. Therefore, duration of this process, the records
should be locked for any update transaction. Otherwise an update transaction
may update a record with a new content while the re-encryption process is in
progress. When the re-encryption is completed the old content, which is encrypted with the new key is inserted back into the database. This would over-
write the updated value of the record causing inconsistency in the database.
Usually the client has limited computational and storage power. In addition, the
encryption and decryption are computationally very expensive operations [8].
Therefore, this may lead to a longer duration of key update procedures. If the
key update blocks out significant amount of user transactions then throughput
of the system may considerably deteriorate.

In addition, we need to be judicious about the system resource usage due to key updates. This includes, network bandwidth and I/O overhead. For example, choosing a finer granularity for processing, could speed-up the key update with lesser interference with the other transactions. This would, however, cause an increased network traffic and message initiation cost since the number of transmission requests increases with the finer granularity.

To address these issues, we devised techniques that observe overall system performance to handle the key updates. In these techniques, our goal is to minimize the interference between the key update procedures and the other user transactions, and to minimize the system resources usage. We describe our techniques in the client networks architectural class, (See Section 2.3), where the requirements we stated above are most pronounced. The applications of the techniques extend to the other classes, namely; standalone clients and the group of clients.

5.1   Key Update (KU) Locks

We introduce a new lock mode called *Key Update (KU) locks* to efficiently handle the the key updates along with the other transactions. This is an additional lock mode for the lock manager run by the server. We assume the lock manager uses shared (S), exclusive (X), and update (U) locks for transaction processing. Other possible lock modes, such as IX, IS, that are used in lock managers are not important for the discussions of this paper. We assume lock manager uses *record locking granularity* [15]. Thus, the lock manager locks a record at a time in a given table.

Shared locks are used to lock a database element for the transactions that access the database element for read-only purposes, e.g., scans. Thus, there can can be any number of shared locks held on a database element. Exclusive locks are used to lock a database element for update operations. Therefore, there can be one exclusive on a database element. Update locks are used to avoid the deadlocks. If it is known that a transaction will update/delete a fetched record, the transaction asks for a U lock to be acquired. U lock is incompatible with U and X, but is compatible with S. Therefore, no other transaction can obtain a U lock on the same record until the current transaction terminates. If only an S lock were to be obtained, then two different transactions could both obtain S locks. Afterward, both may try to obtain X locks and thereby create a deadlock.

Key Update (KU) locks are used lock the reords for key update operations. The lock mode compatibility matrix is given in Table 3. A check mark ("✓") means that the corresponding modes are compatible, which means that two

Table 3. Lock mode compatibility matrix

	S	X	U	KU
S	✓	×	✓	✓
X	×	×	×	×
U	×	×	×	×
KU	✓	✓	✓	×

different transactions may hold a lock simultaneously in those modes on the same record. The rows show the currently held lock and the columns show the requested lock. Let us consider each column of the matrix to explain the new lock mode.

Compatibility with S locks: S locks do not conflict with the KU locks. Because read/scan operations can be executed concurrently with the key update procedure. When a group of *etuples* are brought in to the coordinator node, the original copies of those are still available at the server for querying. Note that, from the query processing -over encrypted data- perspective the only critical attributes in the storage model are the partition indexes. All supported query conditions are handled by making use of the partition indexes [7].

Based on the encrypted data storage model, predicates in the user query are evaluated as described in [7]. This process includes the translation of the query into a form that retrieves the (super)set of *etuples* by evaluating the predicates directly over encrypted data. When the qualified *etuples* (along with RIDs and KIDs) are fetched, the client looks up the key registry and finds out the valid key(s) for each *etuple* and decrypts them. Note that, even the coordinator node runs a key update over the *etuples* that are returned as the answer of the query, the content of the data is the same. The only information the user needs to correctly decrypt is the valid keys and this information is provided by the key registry.

Compatibility with X locks: Unlike the scans, update transactions change the content of the data. There is a clear conflict between the update and key update operations. An update transaction may update a record, encrypted it with the current key, insert it back to the database, and commit while the key update is still running. The key update procedure re-encrypts the old content with the new key and overwrites the updated content, which results in incorrect database state. If the key update transaction commits first, then the update transaction would encrypt the record with the old key and insert it back to the database with the wrong KID value.

However, we can still grant an X lock on a record, which is already locked with a KU lock. The sequence diagram of the protocol to efficiently handle the update transactions is given in Figure 5. The conflicts between the X locks and the KU locks are resolved at the coordinator. The server detects a conflict by using the lock modes. Assume that, a record is locked with KU lock for key update and another transaction requests for an X lock on the same record. The server grants the X lock and sends the conflict information to the client. The coordinator records the conflict information in the log, which is described in Section 4, and stops any processing on the record. At this point, we have two options to process the update.

First, the client asks the coordinator for the new key information. This can be done by using the RIDs. To make the look-up even more efficient, we can store the records in a sorted list or in a tree based data structure based on their RIDs at the coordinator. (As we stated earlier, RIDs are assigned by the client and they

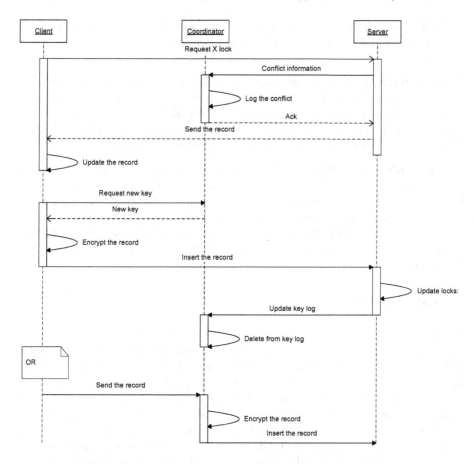

Fig. 5. Lock management protocol for KU and X locks

are not used as references to records by the server.) The client can encrypt the updated record with the new key by itself. Note that, the new key information is placed in the key registry before the coordinator starts the processing. Then the client sends a notification to the coordinator and the coordinator drops the corresponding record from the log. Following this, the client inserts the updated record into the database. Since the coordinator drops the record from the log, the record is not processed by the coordinator anymore thereby preventing the overwriting and inconsistency.

As a second option, the client can transfer the updated record to the coordinator for encryption with the new key. The coordinator first replaces the copy of the record with the updated record, encrypts it with the new key, and inserts it into the database.

The decision between those two alternatives should be made dynamically by considering the performance requirements of the system and the current status

of the processes. This procedure allows the system to handle the record updates
and the key updates together in that way increasing the system's concurrency
performance.

Compatibility with U locks: The U locks are managed in the same way that
the X locks are managed. A transaction that holds a U lock on a record may
escalate the lock mode to X after reading the record. If a KU lock is held on the
same record, the lock manager should consider the escalation. Consequently, the
U lock request is handled the way an X lock request is handled.

Compatibility with New KU lock request: As per the lock mode compatibility matrix in Figure 3, S locks and a new KU lock request do not conflict.
However, new KU locks requests are not compatible with any of the other existing X,U,KU locks on the same record. We may grant a KU lock request if there
is a U lock on the record. Nevertheless, the system's performance doesn't benefit
from this as the coordinator has to wait until the transaction that holds the U
lock terminates.

6   Conclusions

We have studied the efficient key management issues in the encrypted database
environments, specifically in database-as-a-service (DAS) setups. We particularly
observed the importance of the key update procedures and proposed efficient key
update alternatives, which allow the system to update the keys in a concurrent
fashion. Key updates are a fundamental part of any system that uses encryption techniques. Due to the CPU intensive nature encryption/decryption, key
updates may take extended period of time and interfere with the other database
transactions. This could severely affect the systems' concurrency performance.
We have presented specialized techniques, data structures, and protocols to handle the key updates along with the other database transactions to improve the
concurrency performance.

References

1. R. Agrawal, J. Kiernan, R. Srikant, and Y. Xu. Hippocratic databases. In *Proc.
   of VLDB*, 2002.
2. S. Chaudhuri, E. Christensen, G. Graefe, V. R. Narasayya, and M. J. Zwilling. Self-
   tuning technology in microsoft sql server. *Data Engineering Bulletin*, 22(2):20–26,
   1999.
3. Computer Security Institute. CSI/FBI Computer Crime and Security Survey.
   http://www.gocsi.com, 2002.
4. ComputerWorld. Business Process Outsourcing. Jan. 01, 2001.
5. E. Damiani, S. D. C. di Vimercati, S. Jajodia, S. Paraboschi, and P. Samarati.
   Balancing confidentiality and efficiency in untrusted Relational DBMSs. In *Proc.
   of 10th ACM Conf. On Computer and Communications Security*, 2003.
6. B. Fernandez, R. C. Summers, and C. Wood. *Database Security and Integrity*.
   Addison-Wesley, 1981.

7. H. Hacıgümüş, B. Iyer, C. Li, and S. Mehrotra. Executing SQL over Encrypted Data in Database Service Provider Model. In *Proc. of ACM SIGMOD*, 2002.
8. H. Hacıgümüş, B. Iyer, and S. Mehrotra. Providing Database as a Service. In *Proc. of ICDE*, 2002.
9. H. Hacıgümüş, B. Iyer, and S. Mehrotra. Ensuring the Integrity of Encrypted Databases in Database as a Service Model. In *Proc. of 17th IFIP WG 11.3 Conference on Data and Applications Security*, 2003.
10. H. Hacıgümüş, B. Iyer, and S. Mehrotra. Efficient Execution of Aggregation Queries over Encrypted Relational Databases. In *Proc. of International Conference on Database Systems for Advanced Applications (DASFAA)*, 2004.
11. H. Hacıgümüş and S. Mehrotra. Performance-Conscious Key Management in Encrypted Databases. In *Proc. of 18th IFIP WG 11.3 Conference on Data and Applications Security*, 2004.
12. J. He and M. Wang. Cryptography and relational database management systems. In *Proc. of IDEAS '01*, 2001.
13. T. Lunt and E. B. Fernandez. Database Security. *ACM SIGMOD Record*, 19(4), 1990.
14. D. R. Menezes, P. C. van Oorschot, and S. A. Vanstone. *Handbook of Applied Cryptography*. CRC Press, 1997.
15. C. Mohan. ARIES/KVL: A Key-Value Locking Method for Concurrency Control of Multiaction Transactions Operating on B-Tree Indexes. In *Proc. of VLDB*, 1990.

Metadata Management in Outsourced Encrypted Databases

E. Damiani[1], S. De Capitani di Vimercati[1], S. Foresti[1],
S. Jajodia[2], S. Paraboschi[3], and P. Samarati[1]

[1] University of Milan - 26013 Crema, Italy
{damiani, decapita, foresti, samarati}@dti.unimi.it
[2] George Mason University - Fairfax VA 22030-4444, USA
jajodia@gmu.edu
[3] University of Bergamo - 24044 Dalmine, Italy
parabosc@unibg.it

Abstract. Database outsourcing is becoming increasingly popular introducing a new paradigm, called *database-as-a-service*, where a client's database is stored at an external service provider. Outsourcing databases to external providers promises higher availability and more effective disaster protection than in-house operations. This scenario presents new research challenges on which the usability of the system is based. In particular, one important aspect is the *metadata* that must be provided to support the proper working of the system.

In this paper, we illustrate the metadata that are needed, at the client and server, to store and retrieve mapping information for processing a query issued by a client application to the server storing the outsourced database. We also present an approach to develop an efficient access control technique and the corresponding metadata needed for its enforcement.

1 Introduction

Nowadays databases hold a critical concentration of sensitive information and the volume of this information is increasing very quickly. Therefore, many organizations are adding data storage at a high rate. This data explosion is due in part to powerful database applications, deployed by organizations to capture and manage information. In such a scenario, *database outsourcing* is becoming increasingly popular. A client's database is stored at an external service provider that should provide mechanisms for clients to access the outsourced databases. The main advantage of outsourcing is related to the costs of in-house versus outsourced hosting: outsourcing provides *i)* significant cost savings and service benefits and *ii)* promises higher availability and more effective disaster protection than in-house operations. As a consequence of this trend toward outsourcing, highly sensitive data are now stored on systems run in locations that are not under the data owner's control. Therefore, data confidentiality and even integrity can be put at risk. These problems are traditionally addressed by means of encryption [10]. By encrypting the information, the client is guaranteed

W. Jonker and M. Petković (Eds.): SDM 2005, LNCS 3674, pp. 16–32, 2005.

that it alone can observe the data. The problem is then to perform a *selective retrieval* on encrypted information. Since confidentiality demands that data decryption must be possible only at the client side, techniques are needed enabling external servers to execute queries on encrypted data, otherwise the whole relations involved in the query would be sent to the client for query execution. A first proposal toward the solution of this problem was presented in [8,9,12,13,15] where the authors proposed storing, together with the encrypted database, additional indexing information. Such indexes can be used by the DBMS to select the data to be returned in response to a query. In [8,9] the authors propose a hash-based method for database encryption suitable for selection queries. To execute interval-based queries, the B+-tree structures typically used inside DBMSs is adapted. Privacy homomorphism has been also proposed for allowing the execution of aggregation queries over encrypted data [14,16]. In this case the server stores an encrypted table with an index for each aggregation attribute (i.e., an attribute on which the aggregate operator can be applied) obtained from the original attribute with privacy homomorphism. An operation on an aggregation attribute can then be evaluated by computing the aggregation at the server site and by decrypting the result at the client side. Other work on privacy homomorphism illustrates techniques for performing arithmetic operations (+, -, x, /) on encrypted data and does not consider comparison operations [3,11]. In [1] an order preserving encryption schema (OPES) is presented to support equality and range queries over encrypted data. This approach operates only on integer values and the results of a query posed on an attribute encrypted with OPES is complete and does not contain spurious tuples.

However, this scenario, called *database-as-a-service* (DAS), presents new additional research challenges on which the usability of the system is based. One challenge is to develop efficient access control techniques. As a matter of fact, all the existing proposals for designing and querying encrypted/indexing outsourced databases assume the client has complete access to the query result. However, this assumption does not fit real world applications, where different users may have different access privileges. As an example, consider a medical database that includes information about doctors and patients. Each user (doctor/patient) or group thereof should be granted selective access to only a specific subset of data. Enforcing selective access with the explicit definition of authorizations requires the data owner to intercept and process each query request (from the user to the server) and each reply (from the server to the user) to filter out data the requestor is not authorized to access. Such an approach may however cause bottleneck because it increases the processing and communication load at the data owner site. A promising direction to avoid such a bottleneck is represented by selectively encrypting data so that users (or groups thereof) can decrypt only the data they are authorized to access [7]. This solution requires defining and maintaining, both at the client and server, additional information at the level of *metadata* needed to enforce selective access.

In this paper, after a brief summary of our proposal for enforcing access control in the DAS scenario, we focus on the metadata that are needed to access the

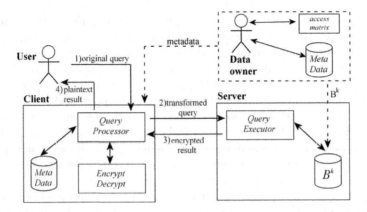

Fig. 1. DAS Scenario

outsourced database according to the policies defined by the data owner. In particular, we describe the metadata and compare different storage strategies each of which is characterized by a different usage in storage and bandwidth capacity. The remainder of this paper is organized as follows. Section 2 describes the DAS scenario and briefly illustrates a solution for enforcing access control through cryptography. Section 3 presents different strategies for storing and managing the metadata necessary to properly use the outsourced database. Section 4 illustrates how a query on a plaintext database is transformed into a query on the corresponding encrypted database. Finally, Section 5 concludes the paper.

2   DAS Scenario

We briefly introduce the considered DAS scenario, the encrypted database structure, and a solution for enforcing an access control policy on which the following metadata analysis is based.

2.1   Data Organization

The DAS scenario involves four entities (see Figure 1):

- *Data owner*: an organization that produces data to be made available for controlled external release;
- *User*: human entity that presents requests (queries) to the system;
- *Client*: front-end that transforms the user queries into queries on the encrypted data stored on the server;
- *Server*: an organization that receives the encrypted data from a data owner and makes them available for distribution to clients.

Clients and data owners are assumed to trust the server to faithfully maintain outsourced data. Specifically, the server is relied upon for the availability of

Patients

PatientId	Surname	Name	Disease	Doctor
125YP894	Carter	Andrew	Tonsillitis	Wayne
5896GT26	Rogers	Mark	Gastritis	Becker
654ED231	Wise	Paul	Hypertension	Wayne
442HN718	Brown	Luke	Hypertension	Lean
942MD745	Fisher	Robert	Tonsillitis	Becker
6271F416	Rogers	Alice	Arthritis	Wayne
058PI175	Brown	Mark	Hypertension	Lean
305EJ186	Rogers	Paul	Gastritis	Morris
276DL557	Fisher	Luke	Hypertension	Lean
364UK784	Rogers	Laura	Tonsillitis	Wayne

(a)

$Patients^k$

Counter	Etuple	IdKey	I_1	I_2	I_3	I_4	I_5
1	r*tso/yui+	AC	ω	γ	δ	π	η
2	hai4de-0q1	AB	ϑ	α	λ	π	μ
3	nag+q8*L	C	ω	γ	ϵ	ρ	η
4	K/ehim*13-	BCD	τ	β	δ	ρ	μ
5	3gia*ni+aL	BD	ω	β	λ	π	μ
6	F0/rab1DW*	BCD	ϑ	α	ϵ	ρ	η
7	Bid2*k1-l0	AB	ϑ	β	λ	ρ	μ
8	/bur21/*-D	BC	τ	α	ϵ	π	η
9	O/c*yd-q2+	C	ω	β	δ	ρ	μ
10	bew0"!DE1a	ACD	ϑ	α	λ	π	η

(b)

Fig. 2. An example of plaintext relation(a) and encrypted relation (b)

outsourced databases. However, the server is assumed not to be trusted with the confidentiality of the actual database content. That is, we want to preserve the server from making unauthorized access to the data stored in the database. To this purpose, the data owner encrypts her data and gives the encrypted database to the sever.

Note that database encryption may be performed at different levels of granularity: relation level, attribute level, tuple level, and element level. Both relation level and attribute level imply the communication to the user of the whole relation involved in a query. On the other hand encrypting at element level would require an excessive workload for data owner and clients in encrypting/decrypting data. For balancing the client workload and query execution efficiency, we assume that the database is encrypted at tuple level.

The main effort of current research in this scenario is the design of a mechanism that makes it possible to directly query an encrypted database [12]. The existing proposals are based on the use of indexing information associated with each relation in the encrypted database [9,15]. Such indexes can be used by the server to select the data to be returned in response to a query. More precisely, the server stores an encrypted table with an index for each attribute on which a query can include a condition. Different types of indexes can be defined, depending on the supported queries. For instance, hash-based methods are suitable for equality queries [15,18] and B+-tree based methods support range queries [9]. For simplicity, in the remainder of this paper we assume that indexes have been created through a hash-based method and that there is an index for each attribute in each relation. Formally, each relation r_i over schema $R_i(A_{i1}, A_{i2}, ..., A_{in})$ in a plaintext database B is mapped onto a relation r_i^k over schema $R_i^k(\texttt{Counter}, \texttt{Etuple}, I_1, I_2, ..., I_n)$ in the encrypted database B^k where, Counter is the primary key; Etuple is an attribute for the encrypted tuple whose value is obtained using an encryption function E_k (k is the key); I_i is the index associated with the i-th attribute. For instance, given relation Patients in Figure 2(a), the corresponding encrypted relation is represented in Figure 2(b).[1] As it is visible from this table, the encrypted table has the same number of rows as the original one.

---

[1] Here, the result of the hash function is represented as a Greek letter. Also, note that the meaning of attribute IdKey will be discussed in Section 3.

The query processing is then performed as follows (see Figure 1): each query (1) is mapped onto a query on encrypted data (2) and is sent to the server that is in charge for executing it. The result of this query is a set of encrypted tuples (3), that are then processed by the client front-end to decrypt data and discard spurious tuples that may be part of the result. The final result (4) is then presented to the user. We will discuss the query processing in more details in Section 4.

2.2 Selective Access on Encrypted Databases

All existing proposals for designing and querying encrypted/indexing outsourced databases focus on the challenges posed by protecting data at the server side, and assume the client has complete access to the query result (e.g., [4,6,15,21]). In other words, tuples are assumed to be encrypted using a single key; knowledge of the key grants complete access to the whole database. Clearly, such an assumption does not fit real world applications, which demand for selective access by different users, sets of users, or applications. Our solution exploits data encryption by including authorizations in the encrypted data themselves. While in principle it is advisable to leave authorization-based access control and cryptographic protection separate, in the DAS scenario such a combination can prove successful. The idea is then to use different encryption keys for different data. To access such encrypted data, users have to decrypt them, which could only be done by knowing the encryption algorithm and the specific decryption key being used. If the access to the decryption keys is limited to certain users of the system, different users are given different access rights. In classical terms, the access rights defined by the data owner can be represented by using an *access matrix* $\mathcal{A}$, where rows correspond to subjects, columns correspond to objects, and entry $\mathcal{A}[s, o]$ is set to 1 if s can read o; 0 otherwise. Given an access matrix $\mathcal{A}$, ACL_i denotes the vector corresponding to the i-th column (i.e., the access control list indicating the subjects that can read tuple t_i), and CAP_j denotes the vector corresponding to the j-th row (i.e., the capability list indicating the objects that user u_j can read). With a slight abuse of notation, in the following we will use ACL_i (CAP_j, resp.) to denote either the bit vector corresponding to a column (a row, resp.) or the set of users (tuples, resp.) whose entry in the access matrix is 1. Let us consider a situation with four users, namely Alice, Bob, Carol, and David, who need to read the tuples of relation Patients. Figure 3 illustrates an example of access matrix.

	t_1	t_2	t_3	t_4	t_5	t_6	t_7	t_8	t_9	t_{10}
Alice	1	1	0	0	0	0	1	0	0	1
Bob	0	1	0	1	1	1	1	1	0	0
Carol	1	0	1	1	0	1	0	1	1	1
David	0	0	0	1	1	1	0	0	0	1

Fig. 3. An example of access matrix

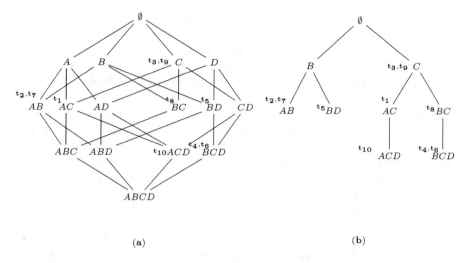

Fig. 4. An example of user hierarchy (a) and the corresponding tree (b)

Different approaches can be taken to enforce the access rights reported in the access matrix. A trivial solution consists in encrypting each tuple with a different key and give users the keys for the tuples they can access. For instance, with respect to the access matrix in Figure 3, user Carol should receive the keys used for encrypting tuples t_1, t_3, t_4, t_6, t_8, t_9, and t_{10}. Obviously, this solution is not efficient and requires the management of too many keys. We propose an alternative solution that consists of collecting users into groups of privileges and encrypt each tuple (set thereof) with the key associated with the set of users who can access it. To this purpose, we base our approach on the definition and use of a *user hierarchy* whose elements are all possible sets of users and on which an order is defined corresponding to the subset relationship between them. Formally, a user hierarchy is defined as follows.

Definition 1. (User Hierarchy) *Given a set $\mathcal{U}$ of users, a user hierarchy, denoted* UH, *is a pair* $(P(\mathcal{U}), \preceq)$, *where* $P(\mathcal{U})$ *is the power set of $\mathcal{U}$ and $\preceq$ is a partial order on* $P(\mathcal{U})$ *such that* $\forall X, Y \in P(\mathcal{U})$, $X \preceq Y$ *iff* $Y \subseteq X$.

The subset relationship between sets of users implies a relationship on their rights. It is trivial to see that, given two sets of users X and Y, if Y is a subset of X (i.e., $X \preceq Y$), then users in Y can access all tuples that users in X can access and the vice versa is not true. With respect to our example in Figure 3, let BCD be the set of users Bob, Carol, David, and let BC be the set of users Bob and Carol. Users in BCD can access tuples t_4 and t_6 and users in BC can access tuples t_4, t_6, and t_8.

By definition the user hierarchy includes all sets of users corresponding to ACL_i. A user hierarchy can be represented through a *directed acyclic graph* (DAG) having a node corresponding to each set of users and a path from node X to node Y if and only if $Y \preceq X$. Figure 4(a) illustrates the user hierarchy corresponding to the access matrix in Figure 3. Here, each node is labeled with the set of initial letters of the users' names belonging to the node, and each tuple t_i is depicted near node ACL_i. Our solution for the determination and assignment of keys exploits the user hierarchy together with a key generation and assignment schema based on the idea of key derivation. Sophisticated key derivation techniques that can be applied to DAGs have been extensively studied in the literature [2,17,19,20]. Intuitively, these key generation schemes operate on the hierarchy computing the keys of lower-level nodes based on the keys of their predecessors. In other words, each node X of a hierarchy is associated with a key that can be used to derive the keys associated with all nodes Y, where $Y \preceq X$ and the opposite is not true. Therefore, using the user hierarchy for key assignment, each user u needs to know only the key associated with the node representing herself and each tuple t has to be encrypted with the key associated with the node representing its ACL. For instance, tuple t_1 is encrypted with the key associated with node AC and Carol knows the key associated with node C (see Figure 4(a)). In this way, Carol can derive the key associated with node AC and can access tuple t_1. Unfortunately, the key generation schemes working on DAGs are complex and they would require a lot of key storage (whose size grows exponentially with the nodes of the hierarchy). To avoid these problems, we decide to apply more simple techniques that work on trees [22]. We develop a greedy *transformation algorithm* from DAG to tree that converts a hierarchy in a corresponding tree [7]. This transformation is performed by first introducing in the tree the nodes corresponding to $ACLs$, and then by selecting, for each node, the "best parent node". This selection is performed by adopting a set of criteria that allow to reduce the number of keys in the system. For instance, a criterion requires the choice of the lowest candidate parent in the hierarchy, that is, the parent node corresponding to the biggest set of users. Another criterion states that it is better to choose as a parent, the node corresponding to an ACL. At the end of the transformation process, the algorithm removes from the structure obtained the nodes that are not necessary neither for encryption nor for key derivation. The resulting *user tree hierarchy* is defined as follows.

Definition 2. (User Tree Hierarchy) *Given a set $\mathcal{U}$ of users, a set $\mathcal{T}$ of tuples, and an access matrix $\mathcal{A}$, the* user tree hierarchy, *denoted* UTH, *is a pair* $(N, \preceq)$, *such that:*

- $N \subseteq P(\mathcal{U})$;
- $\forall t \in \mathcal{T}, \ ACL_t \in N$;
- $\forall X, Y \in N, \ X \preceq Y \ iff \ Y \subseteq X$;
- $\forall X, Y, Z \in N, \ X \preceq Y \ and \ X \preceq Z \Rightarrow Z \preceq Y \ or \ Y \preceq Z$.

The user tree hierarchy uses the same partial order relation as the one defined for the user hierarchy. The data owner has to communicate to each user $u \in \mathcal{U}$ the key associated with element $V \in N$ such that $u \in V$ and $u \notin W$, where W is the parent of V in the UTH. Note that to avoid accesses from untrusted users, the data owner has to check the users' identities before assigning them a key. Figure 4(b) illustrates the UTH corresponding to the user hierarchy in

Figure 4(a). As an example, consider now user `Carol`: she knows key $\{k_C\}$ and can directly derive $\{k_{AC}, k_{BC}\}$ that in turns allows her to derive keys $\{k_{ACD}, k_{BCD}\}$. By using these keys, `Carol` can decrypt the set $\{t_1, t_3, t_4, t_6, t_8, t_9, t_{10}\}$ of tuples corresponding to CAP_{Carol}.

3 Metadata Management in the DAS Scenario

To properly access and manage the outsourced databases, the users, the data owners, and, possibly, the servers have to store some additional information that we call *metadata*. The client and server use these metadata to interpret and execute SQL statements, and to properly manage stored data. The distribution of metadata should follow two principles: *i)* users should know any additional metadata necessary to access the data for which they have a privilege, and *ii)* users should be able to efficiently search and query metadata by saving on bandwidth costs. To this purpose, metadata are stored in relational tables that can be accessed by SQL queries just like any other type of data. Metadata may be as simple as one keyword, or as complex as a derivation path for computing keys. There are three main types of metadata: *authorization metadata*, *descriptive metadata*, and *key management metadata*. Authorization metadata include information about the access control policy defined by the data owner (i.e., the access matrix). Basically, the authorization metadata contain the following tables (as usual, we underline the primary key of each relation).

- `TabUser(`<u>`IdUser`</u>`, Surname, Name)` maintains information about each user in the system. The schema of this table depends on the information needed by the data owner. For simplicity we assume that each user is identified by a unique identifier (attribute `IdUser`) and has a name (attribute `Name`) and surname (attribute `Surname`).
- `AccessMatrix(`<u>`ERelation`</u>`, `<u>`Counter`</u>`, `<u>`IdUser`</u>`)` maintains information about who (attribute `IdUser`) can access what (attributes `ERelation` and `Counter`).

These tables are very sensitive and therefore they have to be stored at the data owner's site. As an example, consider the access matrix in Figure 3: the corresponding authorization metadata are illustrated in Figure 5.

Descriptive metadata are data descriptors and are similar to the system catalogs automatically maintained by relational database systems. Basically, descriptive metadata describe the structure of the encrypted database. The main tables of the descriptive metadata are the following.

- `TabRelation(`<u>`Relation`</u>`, EncryptedRel)` maintains the correspondence between the name of a plaintext relation (attribute `Relation`) and the name of the corresponding encrypted relation (attribute `EncryptedRel`).
- `TabIndex(`<u>`Relation`</u>`, `<u>`Attribute`</u>`, Index, IdMethod)` maintains the correspondence between the name of an attribute (attribute `Attribute`) in a plaintext relation (attribute `Relation`) and the name of the corresponding index (attribute `Index`) together with the index method (attribute `IdMethod`).

Authorization Metadata

TabUser		
IdUser	Surname	Name
A	Harris	Alice
B	Drew	Bob
C	Martin	Carol
D	Muller	David

AccessMatrix(1)		
ERelation	Counter	IdUser
Patients^k	1	A
Patients^k	1	C
Patients^k	2	A
Patients^k	2	B
Patients^k	3	C
Patients^k	4	B
Patients^k	4	C

AccessMatrix(2)		
ERelation	Counter	IdUser
Patients^k	4	D
Patients^k	5	B
Patients^k	5	D
Patients^k	6	B
Patients^k	6	C
Patients^k	6	D
Patients^k	7	A

AccessMatrix(3)		
ERelation	Counter	IdUser
Patients^k	7	B
Patients^k	8	B
Patients^k	8	C
Patients^k	9	C
Patients^k	10	A
Patients^k	10	C
Patients^k	10	D

Descriptive Metadata and Key Metadata

TabRelation	
Relation	EncryptedRel
Patients	Patients^k

TabIndex			
Relation	Attribute	Index	IdMethod
Patient	PatientId	I_1	M1
Patient	Surname	I_2	M2
Patient	Name	I_3	M1
Patient	Disease	I_4	M3
Patient	Doctor	I_5	M2

TabDerivation		
IdKey	IdParent	PublicData
∅	/	Owner
B	∅	Bob
C	∅	Carol
AB	B	AliceBob
BD	B	BobDavid
AC	C	AliceCarol
BC	C	BobCarol
ACD	AC	AliceCarolDavid
BCD	BC	BobCarolDavid

TabKey	
IdKey	Value
∅	gapvv

EncryptAlgo		
Algorithm	IdParameter	Value
One time pad	Start point	273

TabMethod			
IdMethod	Function	IdParameter	Value
M1	Modular	Module	13
M2	Modular	Module	7
M3	Modular	Module	11

KeyDerivationMethod			
IdDerivMethod	MethodDescr	IdParameter	Value
F1	Family of one-way functions	encryption function	Vigenère
F1	Family of one-way functions	key	secret

Data Owner

Descriptive and Key Metadata

TabRelation	
Relation	EncryptedRel
Patients	Patients^k

TabIndex			
Relation	Attribute	Index	IdMethod
Patient	PatientId	I_1	M1
Patient	Surname	I_2	M2
Patient	Name	I_3	M1
Patient	Disease	I_4	M3
Patient	Doctor	I_5	M2

TabDerivation		
IdKey	IdParent	PublicData
C	/	Carol
AC	C	AliceCarol
BC	C	BobCarol
ACD	AC	AliceCarolDavid
BCD	BC	BobCarolDavid

TabKey	
IdKey	Value
C	uetfp

EncryptAlgo		
Algorithm	IdParameter	Value
One time pad	Start point	273

TabMethod			
IdMethod	Function	IdParameter	Value
M1	Modular	Module	13
M2	Modular	Module	7
M3	Modular	Module	11

KeyDerivationMethod			
IdDerivMethod	MethodDescr	IdParameter	Value
F1	Family of one-way functions	encryption function	Vigenère
F1	Family of one-way functions	key	secret

Carol's Client

Fig. 5. Metadata associated with the data owner and `Carol`'s client

- `TabMethod`(<u>`IdMethod`</u>, `Function`, <u>`IdParameter`</u>, `Value`) maintains information about the hash function (attribute `Function`) used with a specific index method (attribute `IdMethod`) together with the value (attribute `Value`) of the corresponding parameters (attribute `IdParameter`).

– EncryptAlgo(Algorithm, IdParameter, Value) maintains information
  about the encryption function (attribute Algorithm) used to encrypt data
  together with the value (attribute Value) of the corresponding parameters
  (attribute IdParameter).

The disclosure of these tables makes it possible for a malicious user to access
the encrypted database. Therefore, the descriptive metadata should never be
stored on the server. Note that each user only knows the portion of the descriptive
metadata corresponding to the relations for which she has a read privilege in
the access matrix; the data owner has instead a complete knowledge of these
metadata. For instance, Figure 5 illustrates the descriptive metadata associated
with Carol and the data owner. Here, we assume that the indexing method is
a hash function implemented through the modular operator, that is, I=A mod
M, where I is the index value corresponding to attribute A and M is a prime
number stored in table TabMethod. We use this specific hash function because
we need collisions.

Key management metadata include information about the key derivation
method, the value of keys directly communicated by the data owner to users,
and the key derivation paths. There are different strategies for storing these
metadata: on clients, on server, or partially on clients and partially on server.
While the client-side strategy saves network bandwidth but uses more client's
memory, the server-side strategy requires more network bandwidth and save
client's storage capacity. We discuss these three strategies more in details in the
following subsections.

3.1   Client-Side Key Metadata Storage

Key management metadata stored at each client include information about the
portion of the user tree hierarchy associated with the corresponding user. Such a
sub-hierarchy allows a user to derive the keys necessary for decrypting the data
for which she has a read privilege. For instance, with respect to the user tree
hierarchy in Figure 4(b), user Carol has to know the portion of the hierarchy
rooted at node C. The relational tables stored at the client-side are therefore
the following.

– TabKey(IdKey, Value) maintains the value of the keys (attribute Value)
  directly communicated to a user.
– TabDerivation(IdKey, IdParent, PublicData) maintains, for each key
  (attribute IdKey) in the considered sub-hierarchy, the identifier of its parent
  (attribute IdParent) and the public information (attribute PublicData)
  necessary to derive the key; if a key corresponds to the root of the sub-
  hierarchy, attribute IdParent is conventionally set to /.
– TabDecryption(EncryptedRelation, Counter, IdKey) maintains, for
  each encrypted relation (attribute EncryptedRelation) and each tuple in
  the relation (attribute Counter), the identifier (attribute IdKey) of the decryption key associated with that tuple.

- KeyDerivationMethod (IdDerivMethod , MethodDescr , IdParameter, Value) maintains information about the key derivation method used for deriving the keys associated with the nodes in the user tree hierarchy[2].

While users have to store the complete sub-hierarchy to which they can access, the data owner may decide to keep track of the information associated with each node of the hierarchy (i.e., the identifier and the public parameters used by the key derivation method) without storing the relationship parent-child. That is, the data owner can decide to store a simplified version of the TabDerivation table that includes only attributes IdKey and PublicData. Although this solution allows the data owner to save storage capacity, it requires to recompute the user tree hierarchy whenever the data owner needs to access the data. Moreover, if the access matrix changes (e.g., a user cannot access a tuple anymore) and the user tree hierarchy is updated without using the transformation algorithm, the new version of the hierarchy could be different from that obtained by applying the algorithm. In this case, also the data owner has to store the TabDerivation table as defined above.

3.2   Server-Side Key Metadata Storage

The client-side approach for storing the key management metadata has the great advantage that each user directly knows the information she needs to properly access the encrypted database. However, by analyzing these data more in details, it is easy to see that this approach requires a duplication of information: the association between a tuple t and the identifier of the key used to encrypt the tuple is duplicated for each user that can access t (table TabDecryption). The same applies for the key derivation paths: two users with non-disjoint user tree sub-hierarchies have a portion of the key derivation paths replicated in table TabDerivation.[3] The only sensitive information that should never be stored on the server is table TabKey. Therefore, to avoid data duplication and to allow the sharing of information among users, the user tree hierarchy and the association tuple-key identifier can be stored on the server. To this purpose, table TabDerivation containing the whole user tree hierarchy is maintained on the server and attribute IdKey defined in the relational schema of an encrypted relation (see Section 2) is used to maintain the association tuple-key identifier. To ensure metadata integrity, message authentication codes, that involve a secret key in the computation of the digest, are used. Obviously, the key used should be known by all users in the system. The main drawback of this solution, however, is that the user tree hierarchy traversal can only be performed by the client. This means that, to derive a key, the client has to perform a sequence of queries that retrieve tree nodes on a derivation path. Another minor drawback of this solution is that, due to the additional attribute IdKey, the result size returned to

---

[2] The schema of this relation may change depending on the key derivation method adopted.

[3] Note that the data inconsistency problem can be avoided by applying the traditional techniques developed in the distributed database area [5].

clients is greater than the result size obtained with the client-side strategy. However, the impact of attribute IdKey on the result size is minimal and therefore can be ignored.

3.3   Client-Side and Server-Side Combined Solution

A hybrid solution for storing the key management metadata can also be adopted thus combining the advantages of the two previous strategies. For instance, the association between tuple-key identifier can be stored on the server by using attribute IdKey as previously discussed, and the information used for the key derivation (i.e., the user tree hierarchy, the derivation method, and the public information associated with each element of the hierarchy) can be stored on the clients. In this way, we avoid a duplication of information and the key derivation process is more efficient because the client can execute it without querying the server.

The choice between a client-side, server-side, or a hybrid solution depends on the storage and bandwidth capacity available to clients. For instance, if the storage capacity is a more critical resource than the bandwidth capacity, a server-side solution is preferable. Otherwise, if the bandwidth capacity is a more critical resource than the storage capacity, a client-side or a hybrid solution is preferable. Note that when specific key derivation methods are used (e.g., the key derivation methods working on tree as in our approach), the size of the public data stored on clients is minimal and therefore the impact on the storage capacity is neglectable. For instance, the key derivation methods based on one-way hash functions [22] require, as public information, a unique name associated with each node of the hierarchy. The size of the public information is therefore of order $O(n \log n)$, where n is the number of elements in the user tree hierarchy. The key derivation methods working on DAGs and based on the modular exponentiation technique [2,20] use as public data associated with an element n of the hierarchy, the product of the prime numbers associated with the nodes in the hierarchy that are not dominated by n. Therefore, in the worst case (i.e., for a leaf of the hierarchy) the size of the public information is of order $O(n(n-1)k) = O(n^2 k)$, where n is the number of elements in the hierarchy and k is the number of bits for representing a prime number.

The computational cost of the derivation mechanism could be reduced if each client keeps a cache of the keys already computed. In this way, if the result of a query includes a tuple encrypted with such a key, it is not necessary recompute the decryption key. Obviously, this cache mechanism requires additional storage capacity on clients. It is also important to note that whenever there is a change in the access matrix, the cache should be cleared because the keys could be changed. Figure 5 illustrates the metadata associated with user Carol and the data owner by using a hybrid solution.

4   Query Processing

We now address the issue of evaluating client queries in the DAS scenario where a hybrid solution for storing the metadata is adopted. For simplicity, we assume that the encrypted database B^k consists of a single relation $\texttt{Patients}^k$ (see Figure 2(b)), and that queries are selection-project expressions.[4] Based on the metadata stored, a query Q on a plaintext relation is split into a query Q_s on the corresponding encrypted relation that is executed on the server, and a client query Q_c for post-processing result of the server query. The transformation between query Q and query Q_s is performed as illustrated in Figure 6. As it is visible from this table, the list of attributes in the SELECT clause is replaced by attributes $\texttt{Counter}$, $\texttt{Etuple}$, and $\texttt{IdKey}$: due to the fact that relations are encrypted at the tuple level, a server can only return the whole encrypted tuple $\texttt{Etuple}$, and therefore the projection operation cannot be executed on the server. Attribute $\texttt{IdKey}$ is necessary to identify the decrypting key. The list of relations in the FROM clause is replaced by the list of corresponding encrypted relations (table $\texttt{TabRelation}$) and conditions in the WHERE clause are transformed according to the index techniques. More precisely, each attribute $\texttt{A}_j$ in the WHERE clause is replaced by the corresponding index (table $\texttt{TabIndex}$) and constant values are transformed by applying the appropriate index technique (table $\texttt{TabMethod}$).

Original Clause (Q)	Transformed Clause (Q_s)
SELECT $\texttt{A}_1, \ldots, \texttt{A}_n$	SELECT $\texttt{Counter, Etuple, IdKey}$
FROM $\quad \texttt{R}_1, \ldots, \texttt{R}_m$	FROM $\quad \texttt{R}_1^k, \ldots, \texttt{R}_m^k$
WHERE $\texttt{A}_j = \text{val}$	WHERE $\texttt{I}_{\texttt{A}_j} = f(\text{val})$
$\texttt{A}_k = \texttt{A}_w$	$\texttt{I}_{\texttt{A}_k} = \texttt{I}_{\texttt{A}_w}$

Fig. 6. Query transformation

As an example, suppose that $\texttt{Carol}$ wants to find the name, surname, and doctor of patients who disease is "Tonsillitis". The SQL query is as follows.

$$Q \equiv \begin{array}{l} \text{SELECT } \texttt{PatientId, Surname, Name, Doctor} \\ \text{FROM } \texttt{Patients} \\ \text{WHERE } \texttt{Disease} = \text{"Tonsillitis"} \end{array}$$

The query processor module retrieves from the metadata the name of the encrypted relation corresponding to $\texttt{Patients}$, the name of the index corresponding to attribute $\texttt{Disease}$ and the hash function (with its parameters) used for creating the index. In this phase, it is also necessary to retrieve both the encryption function and the key derivation method, together with their parameters. To this purpose, the following SQL queries are executed (here, we use an embedded SQL syntax).

---

[4] Note that more complex queries can also be supported (e.g., range queries can be supported by means of indexes based on B+-trees [9]). Details for this, however, are beyond the scope of this paper.

Counter	Etuple	IdKey
1	$r^*tso/yui+$	AC
2	hai4de-0q1	AB
5	3gia*ni+aL	BD
8	$/bur21/^*$-D	BC
10	bew0"!DE1a	ACD

(a)

PatientId	Surname	Name	Doctor
125YP894	Carter	Andrew	Wayne
364UK784	Rogers	Laura	Wayne

(b)

Fig. 7. Encrypted query result (a) and final result returned to Carol (b)

```
SELECT EncryptedRel INTO :R          SELECT Index, IdMethod INTO :I, :M
FROM TabRelation                     FROM TabIndex
WHERE Relation = "Patients"          WHERE Relation = "Patients"
                                     AND Attribute= "Disease"
SELECT Function INTO :h              SELECT Value INTO :P
FROM TabMethod                       FROM TabMethod
WHERE IdMethod = :M                  WHERE IdMethod = :M

SELECT Algorithm, Value INTO :E, :Pe SELECT MethodDescr, Value INTO :DM, :Pm
FROM EncryptAlgo                     FROM KeyDerivationMethod
```

By assuming that the value of variable R is Patients^k, the value of variable I is I_4, and the index value corresponding to "Tonsillitis" is π, the original plaintext query Q is translated as follows:[5]

$$Q_s \equiv \begin{array}{l} \text{SELECT Counter, Etuple, IdKey} \\ \text{FROM Patients}^k \\ \text{WHERE } I_4 = \text{``}\pi\text{''} \end{array}$$

Figure 7(a) illustrates the query result returned to the client. The client has to decrypts all tuples that Carol can access (a tuple is accessible by a user when the corresponding IdKey value appears in table TabKey or table TabDerivation) and to filter out those not matching the actual query predicates in Q. In our example, Carol can access tuples t_1, t_8, and t_{10} and tuples t_2 and t_5 are discarded. The keys to be used for decrypting the tuples are computed as follows. First, for each tuple t of the query result, if table TabKey contains a tuple t' where $t'[\text{IdKey}] = t[\text{IdKey}]$, then the decryption key is already available. Otherwise, the decryption key is obtained by following the key derivation path stored in table TabDerivation.

Figure 8 illustrates the procedure for computing the key derivation path. Intuitively, for each tuple t, by starting from the leaf (i.e., $t[\text{IdKey}]$) of the path, table TabDerivation is queried to determine the parent of the current node of the path. The procedure terminates when root / is reached. Array *Path* stores the key derivation path in reverse order. For instance, consider tuple t_{10}: it is encrypted with key k_{ACD} that can be obtained by following the path $Path[3] =$

---

[5] Note that Q_s is a dynamic embedded SQL statement that is built at run time and placed in a string host variable. For simplicity, we report the final format of the query executed at the server side.

Algorithm 1 (Key derivation path).

KeyDerivationPath($t[\texttt{IdKey}]$)
/* Initializes some variables */
$i:=1;\ Path[i]:= t[\texttt{IdKey}]$
While $Path[i] \neq /$ **do**
    $i := i + 1$
    SELECT **IdParent** INTO $:Path[i]$
    FROM **TabDerivation**
    WHERE **IdKey**$=:Path[i-1]$
return $Path$

Fig. 8. Algorithm for computing the key derivation path

$k_C \rightarrow Path[2] = k_{AC} \rightarrow Path[1] = k_{ACD}$. The decryption key is computed by applying the key derivation method DM along $Path$. Then, the client has to: (1) decrypt the tuples using function E, (2) apply the original condition to discard possibly spurious tuples that do not belong to the result set, and (3) execute the requested projections. Spurious tuples are discarded by applying the following query:

$$Q_c \equiv \begin{array}{l} \text{SELECT } \texttt{PatientId, Surname, Name, Doctor} \\ \text{FROM } \texttt{Result} \\ \text{WHERE } \texttt{Disease=} \text{ ``Tonsillitis''} \end{array}$$

Figure 7(b) reports the final set of tuples that user **Carol** can read. Note that these tuples are a subset of the tuples for which **Carol** has the read privilege (see the access matrix in Figure 3).

As the server returns to the client also tuples that she cannot read, data may be subject to inference attacks. The inference problem in the DAS scenario has been considered in [6,9], where the authors gave a quantitative model for evaluating the robustness of the indexes obtained by applying either the direct encryption or a hash-based method. In summary, they shown that to achieve a higher degree of protection against inference, it is convenient to use a hash function to encode indexes values.

5   Conclusions and Future Work

The management of metadata for accessing a remote encrypted database is of crucial importance in the database-as-a-service scenario. In this paper, we presented the metadata that provide abstract descriptions of the data structures and data formats used in the underlying system. Issues to be investigated will include: *(i)* an effective implementation of the different solutions presented for metadata storage to better evaluate the trade off between storage and bandwidth consumption, and *(ii)* an evaluation of strategies addressing the dynamic updates of the access rights [7].

Acknowledgments

This work was supported in part by the European Union within the PRIME Project in the FP6/IST Programme under contract IST-2002-507591 and by the Italian MIUR within the KIWI and MAPS projects.

References

1. R. Agrawal, J. Kierman, R. Srikant, and Y. Xu. Order preserving encryption for numeric data. In *Proc. of ACM SIGMOND 2004*, Paris, France, June 2004.
2. S. Akl and P. Taylor. Cryptographic solution to a problem of access control in a hierarchy. *ACM Transactions on Computer System*, 1(3):239–248, August 1983.
3. C. Boyens and O. Gunter. Using online services in untrusted environments - a privacy-preserving architecture. In *Proc. of the 11th European Conference on Information Systems (ECIS '03)*, Naples, Italy, June 2003.
4. R. Brinkman, J. Doumen, and W. Jonker. Using secret sharing for searching in encrypted data. In *Proc. of the Secure Data Management Workshop*, Toronto, Canada, August 2004.
5. S. Ceri and G. Pelegatti. *Distributed Database Systems: Principles and Systems*. McGraw-Hill, 1984.
6. A. Ceselli, E. Damiani, S. De Capitani di Vimercati, S. Jajodia, S. Paraboschi, and P. Samarati. Modeling and assessing inference exposure in encrypted databases. *ACM Transactions on Information and System Security (TISSEC)*, 8(1):119–152, February 2005.
7. E. Damiani, S. De Capitani di Vimercati, S. Foresti, S. Jajodia, and P. Samarati. Selective release of information in outsourced encrypted database. Technical report, University of Milan, 2005.
8. E. Damiani, S. De Capitani di Vimercati, M. Finetti, S. Paraboschi, P. Samarati, and S. Jajodia. Implementation of a storage mechanism for untrusted DBMSs. In *Proc. of the Second International IEEE Security in Storage Workshop*, Washington DC, USA, May 2003.
9. E. Damiani, S. De Capitani di Vimercati, S. Jajodia, S. Paraboschi, and P. Samarati. Balancing confidentiality and efficiency in untrusted relational DBMSs. In *Proc. of the 10th ACM Conference on Computer and Communications Security*, Washington, DC, USA, October 27-31 2003.
10. G.I. Davida, D.L. Wells, and J.B. Kam. A database encryption system with sub-keys. *ACM Transactions on Database Systems*, 6(2):312–328, June 1981.
11. J. Domingo-Ferrer and J. Herrera-Joanconmarti. A privacy homomorphism allowing field operations on encrypted data. *Jornades de Matematica Discreta i Algorismica*, March 1998.
12. H. Hacigümüs, B. Iyer, and S. Mehrotra. Providing database as a service. In *Proc. of 18th International Conference on Data Engineering*, San Jose, California, USA, February 2002.
13. H. Hacigümüs, B. Iyer, and S. Mehrotra. Ensuring integrity of encrypted databases in database as a service model. In *Proc. of the IFIP Conference on Data and Applications Security*, Estes Park Colorado, August 2003.
14. H. Hacigumus, B. Iyer, and S. Mehrotra. Efficient execution of aggregation queries over encrypted relational databases. In *Proc. of the 9th International Conference on Database Systems for Advanced Applications*, Jeju Island, Korea, March 2004.

15. H. Hacigümüs, B. Iyer, S. Mehrotra, and C. Li. Executing SQL over encrypted data in the database-service-provider model. In *Proc. of the ACM SIGMOD'2002*, Madison, Wisconsin, USA, June 2002.
16. H. Hacigumus and S. Mehrotra. Performance-conscious key management in encrypted databases. In *Proc. of the 18th Annual IFIP WG 11.3 Working Conference on Data and Applications Security*, Sitges, Catalonia, Spain, July 2004.
17. L. Harn and H. Lin. A cryptographic key generation scheme for multilevel data security. *Computers and Security*, 9(6):539–546, October 1990.
18. B. Hore, S. Mehrotra, and G. Tsudik. A privacy-preserving index for range queries. In *Proc. of the 30th VLDB Conference*, Toronto, Canada, 2004.
19. M. Hwang and W. Yang. Controlling access in large partially ordered hierarchies using cryptographic keys. *The Journal of Systems and Software*, 67(2):99–107, July 2003.
20. S. MacKinnon, P.Taylor, H. Meijer, and S.Akl. An optimal algorithm for assigning cryptographic keys to control access in a hierarchy. *IEEE Transactions on Computers*, 34(9):797–802, September 1985.
21. E. Mykletun, M. Narasimha, and G. Tsudik. Authentication and integrity in outsourced database. In *Proc. of the 11th Annual Network and Distributed System Security Symposium*, San Diego, California, USA, February 2004.
22. R.S. Sandhu. Cryptographic implementation of a tree hierarchy for access control. *Information Processing Letters*, 27(2):95–98, April 1988.

Experiments with Queries over Encrypted Data Using Secret Sharing

Richard Brinkman[1,3], Berry Schoenmakers[2,3], Jeroen Doumen[1], and Willem Jonker[1,3]

[1] University of Twente, The Netherlands
{brinkman, doumen, jonker}@cs.utwente.nl
[2] Technical University of Eindhoven, The Netherlands
berry@win.tue.nl
[3] Philips Research, The Netherlands

Abstract. To avoid insider attacks one cannot rely on access control to protect a database scheme. Encrypting the database is a better option. This paper describes a working prototype of an encrypted database system that allows remote querying over the encrypted data. Experiments with the system show the practical impact of our encoding scheme on storage space and CPU time. Two algorithms, each with two different matching rules, are compared to each other.

1 Introduction

Enterprises often rely on access control to protect their assets. However, a study of the Computer Science Institute and the FBI [1] shows that most successful attacks are conducted by insiders. A possible solution is to replace access control with database encryption where the user keeps the encryption key secret. This shift opens up a new research area of query evaluation over encrypted data.

In this paper we present an extension of our encrypted database system of [2]. We summarise this scheme in section 3. See [2] for further information on the background of searching in encrypted databases. In this paper we present an augmented version of the database system. The former solution lacks the ability to search in the data itself, it only allows searching the XML tags. In the new solution the textual data of an XML document is represented as a *trie* [3], enabling searching tags as well as data. In section 4 we show how to represent the text as a *trie*.

To investigate the practical impact of our database scheme, we have built an implementation. In section 5 we describe some of the implementation issues. In section 6 we use the implementation together with a test database to do several experiments in order to measure the storage space and the influence of the search algorithm and the configuration settings on the CPU time.

2 Related Work

Traditionally, databases are protected against malicious use by means of an access control mechanism. However, the database management system itself is

W. Jonker and M. Petković (Eds.): SDM 2005, LNCS 3674, pp. 33–46, 2005.
© Springer-Verlag Berlin Heidelberg 2005

trusted. When the data is outsourced the database system cannot be trusted anymore to keep the query and the answer secret. Private Information Retrieval [4] aims at letting a user query the database system without leaking to the database which data was queried. The idea behind PIR is to replicate the data among several non-communicating servers. A client can hide his query by asking all servers for a part of the data in such a way that no server will learn the whole query by itself. Chor et al [4] prove that PIR with a single server can only be done by sending all data to the client for each query. In practice database replication is not preferable.

PIR aims at hiding the query from the database leaving the data in the clear. Song, Wagner and Perrig [5] suggest a different technique that supports encrypting the data itself. An encrypted keyword can be found in an encrypted text without the server learning either the keyword or the plaintext. We adapted this work to exploit the tree structure in XML documents in [6].

3   Overview of Our Approach

In our database scheme a plaintext XML document is transformed into an encrypted database by following the steps below. See figure 1 for the encoding of a concrete example.

1. Define a function $map : node \rightarrow \mathbb{F}_{p^e}$, which maps the tag names of the nodes to values of the finite field $\mathbb{F}_{p^e}$, where p^e is a prime power (p prime and e a positive integer) which is larger than the total number of different tag names (figure 1(b)).
2. Transform the tree of tag names (figure 1(a)) into a tree of polynomials (figure 1(d)) of the same structure where each $node$ is transformed to $f(node)$ where function $f : node \rightarrow \mathbb{F}_{p^e}[x]/(x^{p-1} - 1)$ is defined recursively:

$$f(node) = \begin{cases} x - map(node) & \text{if } node \text{ is a leaf node} \\ (x - map(node)) \prod_{d \in child(node)} f(d) & \text{otherwise} \end{cases}$$

   Here $child(node)$ returns all children of a $node$.
3. Split the resulting tree into a client (figure 1(e)) and a server tree (figure 1(f)). Both trees have the same structure as the original one. The polynomials in the client tree are generated by a pseudorandom generator. The polynomials of the server tree are chosen such that the sum of a client node and the corresponding server node equals the original polynomial.
4. Since the client tree is generated by a pseudorandom generator it suffices to store the seed on the client. The client tree can be discarded. When necessary, it can be regenerated using the pseudorandom generator and the seed value.

It is simple to check whether a node N is stored somewhere in a subtree by evaluating the polynomials of both the server and the client at $map(N)$. If the sum of these evaluations equals zero, this means that N can be found somewhere in the subtree N. To find out whether N is the root node of this subtree, you have to divide the unshared polynomial by the product of all its direct children. The result will be a monomial $(x - t)$ where t is the mapped value of the node.

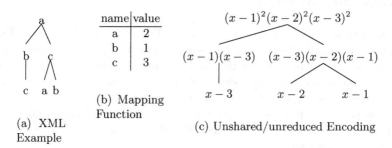

(a) XML
Example

(b) Mapping
Function

(c) Unshared/unreduced Encoding

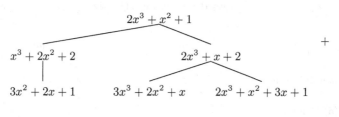

(d) Unshared/reduced Encoding

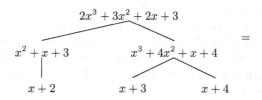

(e) Client Encoding

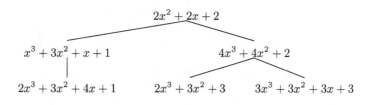

(f) Server Encoding

Fig. 1. The mapping function (1(b)) maps each name of an input document (1(a)) to an integer. The XML document is first encoded to a tree of polynomials (1(c)) before it is reduced to the finite field $\mathbb{F}_5[x]/(x^4 - 1)$ (1(d)) and split into a client (1(e)) and a server (1(f)) part.

4   *Trie* Enhancement

The approach sketched in section 3 is only efficient when p^e is small. This is no problem for tag names that are chosen from a fixed sized set (described in a DTD), but cannot be used for the data because the number of different data nodes is unbounded. And since each polynomial takes $(p^e - 1)\log_2 p^e$ bits of storage space, it is important to keep p^e as small as possible.

In this paper we propose a representation of XML documents allowing for efficient searching in data nodes. Basically, all data nodes are transformed to their *trie* representation [3].

A data string in the original XML document is translated to a path of nodes where each node is chosen from a small set. Assume this set contains $a, b, \ldots, z$. With this set we can translate the tree shown in figure 2(a) to an equivalent *trie* 2(b) or an uncompressed *trie* 2(c). An uncompressed *trie* stores exactly the same information as the original data string, whereas the compressed *trie* loses the order and cardinality of the words. If this is a problem an encryption of the data string may be added to the node. In this example we first split a string into words, represented by paths, and then each path is split into several characters. Other ways of splitting the string into nodes are possible.

On average removing duplicate words from a text reduces the size by 50%. Reducing a text into a compressed *trie* reduces the size by 75-80%. However each

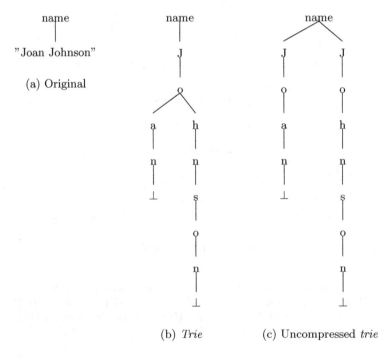

(a) Original

(b) *Trie*   (c) Uncompressed *trie*

Fig. 2.   Transformation of an XML document tree into either a compressed or an uncompressed *trie*

node is converted into a polynomial of size $(p^e - 1) \log_2 p^e$ bits. In case $p = 29$ a polynomial costs 17 bytes. Due to the *trie* compression the 'encryption' of a single letter will cost approximately $3\frac{1}{2} - 4\frac{1}{2}$ bytes.

Having translated the original XML tree into a (compressed) *trie*, the same strategy of [2] can be used to encode the document. Like the document, also the queries should be pre-tuned to the new scheme. A query like

$$\texttt{/name[contains(text(), "Joan")]}$$

is first translated to

$$\texttt{/name[//J/o/a/n]}$$

before it is translated to

$$\texttt{/}map(\texttt{name})\texttt{[//}map(\texttt{J})\texttt{/}map(\texttt{o})\texttt{/}map(\texttt{a})\texttt{/}map(\texttt{n})\texttt{]}.$$

Simple regular expressions like . and .* can be mapped to their *trie*-equivalents * and //.

5 Implementation

In the previous sections we described our theory of searching in encrypted data by using secret sharing and a special kind of encoding/encryption. To demonstrate that searching in encrypted data is not only possible in theory, but also

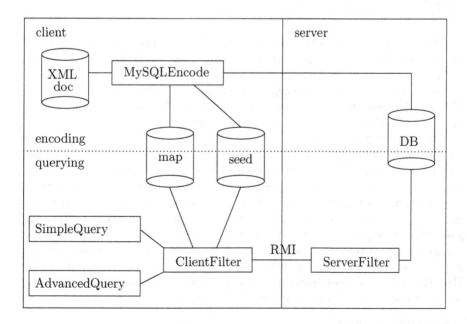

Fig. 3. Client/Server Architecture

in practice, we have built a prototype implementing the encoding and search strategy described in section 3.

The implementation is written in Java and set up using a client/server model. Figure 3 shows the architecture. We will elaborate on each component in the following sections.

The server stores all the polynomials in a database. The database is not protected and can be considered publicly readable. However, the client encodes the original plaintext XML document into encoded polynomials by using the `MySQLEncode` class. The encoder needs a private seed and a private map file which will be re-used by the query engines. The map file is just a text file which stores the mapping between tag names and corresponding values from $\mathbb{F}_{p^e}$.

The prototype consists of two different query engines: `SimpleQuery` and `AdvancedQuery`. Both engines share the same filtering technique. The filter is distributed over the client and the server. The filter classes perform basic operations like function evaluation and tree reconstruction.

5.1 MySQLEncode

Since the server should not learn the information it is storing, it is the client's responsibility to fill the database.

The `MySQLEncode` class acts on three files which are provided on the command-line:

1. A map file
2. A seed file
3. The original XML document

The map file is a property file where each line is of the form $name = value$, where $name$ is one of the tag-names as specified by the DTD or XML schema and $value \in \mathbb{F}_{p^e}$ is the value it is mapped to.

The seed file acts as the encryption key and should therefore be kept secure. Without the seed file it is impossible to regenerate the client tree, and without the client tree the data on the server is meaningless.

The original XML document is parsed by a SAX parser[1]. This means that there is no need for a big client machine with lots of memory. This fits nicely into our philosophy of small clients (cell phones, for example) and big servers. The parser linearly reads the document and constructs the tree on the fly. It only needs memory proportional to the depth of the tree. The tree structure is stored by adding *pre*, *post* and *parent* values to each polynomial. The *pre* and *post* fields are sequence number that count the open tags respectively close tags. The *parent* fields refers to the *pre* value of its parent. This is a common way to store a tree structure into a flat relational table [2,7]. In our prototype we use MySQL[2] as the database back-end. In order to speed up the search process the *pre*, *post* and *parent* fields are indexed by a B-tree.

---

[1] `www.saxproject.org/`

[2] `www.mysql.com`

5.2   The Filter Implementation

Each different query engine (see section 5.3) will use the same set of basic operations. These operations are offered by `ServerFilter` and `ClientFilter`. Both classes implement a common interface `Filter` but are adapted to work on the server site respectively the client site. The two objects communicate with each other using Java's Remote Method Invocation (RMI). The operations consist of functions to query the tree structure as well as to evaluate the polynomials. `ServerFilter` will evaluate the polynomials stored in the database for the given values. `ClientFilter` first regenerates the client polynomial by using the pseudorandom generator with the secret seed and the *pre* location of the polynomial. After the evaluation of its generated polynomial it will add the result to the retrieved value from the server. Only when the sum equals zero, the location is returned to the invoking query engine, otherwise the next candidate node is generated/retrieved, evaluated and added together.

With the evaluation method only the *containment* of a node in a subtree is tested. To be sure that the node is *equal* to the root of the subtree there is an option to check the first factor of a node. To retrieve the factor $(x - t)$ in $f(x) = (x - t)\prod c(x)_{c \in children(f)}$ it is necessary to reconstruct the node's polynomial and all its child polynomials. Because the equality test is expensive it should only be invoked when absolutely necessary.

The operator `nextNode()` acts as a pipeline. The thin client only needs to have one node in memory at a time. The big server will do the buffering of the intermediate results.

5.3   Query Engines

Since it was not a priori clear which search strategy is the best, we have decided to implement two query engines, called `SimpleQuery` and `AdvancedQuery`, each using a different search strategy, as explained below.

SimpleQuery. The most simple search strategy parses the XPath[3] query into steps where each step consists of a direction (child (/) or descendant (//)) and a tag name. Two special tag names exist: `..` matches the parent and `*` matches every child.

In this example we make use of the containment test only. In section 6 we will also use the equality test. There we will compare the two tests to see whether one is preferable to the other. We will sketch the algorithm by using an XML document generated by the XMark benchmark [8] and the example query `/site/*/person//city`. See appendix A for the DTD. This query is parsed into the following steps:

`/site` The first slash instructs the search engine to locate the root node (i.e. the only node without a parent (parent=0)). Since the parent field is indexed this is done in constant time. After the root node has been located both the

---

[3] `www.w3.org/TR/xpath`

stored polynomial on the server and the generated polynomial on the client are being evaluated at $map(site)$. Only when the sum equals zero the next steps are carried out.

/* At this point the preliminary result set (implemented as a `Queue` on the server) will consist of only a single element. This step will change the result set into all children of the root node (i.e. regions, categories, catgraph, people, open_auctions and closed_auctions). The * reduces the workload because no additional filtering is needed.

/person All children of the 6 nodes in the result set are being examined in this step. Evaluation at $map(person)$ is done for all the polynomials found. Only those nodes for which the sum of the server and client evaluations equals zero remain in the result set.

//city This step is quite expensive in terms of execution time. The result of the previous step is already quite large and this step even increases the number of possible nodes that have to be checked. All the descendants of the person-nodes (i.e. name, emailaddress, phone, address, homepage, credit-card, profile, watches, street, city, country, province, zipcode, interest, education, gender, business, age, watch, category, open_auction and description) have to be checked against $map(city)$.

AdvancedQuery. In contrast to the `SimpleQuery` the `AdvancedQuery` takes the tree as the starting point and parses it from root to leaf nodes. At each step the whole remaining query is taken into account. We take advantage of the fact that nodes have knowledge of all descendants. This way it is possible to identify dead branches early in the search process at the cost of more evaluations for each node.

For easy comparison we use the same query and the same test (containment) as before.

/site/*/person//city The `AdvancedQuery` engine always starts at the root node. This node is checked against $map(site)$, $map(person)$ and $map(city)$. Only when all three sums are zero the next steps are carried out. Note that we can only check for the existence of a node. The structure of the query cannot be taken into account since the nodes don't store the structure of the subtree.

/*/person//city The engine proceeds by consuming the /site part of the query and traversing the tree one step down to find the root's children. This unfiltered set of nodes are regions, categories, catgraph, people, open_auctions and closed_auctions. After filtering only the people, open_auctions and closed_auctions remain; all the other nodes do not contain person or city nodes. Thus we may skip these branches.

/person//city In this step the /* has been removed. This means we traversed the tree one step downwards. The children of people, open_auctions and closed_auctions are person, open_auction and closed_auction. Because open_auction and closed_auction contain person and city nodes they remain in the result set even after filtering. The implementation does not check if the node *is* a person but if it *contains* it. This is done because we chose to use the containment test instead of the equality test. In section 6 we investigate whether this was a good choice or not.

//city From the person, open_auction and closed_auction nodes we interactively walk downwards in the tree evaluating the polynomials at $map(city)$ until this results in a non-zero sum. The result set now contains all nodes having a city inside. If we had chosen the equality test only the city nodes would have been in the result set.

6   Experiments

The prototype is an ideal instrument to perform experiments with. With the experiments described in this section we would like to find out what the practical impact of our encrypted database scheme is. We investigated the storage space overhead (section 6.1), the influence of the different search engine algorithms (section 6.2) and the difference between the equality and containment tests (section 6.3). All experiments act on an auction database synthesized by the XMark benchmark [8]. The DTD (see appendix A) contains 77 elements. We chose $p = 83$ and $e = 1$ throughout this section.

6.1   Encoding

Encoding an XML document as polynomials requires extra storage space. This is due to the fact that each polynomial not only stores the information of its own node but also of all its descendants. Figure 4 plots the encoded database size

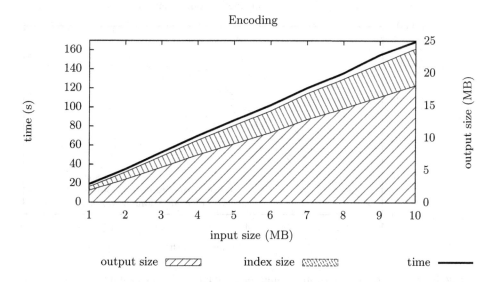

Fig. 4. Encoding

against the input XML size. Approximately 17% of the output size is caused by the pre, post and parent values (not plotted in the figure). The remainder is thus approximately 1.5 times the size of the input. To speed up the search process we added indices to the pre, post and parent fields using B-trees. The size of these indices is added on top of the output size. As expected both the storage space and the encoding time are strictly linear in the input size.

6.2 Query Engines

One of the main reasons for building the prototype was because it was not a priori clear what the most efficient query engine algorithm is. Is it best to evaluate a polynomial at as many points as possible at each node to find an early dead branch or should you evaluate at a single point at a time? To answer this question we performed two tests: one with the simplest of all queries at increasing length and one with more advanced queries containing // and *.

The first test is the worst case scenario for the advanced query engine. The queries in table 1 are chosen in such a way that there is no gain for the advanced algorithm. For instance it is a waste of effort to check whether a europe node contains an item, description, parlist, listitem, text and keyword node, because the DTD (see appendix A) dictates it to be always the case.

As can be seen in figure 5, where the number of evaluations is plotted against the queries of increasing length shown in table 1, the two search algorithms are comparable. They differ by at most a constant factor.

The second test with queries containing // and * was performed in conjunction with the strictness test. The test result are given in the next section.

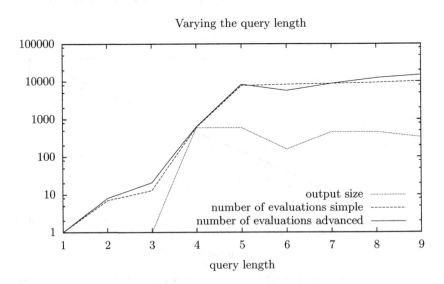

Fig. 5. Several queries with increasing query length. The query numbers refer to the queries summed up in table 1.

Table 1. Queries with increasing length. The numbers correspond to figure 5.

```
1 /site
2 /site/regions
3 /site/regions/europe
4 /site/regions/europe/item
5 /site/regions/europe/item/description
6 /site/regions/europe/item/description/parlist
7 /site/regions/europe/item/description/parlist/listitem
8 /site/regions/europe/item/description/parlist/listitem/text
9 /site/regions/europe/item/description/parlist/listitem/text/keyword
```

6.3   Strictness

Another aspect that is hard to predict is the difference between the equality
test and the containment test. On the one hand, it can be argued that, since
the reconstruction of the first factor of a polynomial is computationally more
expensive than a simple function evaluation, it is preferable to use the containment test. On the other hand, the reduced accuracy causes more nodes to be
examined. Therefore we used our prototype to compare the two tests using both
search algorithms.

For each query in Table 2 four experiments were performed. Each algorithm
(simple and advanced) was run twice: once with the equality test (strict checking) and once with the containment test (non-strict checking). The results are
plotted in figure 6. For all queries the advanced algorithm outperforms the simple algorithm. Furthermore, it can be noticed that sometimes the strict checking
pays off and sometimes it does not. In general, the equality test may cause a
slight overhead or a major improvement.

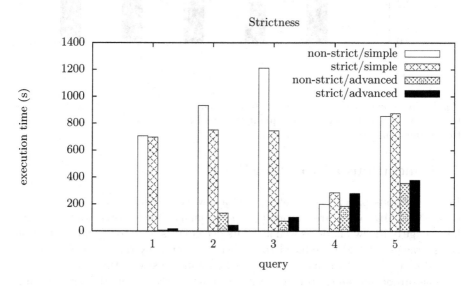

Fig. 6. Equality test versus containment test

Of course it is unfair to compare the equality test, which always gives the exact answer, with the containment test without considering the accuracy. Figure 7 shows the accuracy of the containment test. It plots the percentage of the nodes in the containment test's result that also pass the equality test. Notice that the accuracy drops for each // in the query. For absolute queries which do not contain //, the accuracy of the containment test reaches 100%.

Table 2. Queries for the strictness checks. The numbers correspond to figure 6.

```
1 /site//europe/item
2 /site//europe//item
3 /site/*/person//city
4 /*/*/open_auction/bidder/date
5 //bidder/date
```

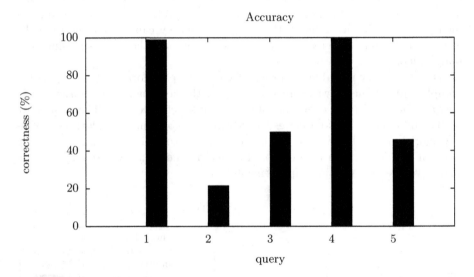

Fig. 7. Accuracy of the containment test as defined by the quotient $\frac{E}{C}$, where E is the size of the result set using the equality test and C is the size of the result set using the containment test

7   Conclusions and Future Work

In our previous paper [2] we introduced a new search strategy over encrypted data. All XML nodes are encoded as polynomials. Each polynomial contains knowledge of its own node as well as all its decendants. Due to a smart reduction the storage overhead is reduced to 50% as measured by our prototype (using $p = 83$ and $e = 1$). The encoding time is linear in the size of the input.

The prototype can choose between two different search algorithms. The simple algorithm reads a query from left to right carrying out a single evaluation at each node. The more advanced algorithm uses a look-ahead strategy where the whole remaining query is taken into account. Experiments show that the advanced algorithm outperforms the simple algorithm in the majority of cases. Only for the most simple queries it is slightly slower.

The search algorithms can use two comparison tests: the equality test and the containment test. The containment test is just a cheap evaluation whereas the equality test is more expensive because a node's own polynomial should be divided by all its child polynomials. The cost of a single equality test depends on the number of children, whereas the costs of a containment test is always constant. All the child nodes should be retrieved from the server and added to the pseudorandomly generated client polynomials. The accuracy of the containment test is reasonable but it does not result in a major improvement in the running time. On the contrary, it is often better to use the equality test to reduce the number of nodes to check, especially for the simple algorithm.

Using a *trie* to represent data content enables querying of the data inside the XML tags. The *trie*-representation is not yet part of the current prototype but we expect a major improvement especially in the advanced algorithm. Queries over the data are more precise than those over the tag labels and thus the number of nodes to be examined is being reduced. Since knowledge of the data is present at high level nodes, the query engine can find the path to the answer almost immediately.

References

1. Computer Science Institute. CSI/FBI computer crime and security survey. http://i.cmpnet.com/gocsi/db_area/pdfs/fbi/FBI2004.pdf.
2. R. Brinkman, J.M. Doumen, P.H. Hartel, and W. Jonker. Using secret sharing for searching in encrypted data. In W. Jonker and M. Petković, editors, *Secure Data Management VLDB 2004 workshop*, volume LNCS 3178, pages 18–27, Toronto, Canada, August 2004. Springer-Verlag, Berlin. http://www.ub.utwente.nl/webdocs/ctit/1/00000106.pdf.
3. Edward Fredkin, Bolt Beranek, and Newman. Trie memory. *Communications of the ACM*, 3(9):490–499, September 1960.
4. B. Chor, O. Goldreich, E. Kushilevitz, and M. Sudan. Private information retrieval. In *FOCS*, pages 41–50, 1995.
5. Dawn Xiaodong Song, David Wagner, and Adrian Perrig. Practical techniques for searches on encrypted data. In *IEEE Symposium on Security and Privacy*, pages 44–55, 2000. http://citeseer.nj.nec.com/song00practical.html.
6. R. Brinkman, L. Feng, J.M. Doumen, P.H. Hartel, and W. Jonker. Efficient tree search in encrypted data. *Information Systems Security Journal*, 13(3):14–21, July 2004. http://www.ub.utwente.nl/webdocs/ctit/1/000000f3.pdf.
7. Torsten Grust. Accelerating xpath location steps. In *Proceedings of the 21st ACM International Conference on Management of Data (SIGMOD 2002)*, pages 109–120. ACM Press, Madison, Wisconsin, USA, June 2002. http://www.informatik.uni-konstanz.de/~grust/files/xpath-accel.pdf.
8. A. R. Schmidt, F. Waas, M. L. Kersten, D. Florescu, I. Manolescu, M. J. Carey, and R. Busse. The XML Benchmark Project. Technical Report INS-R0103, CWI, Amsterdam, The Netherlands, April 2001. http://monetdb.cwi.nl/xml/index.html.

A   Appendix: XMark's Auction DTD

```
<!ELEMENT site            (regions, categories, catgraph, people, open_auctions, closed_auctions)>
<!ELEMENT categories      (category+)>
<!ELEMENT category        (name, description)>
<!ELEMENT name            (#PCDATA)>
<!ELEMENT description     (text | parlist)>
<!ELEMENT text            (#PCDATA | bold | keyword | emph)*>
<!ELEMENT bold            (#PCDATA | bold | keyword | emph)*>
<!ELEMENT keyword         (#PCDATA | bold | keyword | emph)*>
<!ELEMENT emph            (#PCDATA | bold | keyword | emph)*>
<!ELEMENT parlist         (listitem)*>
<!ELEMENT listitem        (text | parlist)*>
<!ELEMENT catgraph        (edge*)>
<!ELEMENT edge            EMPTY>
<!ELEMENT regions         (africa, asia, australia, europe, namerica, samerica)>
<!ELEMENT africa          (item*)>
<!ELEMENT asia            (item*)>
<!ELEMENT australia       (item*)>
<!ELEMENT namerica        (item*)>
<!ELEMENT samerica        (item*)>
<!ELEMENT europe          (item*)>
<!ELEMENT item            (location, quantity, name, payment, description, shipping, incategory+, mailbox)>
<!ELEMENT location        (#PCDATA)>
<!ELEMENT quantity        (#PCDATA)>
<!ELEMENT payment         (#PCDATA)>
<!ELEMENT shipping        (#PCDATA)>
<!ELEMENT reserve         (#PCDATA)>
<!ELEMENT incategory      EMPTY>
<!ELEMENT mailbox         (mail*)>
<!ELEMENT mail            (from, to, date, text)>
<!ELEMENT from            (#PCDATA)>
<!ELEMENT to              (#PCDATA)>
<!ELEMENT date            (#PCDATA)>
<!ELEMENT itemref         EMPTY>
<!ELEMENT personref       EMPTY>
<!ELEMENT people          (person*)>
<!ELEMENT person          (name, emailaddress, phone?, address?, homepage?, creditcard?, profile?, watches?)>
<!ELEMENT emailaddress    (#PCDATA)>
<!ELEMENT phone           (#PCDATA)>
<!ELEMENT address         (street, city, country, province?, zipcode)>
<!ELEMENT street          (#PCDATA)>
<!ELEMENT city            (#PCDATA)>
<!ELEMENT province        (#PCDATA)>
<!ELEMENT zipcode         (#PCDATA)>
<!ELEMENT country         (#PCDATA)>
<!ELEMENT homepage        (#PCDATA)>
<!ELEMENT creditcard      (#PCDATA)>
<!ELEMENT profile         (interest*, education?, gender?, business, age?)>
<!ELEMENT interest        EMPTY>
<!ELEMENT education       (#PCDATA)>
<!ELEMENT income          (#PCDATA)>
<!ELEMENT gender          (#PCDATA)>
<!ELEMENT business        (#PCDATA)>
<!ELEMENT age             (#PCDATA)>
<!ELEMENT watches         (watch*)>
<!ELEMENT watch           EMPTY>
<!ELEMENT open_auctions   (open_auction*)>
<!ELEMENT open_auction    (initial, reserve?, bidder*, current, privacy?, itemref, seller, annotation, quantity, type, interval)>
<!ELEMENT privacy         (#PCDATA)>
<!ELEMENT initial         (#PCDATA)>
<!ELEMENT bidder          (date, time, personref, increase)>
<!ELEMENT seller          EMPTY>
<!ELEMENT current         (#PCDATA)>
<!ELEMENT increase        (#PCDATA)>
<!ELEMENT type            (#PCDATA)>
<!ELEMENT interval        (start, end)>
<!ELEMENT start           (#PCDATA)>
<!ELEMENT end             (#PCDATA)>
<!ELEMENT time            (#PCDATA)>
<!ELEMENT status          (#PCDATA)>
<!ELEMENT amount          (#PCDATA)>
<!ELEMENT closed_auctions (closed_auction*)>
<!ELEMENT closed_auction  (seller, buyer, itemref, price, date, quantity, type, annotation?)>
<!ELEMENT buyer           EMPTY>
<!ELEMENT price           (#PCDATA)>
<!ELEMENT annotation      (author, description?, happiness)>
<!ELEMENT author          EMPTY>
<!ELEMENT happiness       (#PCDATA)>
```

An Authorization Framework for Sharing Data in Web Service Federations

Martin Wimmer and Alfons Kemper

Technische Universität München,
D-85748 Garching bei München, Germany
{martin.wimmer, alfons.kemper}@in.tum.de

Abstract. In this paper we present our authorization framework that supports the dynamic set-up of Web service federations for sharing data within virtual federations. Building on previous work, where we showed how the access control of Web services can be consolidated with the access control of the underlying database systems, we focus on the delegation of trust across administrative boundaries, thus enabling inter-organizational collaboration. In order to restrict the flow of (possibly sensitive) access control information, authorization proceeds as an interplay of local and distributed policy enforcement. Scalability and performance of distributed policy enforcement are provided through caching techniques, which have to ensure strong cache consistency.

1 Introduction

In areas like e-science, e-business, and e-health, inter-organizational collaborations are becoming more and more prevalent. Thereby, tightly and loosely coupled systems are differentiated. Considering e-health, an example for a tightly coupled system is a collaboration network built of hospitals for providing shared access on medical records. Collaboration might also be established and again be terminated dynamically, i.e., in a loosely coupled manner. As an example consider the exchange of therapy results for testing new medications for a research project. These scenarios have in common that data has to be shared among users of different organizations participating in a collaboration network. As each organization is considered to act autonomously regarding the management of its data, the dynamic setup of database federations with a consolidated schema is inflexible and can hardly be realized. Service oriented architectures (SOAs) provide a remedy for this integration task. As SOAs are based upon widely adopted Web service standards, they are well suited for the integration of heterogeneous applications supplied by different providers.

Providing access on data within a Web service federation poses two challenges on access control. On the one hand, access control of the Web service interfaces has to be consolidated with the security policies of the underlying database systems. On the other hand, inter-organizational privilege delegation and policy enforcement have to be realized.

W. Jonker and M. Petković (Eds.): SDM 2005, LNCS 3674, pp. 47–62, 2005.

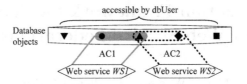

Fig. 1. Illustration of access corridors (AC1 and AC2)

Foregoing Work. When Web services are used as interfaces for database systems, access control proceeds in two stages. First, the authorization of requests is checked on the side of the Web services, e.g., by employing security standards and protocols like SAML, XACML and WS-Security. Second, when services execute queries, access control is performed by the underlying database systems. In the general case, these authorization steps are done independently. With regard to this, we presented engineering techniques addressing the consolidation of the access control frameworks for Web services and databases in [1]. We further introduced a partial order on policies, allowing the verification of access control dependencies, i.e., ensuring that database policies embrace the access rights required by the depending Web services. Mainly due to restrictions of SQL, access control provided by database systems is not as fine-grained as required by today's (Web) applications. By proceeding the way as described in [1], effective security gatekeepers for database systems can be realized on the application layer.

A central aspect of the access control consolidation is the adjustment of database profiles. Today it is common practice to access databases via powerful (and potentially dangerous) super-user accounts. This might be reasonable for large software installations like SAP R/3 running within closed trust domains. But at the latest if data is made accessible via lightweight software components like Web services, the same does not hold. Figure 1 illustrates an abstract example of two services that access the same database. Each service requires only access to an extract of the database content, expressed via the access corridors AC1 and AC2. As both corridors overlap, it seems preferable to use the account dbUser for both applications. In case of services or the service platform being attacked, information not provided through the service interfaces will also be accessible, e.g., ▼ and ■ in the figure. We avoid this risk by automatically generating adequate database profiles from the service specifications and policies. Thus, we follow the least privilege principle according to which accounts are only granted those privileges needed to provide the service functionality.

Focus of This Contribution. Based on our previous work for the reliable design of Web service interfaces for database systems, we concentrate on our authorization framework that enables the set-up of tightly as well as loosely coupled collaboration networks. Our approach relies on an interplay of local and distributed policy enforcement. While local authorization enforces policies within one closed trust domain, distributed authorization is required for verifying privilege and role assignments that span several organizations. In order to optimize distributed policy enforcement, i.e., reduce communication costs and achieve low execution times, we devise a caching strategy for the goal-oriented validation of assignments. As authorizations must not succeed based on outdated cache entries, we employ caching techniques that provide the required strong cache consistency and analyze them with regard to their applicability in the authorization context. The tight integration of these techniques in our Web service platform ServiceGlobe [2] supports the secure sharing of data in Web service federations.

Document Structure. The remainder of this paper is structured as follows: In Section 2 the employed notation and policy representation is introduced. In Section 3 the algorithms for local and distributed policy evaluation are described. The optimization of distributed policy evaluation through caching is shown in Section 4. Related work is presented in Section 5 and Section 6 provides a summary of the paper.

2   Policy Representation

2.1   Notation

Privilege assignments define relations between principals (the subjects) and resources (the objects). In our authorization model any access is denied unless a privilege granting a certain type of access can be inferred. This so-called closed world assumption in combination with positive authorization is reasonable for modeling access control of dynamic collaboration networks with trust relationships being existent only temporarily.

The assignment of an access right to a subject is represented by use of the following notation:

$$[\texttt{Subject} \rightarrow_P \texttt{Privilege}]_{\texttt{Condition}} \ \texttt{Issuer} \tag{2.1}$$

A `Privilege` summarizes information about a particular resource and the way it can be accessed. An Issuer is an entity that is granted the administrative rights to declare an assignment. The validity of an assignment can further depend on a `Condition` like a temporal constraint. But it is also possible to define constraints on the `Subject`'s context. For example, the access to the medical record of a certain patient can be restricted to his/her attending physicians. In addition to this common discretionary access control model, we integrated role based access control (RBAC [3]) concepts in our authorization framework. Privileges are associated with roles through privileges-to-roles assignments in the meaning of assignment (2.1) with the subject being a `Role`. Subjects are granted privileges through the indirection of assigning roles to them. As roles constitute subjects themselves, hierarchical RBAC is realized, too. Similar to the previous assignment, role assignments can be constrained as well:

$$[\texttt{Subject} \rightarrow_R \texttt{Role}]_{\texttt{Condition}} \ \texttt{Issuer} \tag{2.2}$$

Assignments (2.1) and (2.2) support a static rights management. The following assertions enable the delegation and revocation of privilege and role assignments, which provide a dynamic rights management.

$$[\text{Subject} \rightarrow_P^{(\text{assign}|\text{revoke})} \text{Privilege}]_{\text{Condition}} \text{ Issuer} \qquad (2.3)$$

$$[\text{Subject} \rightarrow_R^{(\text{assign}|\text{revoke})} \text{Role}]_{\text{Conditon}} \text{ Issuer} \qquad (2.4)$$

Prefix notation is used to denominate organization affiliations of subjects, roles and privileges. In the case of the subject's affiliation varying from the granted privilege's one, we talk about an inter-organizational privilege assignment or delegation. Analogous considerations apply to the assignment of roles. The right to assign a privilege, respectively role, to a subject does not presuppose the issuer to possess the privilege (role) himself/herself. A self-assignment can be prohibited via appropriate conditions.

Though entities in the subsequent examples are represented by names (e.g., Kerry Weaver as a subject or physician as a role), the introduced access control model is not restricted to identities. In general, an entity, i.e., a subject or an object, is described via a set of attributes. To give an example, physicians are characterized by their names, field of activity, social security number (SSN), age and so on. Thus, if Kerry Weaver is a chief physician at the Cook County General Hospital (CCG), the following role assignment may be used:

$$[\{\text{name} = \text{K.Weaver} \wedge \text{SSN} = 1234\} \rightarrow_R \{\text{role} = \text{CCG.ChiefPhysician}\}] \text{ CCG}$$

2.2 Implementation Details

The above notation constitutes a representation of the rights management we realized in our authorization framework. We chose XACML [4,5] as policy language for several reasons. One is its usability in the Web services context as both, XACML and the Web services technology, are based upon XML. Thus, no new terminology or processing technology is required. Moreover, the introduced formal notation can seamlessly be realized in XACML. We distinguish three types of policies.

- *Permission policies* specify access rights, i.e., objects and the way they can be accessed. They are not restricted to certain subjects. Subcategories of this type of policy exist for the assignment, respectively revocation of privileges and roles. In these cases, other permission policies (i.e., privileges) or roles constitute the objects and actions are in {assign, revoke}.
- By means of *base policies*, privileges (defined as permission policies) are assigned to subjects. Thus, this type of policy is used to express assignments (2.1), (2.3) and (2.4).
- *Role assignment policies* are used to assign roles to subjects in the meaning of assertion (2.2).

The strict separation of privilege definitions and their assignment to users, respectively roles, enable the system's scalability: The administrative effort is kept at a low level and the rights management remains concise and flexible. We integrated the described policy management into our research Web service platform ServiceGlobe. ServiceGlobe [2] is a lightweight, distributed and extensible Service Oriented Architecture. It is completely implemented in Java and based on standards like XML, SOAP, WSDL and UDDI. Services in ServiceGlobe are mobile code that can be executed on arbitrary service hosts participating in the ServiceGlobe federation. Access control functionality is supplied by separate authorization components provided by the service platform. So-called Delegation Services supervise the policy repositories of organizations, provide the functionality for privilege and role delegation, respectively revocation, and can be used to evaluate authorization requests.

3   Policy Evaluation

We distinguish between local and distributed authorization. In case subject s of organization D_s, denoted $D_s.s$, invokes a Web service of organization D, first of all the policies of D are evaluated. This is what we refer to as local policy evaluation. If the requested access cannot be granted solely based on the access control information available at D, it is checked whether D and D_s are part of a collaboration network which grants $D_s.s$ the required privileges. As we do not rely on central authorities, i.e., each organization administers and enforces access rules locally, this step refers to distributed policy evaluation.

3.1   Local Policy Evaluation

Local policy evaluation is employed to check whether a subject $D_s.s$ is granted a privilege (to execute a respective Web service) within a closed trust domain D, based only on D-local access rules. As introduced in the previous section, the policies of D are separated into three categories: permission policies, base policies and role assignment policies. Thus, local policy evaluation proceeds in three steps:

1. Determine the set of local roles $\mathcal{R}^{(l)}$ that are granted to $D_s.s$, defined as

$$\mathcal{R}^{(l)} \stackrel{def}{=} \{D.r \mid D.r \text{ is a role} : \exists \left[D_s.s \to_R D.r' \right]_c X, \text{ with } D.r' \succeq D.r\}$$

   In the above equation, X is a placeholder for an issuer and c for a condition. Through $\succeq$ a partial order on roles is defined. $D.r' \succeq D.r$, iff every privilege that is granted to D.r is also granted to D.r'. On the other hand, every subject that possesses the role D.r' is implicitly granted the role D.r, too. In the terminology of role hierarchies [3], D.r' is said to be a senior role of D.r. In return, D.r is called a junior role of D.r'.
2. Determine the set $\mathcal{P}$ of privileges that are granted to $D_s.s$ directly or to any role $r \in \mathcal{R}^{(l)}$.

3. If any privilege $D.p \in \mathcal{P}$ applies, the request is permitted. Thereby, $D.p$ applies to the request req, iff $D.p$ addresses a resource that includes or is equal to the resource addressed by req and the action allowed by $D.p$ is equal to or more comprehensive than the action expressed by req.

3.2 Distributed Policy Evaluation

Collaboration networks are established by assigning roles and/or privileges to entities of foreign trust domains. For example, if two organizations D and D′ intend to collaborate, roles and/or access rights of organization D are assigned to principals (i.e., subjects like users or roles) of D′ and vice versa. As mentioned before, the respective assignment policies are administered and enforced at the organization that is the owner of the granted privileges and roles. Consequently, access control for collaboration networks relies on distributed policy evaluation that proceeds as follows:

1. First of all the set $\mathcal{P}$ of privileges that grant the requested service execution is determined.
2. Authorization will succeed, if $D_s.s$ possesses a role that is granted at least one of the privileges in $\mathcal{P}$ and which is defined in a trust domain that cooperates with D. Let $\mathcal{R}$ be the set of roles that fulfill these requirements, defined as

$$\mathcal{R} \overset{def}{=} \{D_i.r_i \mid D_i.r_i \text{ is a role}, D_i \neq D, \exists D.p \in \mathcal{P} : [D_i.r_i \rightarrow_P D.p]_{c_i} X \vee$$
$$(\exists D.r \text{ is a role} : [D_i.r_i \rightarrow_R D.r]_{c_i} X \wedge [D.r \rightarrow_P D.p]_{c'} X')\}$$

X and X′ represent arbitrary issuers and c_i, c' conditions of assignments. $D.r \rightarrow_P D.p$ stands for the assignment of the privilege $D.p$ to $D.r$, whereby $D.p$ is granted to $D.r$ either directly (referring to assertion (2.1) in Section 2.1) or via role inheritance according to the D-local role hierarchy. For each $D_i.r_i \in \mathcal{R}$ it is checked whether the role is assigned to $D_s.s$.
3. In case this assumption holds for any $D_i.r_i$, authorization succeeds. In order to verify this, the Delegation Service of organization D_i is queried, which evaluates the policies of D_i. This proceeds analogously to a D_i-local policy evaluation that either succeeds or requires further distributed evaluation.
   (a) If successful, the Delegation Service of D_i returns a positive response and the initial request for executing D's Web service can be granted.
   (b) Otherwise, the set $\mathcal{R}_i^{(f)}$ of roles that are granted $D_i.r_i$ or any senior role of $D_i.r_i$ is determined. $\mathcal{R}_i^{(f)}$ is defined as

$$\mathcal{R}_i^{(f)} \overset{def}{=} \{D_f.r_f \mid D_f.r_f \text{ is a role}, D_f \neq D_i \wedge$$
$$[D_f.r_f \rightarrow_R D_i.r_i']_c X \text{ with } D_i.r_i' \succeq D_i.r_i\}$$

Distributed evaluation branches by invoking the Delegation Services of the trust domains D_f with $D_f.r_f \in \mathcal{R}_i^{(f)}$. The services are called, querying whether $D_s.s$ is granted $D_f.r_f$. Each of these invocations can lead to further distributed policy evaluation calls, i.e., step 3 can be executed repeatedly.

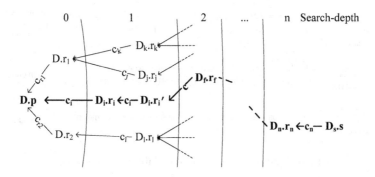

Fig. 2. Graphical representation of distributed evaluation

The evaluation terminates at organization D_i, in case of $D_i.r_i$ being assigned to $D_s.s$ or the set $\mathcal{R}_i^{(f)} = \varnothing$. A chain of distributed role assignments that applies to the subject $D_s.s$ is called *authorization path*. If at least one authorization path exists, the execution of the Web service of D requested by $D_s.s$ is permitted.

Distributed policy evaluation thus corresponds to a browsing of a distributed role hierarchy. As illustrated in Figure 2, this is equivalent to a backwards oriented depth first search (DFS) in the distributed role assignments graph, with roles constituting the nodes of the graph and the edges being annotated with conditions. In other words, there is a directed edge from $D_f.r_f$ to $D_i.r_i'$ annotated with c, if and only if there exists a role assignment policy $[D_f.r_f \rightarrow_R D_i.r_i']_c X$. An increase of the search-depth proceeds by invocations of collaborating Delegation Services. It can be assumed that real-world collaborations tend to have a quite short delegation depth, denoting that collaboration networks are likely to span only few trust domains. At the same time, organizations tend to directly cooperate with other organizations. Consequently, a breadth first search (BFS) algorithm is supposed to be particularly suitable by providing lower response times than DFS. Unfortunately, a BFS-variant can hardly be realized due to the distributed characteristics of the graph. For BFS, the role assignment graph either has to be traversed with an initial depth bound that is increased successively – which would lead to higher network traffic –, or the complete access control information has to be available at a central authority, which would contradict security considerations of loosely coupled systems. Techniques for enhancing the evaluation process are discussed in more detail in Section 4.

Sensitivity of access control information is also the reason for the pull characteristic of distributed policy evaluation. According to the pull model, the requestor provides only his/her identifying attributes (and/or context information), i.e., $D_s.s$, while his/her privileges are determined by the framework. On the other hand, following a push model, $D_s.s$ would have to provide all security credentials that are required to execute the particular Web service in advance. These security credentials for example consist of the public keys of the roles $D_s.s$ possesses. On the one hand $D_s.s$ has to know which set of keys is required for executing the service method. This information has to be provided by the

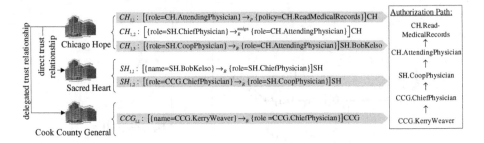

Fig. 3. Example of a hospital collaboration network

Web service but can only be given to D_s.s under the precondition of D_s.s being trusted. D_s.s (or the application calling the service acting in D_s.s' place) on the other hand has to provide the required security credentials. In general, these have to be collected in a distributed manner, as storing all role information with D_s.s would contradict RBAC principles. In our approach, the service platform is responsible for verifying the authorization based only on D_s.s' identity and context information.

3.3   Example Evaluation

Figure 3 illustrates an example of a hospital collaboration network. The Chicago Hope Hospital (CH), the Sacred Heart Hospital (SH) and the Cook County General Hospital (CCG) form a federation that allows physicians to read medical records of patients that are housed in collaborating hospitals, e.g., the Chicago Hope Hospital. This privilege is represented through the permission policy CH.ReadMedicalRecords. Figure 3 shows an extract of the access control rules. For keeping the example concise, we disregarded further conditions, like the restriction that only medical records of patients that agreed to publish their data within the federation would be accessible. The policies contain rules for the organization spanning assignment of roles. Rule $CH_{1,2}$ states that chief physicians of SH are allowed to delegate the role CH.AttendingPhysician, which is applied by rule $CH_{1,3}$. Through $SH_{1,2}$ this role is assigned to chief physicians of the CCG and, according to $CCG_{1,1}$, also to Kerry Weaver. If Kerry Weaver requests to read a medical record of a patient housed at the Chicago Hope Hopital, the authorization chain $CCG_{1,1}$, $SH_{1,2}$, $CH_{1,3}$ to $CH_{1,1}$ has to be traversed in reverse order. Foremost, as local evaluation at CH fails, the roles that are granted CH.ReadMedicalRecords are determined. This applies to CH.AttendingPhysician. As Kerry Weaver is not granted the role based on the local policies, the Delegation Service of SH is invoked, querying whether she possesses the role SH.CoopPhysician. Again, this cannot be answered SH-locally, so that the Delegation Service of CCG is invoked, asking for the assignment of CCG.ChiefPhysician. Due to $CCG_{1,1}$ the request is granted.

3.4   Inter-organizational Assignments

Collaboration networks based on Web services technology can be highly dynamic. This especially applies to short-term interactions. ServiceGlobe as the underlying authorization middleware provides the required level of flexibility through the support of inter-organizational assignments. Privileges for the assingment or revocation of access rights or roles are expressed via permission policies in the meaning of assertions (2.3) and (2.4) in Section 2.1. If a subject $D_{s1}.s1$ intends to assign the privilege D.p (respectively role D.r) to a subject $D_{s2}.s2$, it invokes the Delegation Service of D. If $D_{s1}.s1$ is authorized, particular policies are generated. In case of a privilege assignment, a base policy representing $[D_{s2}.s2 \rightarrow_P D.p] D_{s1}.s1$ is created. A role assignment is represented through a role assignment policy $[D_{s2}.s2 \rightarrow_R D.r] D_{s1}.s1$.

Revocations of assignments lead to the deletions of the respective policies. We distinguish between conservative and destructive revocation. If, for example, $D_{s1}.s1$ revokes the role assignment $[D_{s2}.s2 \rightarrow_R D.r] D_{s1}.s1$, only the associated role assignment policy will be deleted in case of conservative revocation. If the destructive approach is applied, it is analyzed if D.r authorizes to delegate roles or privileges, and every applied assignment will be revoked, too. Consequently, the destructive approach cascades and involves the reorganization of the policy repositories of the cooperating organizations, in general. Beneath its complexity, destructive revocation might not be used depending on the application, e.g., if an administrative officer of a hospital, who was responsible for the arrangement of attending physicians, retires, his/her assignments shall not get lost.

A policy repository has to be modified exclusively, i.e., has to be locked in case of updates. Otherwise, concurrency can cause inconsistencies. Considering two requests with the first one performing a delegation of any role r, while the second initiates the revocation of the respective delegation permission, isolation of requests has to be ensured to avoid conflicts.

For some applications it might be required that (long-lasting) inter-organizational transactions perform a rollback if any required privilege is revoked in the meantime. This is realized by integrating Delegation Services into the transaction workflow. Prior to the start of a particular transaction, authorization proceeds as described above. Before the services commit, access control is performed once again, e.g., by verifying the authorization path that was found during the initial authorization check. If authorization fails, the Delegation Service sends an abort message to the coordinator, initiating a rollback of the transaction.

4   Caching of Authorization Paths

The described policy enforcement technique performs a DFS on the distributed role assignment graph. Thus, in the worst case the complete collaboration network has to be analyzed sequentially. While long execution times of unsuccessful policy enforcements might be tolerable, successful authorizations have to proceed as quickly as possible. Most collaborations can be assumed to span only few organizations, i.e., role assignment chains are rather short. However, as outlined before, BFS can hardly be applied as the distributed role assignment graph cannot be provided at a central authority in order to preserve autonomy of authorization and ensure scalability. But the response times of the DFS variant can be reduced substantially through parallelizing the search, i.e., asynchronously querying the Delegation Services of cooperating organizations. Unfortunately, lower response times then have to be traded for an increase of network traffic. Both objectives, i.e., low response times and low network traffic can be obtained by caching authorization paths of frequently and/or recently used requests. More precisely, paths cached at a domain D look as follows:

$$\left\langle D_s.s \xrightarrow{c_n} D_n.r_n \xrightarrow{c_{n-1}} D_{n-1}.r_{n-1} \dots \xrightarrow{c_1} D_1.r_1 \xrightarrow{c} D.r \right\rangle$$

This represents the delegation chain that asserts that the role $D.r$ is assigned to the subject $D_s.s$ – if the conditions $\{c_n, c_{n-1}, \dots, c_1, c\}$ are fulfilled. Such a cache entry is created when $D_s.s$ invokes a Web service of D for which the privileges of $D.r$ are required and $D_s.s$ is granted $D.r$. We refer to a Delegation Service as a client, in case it consumes information, i.e., caches results of authorization queries. If a Delegation Service returns successful evaluation results that can be cached at collaborating organizations, the service is characterized as a server.

Caches are evaluated prior to a distributed policy evaluation query. If $D_s.s$ requires privileges that are granted to $D.r$, the cache entries starting with $D_s.s$ and ending with $D.r'$ are determined. In this regard, $D.r'$ has to be a senior role of $D.r$ or equal to $D.r$, i.e., $D.r' \succeq D.r$. Thus, not only exact matches can be handled. If no applicable path is found, distributed policy evaluation takes place as described above. Caching of access control information requires strong cache consistency [6], meaning that authorization must not succeed based on outdated, i.e., invalidated access control information. In the following we describe three strategies that ensure strong cache consistency and are thus applicable for caching authorization paths.

4.1   Client Validation

Client validation denotes that client-Delegation Services have to ensure the validity of cached entries. Therefore, a cache hit, i.e., an applicable authorization path, is validated before authorization succeeds. Considering the introduced formal representation of a delegation path, the Delegation Service of D first checks whether $D_1.r_1 \xrightarrow{c} D.r$ is still valid by evaluating the D-local policies and the requestor's context ($D.r$ is assigned to $D_1.r_1$ via a D-local role assignment policy). Subsequently, the evaluation is continued at the Delegation Service of D_1 for verifying the next extract of the authorization path ($D_2.r_2 \xrightarrow{c_1} D_1.r_1$) and so on. Verification succeeds, if every assertion of the delegation path holds. Otherwise, the authorization path is removed from the cache and further applicable entries of the cache are evaluated, i.e., validated. Common distributed policy evaluation proceeds if no applicable entry could be validated.

Compared to the introduced DFS-like distributed policy enforcement, the validation of authorization paths significantly reduces run time. Client validation in the authorization context differs from common Web caching scenarios: In the general case, the location of the requested Web content remains unchanged and performance there is enhanced by reducing data transfer. Here, execution time is saved as the validation of authorization paths corresponds to a goal-oriented "walk" through the distributed role assignment graph, rather than a complete browsing of the graph in the worst case.

According to the above description, a cache entry represents a complete delegation path. This design enables the efficient validation of cache entries, but it requires that all cooperating organizations agree in the exchange of access control information. In many cases, this assumption holds, because the cooperating organizations are supposed to trust each other. Nevertheless, the information flow is kept at minimum by caching authorization path fragments of the form $\langle D_s.s \twoheadrightarrow D_1.r_1 \xrightarrow{c} D.r \rangle$ at D. As the assignment $D_1.r_1 \xrightarrow{c} D.r$ is contained in the repository of D, no security relevant data disperses to other organizations. The complete authorization path is restored by starting a goal-oriented search at D_1. The Delegation Service of D_1 either determines the subsequent fragment of the authorization path in its local cache, or – in the worst case – triggers distributed policy enforcement. With this modification, caching within dynamic collaboration networks, with trust being existent only temporarily, is enabled.

4.2 Server Invalidation

When using server invalidation, Delegation Services inform adjacent clients in case of policy updates that lead to an invalidation of cache entries. Therefore, a Delegation Service has to log the requests of clients that received positive authorization responses. A modification of policies must not proceed before all affected cache entries have been invalidated and the invalidation has been acknowledged by the clients. Consequently, this approach is vulnerable regarding the unreachability of services, e.g., because of network failures. This clearly disqualifies this caching technique for highly dynamic federations.

One further disadvantage of server invalidation is its limited scalability. A Delegation Service has to log requests of clients, in order to notify them of policy updates. But as in most use cases the size of collaboration networks is restricted, this is not considered to be a crucial drawback.

4.3 Lease-Based Approach

Lease-based caching [7] is situated between client validation and server invalidation. A lease is a contract between client and server-Delegation Service. The server asserts not to modify the administered access control policies as long as the lease is valid. After the lease has expired, this task is shifted to the client. When updating policies, a server has to wait until each client has acknowledged the invalidation of cache entries, or in case of any of them being unreachable, until the respective leases have expired. Consequently, the lease-based approach is parameterizable by the validity periods of leases. Setting them close to zero, it behaves quite similar to client validation. On the other hand, server invalidation is approximated by setting the periods near infinity. Thus, depending on the parametrization, the pros and cons of client validation and server invalidation more or less apply to this caching technique, too.

4.4   Experimental Results

To the best of our knowledge, there do not exist any standardized benchmarks for measuring and comparing the performance of caching access control information. Therefore, we developed several test cases varying the dimensions (i.e., width and depth) of collaboration networks, the frequency of policy updates, and the request characteristics. Due to space limitations, we only present experimental results regarding the variation of the request characteristics. Figure 4 illustrates the results of a benchmark that was performed varying the relation of local and distributed policy enforcement. p is the proportion of requests that are handled by local policy evaluation. We simulated a static collaboration network with branching degree 2 and maximum delegation depth 5. That means, every domain represented by a Delegation Service delegates trust to 2 other domains and the maximum length of role delegations is 5. Thus, a network of 63 collaborating organizations was simulated.

The benchmark was performed on ServiceGlobe installations running on a cluster of 2.8 GHz Intel Xeon systems with up to 4GB of main memory. For the test scenario we measured the performance of authorization when no caching, client validation, and server invalidation were used. The performance of the lease-based approach depends on the expiration period of leases and resides between the performance of client validation and server invalidation. Therefore, results for this kind of caching technique are not listed for the following experiments. On average, the execution of a Delegation Service lasted 650ms. About 30% of this time are required for local policy evaluation and cache examination (with policies and caches being realized as XML documents), while the predominant amount is needed for service loading and initialization.

In the experiment, 50 different request types were simulated with $p \cdot 50$ positive access rules being inserted in the topmost policy repository, i.e., a portion of p requests require local policy evaluation. The $(1 - p) \cdot 50$ access rules that apply to the remaining part of request types were inserted in the other repositories according to a Zipf distribution. When sorting the levels of the collaboration network according to the frequency with which access rights are assigned to them, Zipf's law states that the frequency of rights being assigned to a level l ($\mathrm{frq}\,(l)$) is inversely proportional to its ranking following a power law: $\mathrm{frq}(l) \sim 1/l^{\alpha}$. Typically, $\alpha \in [0, 1]$. A uniform distribution is modeled through $\alpha = 0$, while a highly skewed distribution is achieved at $\alpha = 1$. By setting $\alpha = 0.85$, we simulated a scenario with the predominant part of requests being authorized after a few delegation steps, while only some require the enforcement of policies of the undermost policy repositories. For each value of p, 2000 requests were posted to the root Delegation Service and the mean evaluation time was determined.

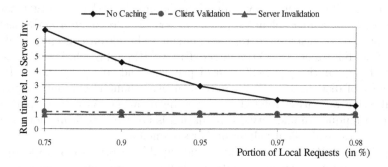

Fig. 4. Variation of the request characteristic

The 2000 requests are separated into clusters of those requiring local policy evaluation and those requiring distributed policy evaluation with a ratio of p to $(1-p)$ – analogously to the distribution of access rights. For each cluster, the request types were chosen according to a Zipf distribution with $\alpha = 0.85$, as the authors of [8] showed that Zipf-like distributions are useful for modeling the request characteristics of many Web applications.

In contrast to the caching of arbitrary Web content, the space requirements for the caching of authorization paths can be estimated quite well in advance. Thus, cache replacement strategies are of minor interest and were not considered in these experiments. In many real-world applications, p is assumed to be quite close to 1. Figure 4 illustrates the performance measurements relative to the results for server invalidation. As the presented experimental results show, response times for requests requiring distributed policy enforcement can be reduced significantly, thus justifying the use of authorization caches.

5 Related Work

There has been substantial effort in the research community for providing security for distributed applications. The Community Authorization Service (CAS) [9] of the Globus Project manages access control for resources that are available within larger communities. The CAS plays the part of a central authority. In contrast to this, our framework is suitable for both, centralized and decentralized authorization. We presented our algorithm for distributed policy evaluation, supporting loosely coupled systems. Tightly coupled federations building upon centralized authorization can seamlessly be realized by shifting policy enforcement to a trusted authority, thus breaking authorization down to local policy enforcement. The CAS uses a push model for inferring granted access rights, while we use a pull model to determine the roles and privileges that are granted to users. A pull model is also used in Akenti [10] that is related to X.509 certification technique. Policies, conditions, and attribute statements can be encapsulated into certificates. Akenti allows access control for one resource to be administered by multiple authorities. Our framework supports this through delegation privileges, but policy evaluation remains the task of the organizations the respective resource belongs to, thus preserving autonomy of authorization. Our approach for distributed role assignment is based on concepts similar to those of the RT-framework [11] and the dRBAC [12] approach. We adapted the syntax of [12] for the representation of privilege and role assignments. In [12] complexity of distributed policy enforcement was countered through a publish-and-subscribe algorithm related to server invalidation. As our comparison of caching techniques shows, server invalidation is not well applicable for dynamic federations. Instead, client validation is recommended.

Jajodia et al. [13] present a flexible and capable security framework supporting positive and negative authorization. They introduce conflict resolution techniques as they are also provided by XACML [4,5]. Both, XACML and the Web services technology are based upon XML. Thus, its integration into the security system of a service platform that is based on SAML [14] and/or WS-Security [15] like the one of ServiceGlobe is supported. As our formal notation can seamlessly be realized in XACML we chose it as policy language and extended it by integrating database specific object types and functions for attribute comparisons and the evaluation of conditions. In earlier work [1] we presented a technique for comparing XACML policies. More details and a definition of a partial order on policies are presented there.

6   Conclusion and Future Work

The Web services technology provides the basis for sharing data in organization-spanning collaboration networks and future database related applications are likely to be realized as distributed Web service federations. But the sharing of data requires a capable and flexible security system coping with authorization within tightly and especially loosely coupled collaboration networks. This is offered by our authorization framework that can be applied for both types of federation systems. By employing a central authority responsible for administering the resources within a virtual organization through performing access control in a centralized manner, tightly coupled federations are realized. We also presented an algorithm for distributed, i.e., decentralized policy enforcement. This allows the set-up of loosely coupled federations with trust relationships being established only temporarily. Thereby, the flow of information within the federation is restricted and the collaborating organizations preserve their authorization autonomy by policies being administered and evaluated locally. In order to optimize distributed policy enforcement, we devised caching strategies that allow the efficient evaluation of frequently and repeatedly occurring authorization requests – again by ensuring a minimum flow of information.

Future research proceeds in the following directions: On the one hand, caching of authorization paths is examined further, e.g., by the evaluation of different cache replacement strategies and usage of cryptography for securing cache entries. On the other hand, we intend to examine negative authorization, i.e., the evaluation of prohibitions in the context of loosely coupled federations.

References

1. M. Wimmer, D. Eberhardt, P. Ehrnlechner, and A. Kemper, "Reliable and Adaptable Security Engineering for Database-Web Services," in *Proceedings of the Fourth International Conference on Web Engineering*, vol. 3140 of *Lecture Notes in Computer Science (LNCS)*, (Munich, Germany), pp. 502–515, July 2004.
2. M. Keidl, S. Seltzsam, K. Stocker, and A. Kemper, "ServiceGlobe: Distributing E-Services across the Internet (Demonstration)," in *Proceedings of the International Conference on Very Large Data Bases (VLDB)*, (Hong Kong, China), pp. 1047–1050, Aug. 2002.
3. D. F. Ferraiolo, R. Sandhu, S. Gavrila, D. R. Kuhn, and R. Chandramouli, "Proposed NIST standard for Role-Based Access Control," *ACM Trans. Inf. Syst. Secur.*, vol. 4, no. 3, pp. 224–274, 2001.
4. T. Moses, A. Anderson, A. Nadalin, B. Parducci, D. Engovatov, *et al.*, "eXtensible Access Control Markup Language (XACML) version 2.0." http://www.org/committees/tc_home.php?wg_abbrev=xacml (last visited 06/20/05), Dec. 2004.
5. A. Anderson, "Core and Hierarchical Role Based Access Control RBAC Profile of XACML version 2.0." http://www.oasis-open.org/committees/tc_home.php?wg_abbrev=xacml (last visited 06/20/05), Sept. 2004.
6. L. Y. Cao and M. T. Özsu, "Evaluation of Strong Consistency Web Caching Techniques," *World Wide Web*, vol. 5, no. 2, pp. 95–124, 2002.
7. C. Gray and D. Cheriton, "Leases: An Efficient Fault-tolerant Mechanism for Distributed File Cache Consistency," in *Proceedings of the Twelfth ACM Symposium on Operating Systems Srinciples*, pp. 202–210, ACM Press, 1989.
8. L. A. Adamic and B. A. Huberman, "Zipf's Law and the Internet," *Glottometrics*, vol. 3, pp. 143–150, 2002.
9. L. Pearlman, I. F. V. Welch, C. Kesselman, and S. Tuecke, "A Community Authorization Service for Group Collaboration," in *3rd International Workshop on Policies for Distributed Systems and Networks (POLICY)*, (Monterey, CA, USA), pp. 50–59, IEEE Computer Society, June 2002.
10. M. R. Thompson, A. Essiari, and S. Mudumbai, "Certificate-based Authorization Policy in a PKI Environment," *ACM Trans. Inf. Syst. Secur.*, vol. 6, no. 4, pp. 566–588, 2003.
11. N. Li, J. C. Mitchell, and W. H. Winsborough, "Design of a Role-based Trust Management Framework," in *Proc. IEEE Symposium on Security and Privacy*, (Oakland), pp. 114–130, May 2002.
12. E. Freudenthal, T. Pesin, L. Port, E. Keenan, and V. Karamcheti, "dRBAC: Distributed Role-Based Access Control for Dynamic Coalition Environments," in *Proceedings of the Twenty-second IEEE International Conference on Distributed Computing Systems (ICDCS)*, (Vienna, Austria), pp. 411–420, July 2002.
13. S. Jajodia, P. Samarati, M. L. Sapino, and V. S. Subrahmanian, "Flexible Support for Multiple Access Control Policies," *ACM Trans. Database Syst.*, vol. 26, no. 2, pp. 214–260, 2001.

14. S. Cantor, J. Kemp, R. Philpott, and E. Maler, "Assertions and Protocols for the OASIS Security Assertion Markup Language (SAML)." `http://www.oasis-open.org/committees/tc_home.php?wg_abbrev=security` (last visited 06/20/05), Mar. 2005.

15. A. Nadalin, C. Kahler, P. Hallam-Baker, R.Monzillo, *et al.*, "Web Services Security (WS-Security)." `http://www.oasis-open.org/committees/tc_home.php?wg_abbrev=wss` (last visited 06/20/05), Mar. 2004.

User-Managed Access Control for Health Care Systems

Amir H. Chinaei and Frank Wm. Tompa

School of Computer Science,
University of Waterloo, Canada
{ahchinaei, fwtompa}@uwaterloo.ca

Abstract. The requirements and technologies supporting shared health record databases pose new access control challenges. This paper proposes a decentralized access control system in which corporate policy can allow all health record owners to administer access control over their own objects, and at the same time, all objects are reasonably secure. We exploit various concepts of Rule Based Access Control, Role Based Access Control, XML structures, and object databases in our model.

1 Introduction

The complex base of sensitive objects in health record databases poses new access control challenges. Much work has been done to address access control problems. However in practice, there are several factors that affect access control efficiency in health care systems. First, health records are sensitive personal objects that should be secure all the time yet easily accessible to authorized subjects in emergency situations. Second, querying the access control mechanism must be relatively fast even in non-emergency cases. Third, similar to other applications, access control in health care must be provided for the access control specification itself. Fourth, delegating privileges must be efficiently controllable and selectively revocable; patients often and temporarily have to reveal their personal data to particular appropriate parties such as physicians, hospitals, and laboratories.

User-Managed Access Control (UMAC) in medical record databases is required when several parties, usually without administrative control over one another, need to share the medical data. UMAC reduces the bottleneck of access administration in situations where health data is distributed among various parties.

This paper considers access control within a large shared medical document server. Such an environment entails a decentralized access control administration within which each subject possesses two faces: the administrator of its own objects, and at the same time, a user of others' objects. With their administration face, subjects require full access control over their own objects, but as users they are typically licensed to more limited levels of access. The problem is complicated when the hierarchy of subjects is not consistent with the hierarchy of objects. In other words, subjects (e.g. technicians) may have access to many small parts of objects (their patients' relevant personal data). Moreover, accessible domains of various subjects

W. Jonker and M. Petković (Eds.): SDM 2005, LNCS 3674, pp. 63–72, 2005.
© Springer-Verlag Berlin Heidelberg 2005

form diverse structures that should be recognized for optimization purposes. For instance, a physician's accessible data mainly consists of a collection of disconnected nodes each of which corresponds to a particular patient treated in various clinics; while, a technician's accessible data is basically medical data of patients treated in a particular laboratory.

Delegation is a significant open issue, which is not well addressed in the literature of decentralized medical data administration. Data administrators (e.g. medical data owners) often need to delegate some of their privileges to other users (e.g. other health care parties). Furthermore users may delegate their privileges to third parties, but the owners of the data must be able to efficiently control access with selective revocation. This means that the UMAC mechanism must enforce owners' arbitrary restrictions.

An access control matrix [20] is the underlying logical model for implementing access control. We exploit the *role* concept of Role Based Access Control (RBAC) to group particular operations on the matrix. More specifically, since roles map a many-to-many relationship between subjects and objects, assigning either a new subject or object to a role is one operation corresponding to multiple operations on the access data.

The major contribution of this work is our UMAC model for very large systems such as health care document servers. We provide access control flexibility and efficiency for environments in which hundreds of thousands of subjects and objects exist. We assume that users may belong to groups and that groups of users may belong to higher level groups in a hierarchy. We also assume that objects are arranged in a "part of" hierarchy and that roles are arranged in an inheritance hierarchy. To establish a dynamic model in which some operations are done implicitly, we exploit *rules* to define both the hierarchies and the assignments of subjects or objects to roles. Also, to control delegation, we exploit import/export mechanisms to support role inheritance. To the best of our knowledge, such a UMAC model for medical environments has not been addressed in the literature.

We propose a flexible model for decentralized administration by which health care organizations are able to adjust the central power by defining precisely what actions are to be taken centrally. At one end of the spectrum, access control can be completely anarchistic, with the owners of each item of data maintaining complete control over which subjects may access that data using which methods. At the other end, access control can be absolutely autocratic, with a central administrative authority dictating which subjects may access which objects. We assume a central mechanism that enforces access control policies defined by arbitrarily many subjects but does not necessarily dictate those policies itself.

The rest of this paper is organized as follows. Section 2 reviews the literature of access control models. In Section 3, the specification of the UMAC model is discussed. Section 4 illustrates our model by focusing on a use case for medical records. Finally in Section 5, our contributions and future work are discussed.

2 Literature Review

Access control enforcements are traditionally divided into Discretionary Access Control (DAC) and Mandatory Access Control (MAC). While DAC concerns predefined (by users) discretionary rules and access control based on users' identity, MAC is mainly based on the classification of subjects and objects in a system; in such environments, access control rules are decided by only the system policies not by the owners of objects. Both DAC and MAC frameworks have been of interest to researchers, and they have been supported by later models as well. In this section, we review the literature of access control based on mechanisms, administration, granularity, and properties.

Access control mechanisms are required to enforce access control policies. An access control model is conceptually viewed as maintaining an access control matrix [20], which is a function with three components: *subject*, *right*, and *object*. Despite its popularity due to simplicity and elegance, an access control matrix is actually an abstract formulation, and needs to be refined for many practical systems. A major approach is to implement the access control matrix implicitly by rules [11, 13]. Also, the Take-Grant model [15] based on directed graphs is another improved version of the matrix model, which provides a compact way of representing the access control data as well as supporting the transfer of rights. Typically, the access control matrix is large and sparse. Hence, storage techniques such as access control lists and capabilities improve the storage efficiency. For example, the Compressed Accessibility Map (CAM) is an enhanced technique based on capability lists [25]. The CAM algorithms exploit structural locality of subjects' accessibility on hierarchical data to construct a more efficient representation.

The administration of access control manages subjects' activities to enforce access control policies. MAC is an example of fully centralized administration. The Multilevel Security model [2] is a well-known MAC model, which has been used over the years. MAC has no flexibility, and it is not applicable when subjects or objects may not be classified to a limited number of groups.

Regardless of whether the access control structure is centralized or distributed, administration for DAC may still be centralized or decentralized. For example, RBAC is a mechanism that typically provides central administration of access control for an organization [22]. The central administration is implemented by defining roles, which correspond to the job titles of the organization. Although RBAC can be used to model arbitrary DAC systems, the decision of which subjects and objects are to be assigned to which roles is centrally controlled. This not only causes a potential efficiency bottleneck when new subjects and objects are added to the system, but it restricts the subjects' ability to manage the access controls themselves. If there were truly decentralized Discretionary Access Control, owners would fully manage the formation of groups and roles and the assignment of rights without interfering with one another and without requiring a centralized administration to update the access control structure.

Since the first publication of the RBAC model [8], many researchers have investigated various issues of RBAC, such as the roles hierarchy [1, 7, 14] and separation of duties [5, 17, 19]. Furthermore, some enhancements have been proposed to the RBAC model for distributed environments [21, 24]. There have been several restrictions on the use of RBAC in practice. First, it is not normally suggested for applications in which a natural roles hierarchy does not exist. Second, delegation and revocation are not clearly discussed in the RBAC literature. Scalability in the number of subjects and objects is also a problem due to the central administration of the model.

Decentralized access control mechanisms were first proposed for System R to permit users to share and control their data in multi-user databases systems [12]. However, it does not support negative rights nor provide an expressive revocation algorithm. Later, a more powerful model was proposed for relational data management systems [3], but it is too complex to be practical.

Access control granularity, in the context of a hierarchically organized database, refers to the extent to which different levels of access can be defined on objects or parts of objects. Fine-grained access control manages access rights on small pieces of objects. Many proposed models [11, 13, 15, 20] assume access control at the object level only and ignore any internal structure within objects. However, if objects entail a hierarchy, the distinction between objects and sub-objects becomes meaningful. Jones examined an object-level access control model for client-server object databases [16]. He provided a fine-grained access control model, which supports navigating the data structure by inter-object references. Also Zhou introduced access control vectors and slabs for fine-grained access control based on a code-based scheme to represent a more compact structure for control data [26].

To evaluate whether an access control instance conforms to an access control policy, one may check the mechanism's properties such as safety, invulnerability, no-information-flow, non-interference, and revocation [2, 4, 9, 10]. The safety property is defined as the determination of whether or not a given subject can ever acquire a particular right on a given object [13]. For example, both Graham-Denning and Harrison-Ruzzo-Ullman models have weak safety properties [11, 13]. Introducing strong typing into the latter model, the typed access control matrix model has stronger safety properties [23]. As another example, retaining a limited expressive power, the Take-Grant model does not exhibit the undecidable safety of the Harrison-Ruzzo-Ullman model [15].

3 Problem Specification

We wish to design an access control system for health care systems in which the decentralization degree is adjustable anywhere from completely anarchistic to absolutely autocratic; and of course, all users' sensitive documents must remain secure. Our model exploits different concepts such as roles, rules, XML structure, and object databases. Similar to RBAC, our model consists of three layers; each is a Directed Acyclic Graph namely SDAG, ODAG, and RDAG corresponding to subjects, objects, and a layer of roles, respectively.

We concentrate on RDAG in which nodes correspond to the roles, and edges represent an inheritance hierarchy among the roles. A role is a special object containing a set of privileges on a set of objects. For instance, in Figure 1, role r_3 contains a privilege to run method M_1 on document d1 with grant option (+). The set of objects is determined by rules, e.g. specified as XPath expressions that identify components of the data represented in XML. The licensing hierarchy between roles (indicated by arrows) represents implicit privileges, which are imported from "senior" roles (higher in the hierarchy). RDAG is an intermediate graph between subjects and objects; on one hand, a set of subjects (either individual users or groups) from SDAG is assigned to each node of RDAG (indicated by dot-dashed lines). On the other hand, each role contains a set of permissions on a set of objects of ODAG (indicated by dashed lines). We note that objects can be of any type (with arbitrary associated methods), including documents or document fragments, groups in the subject hierarchy, or even roles.

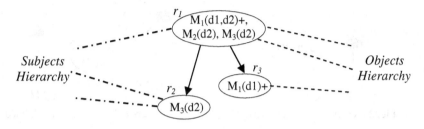

Fig. 1. Roles Hierarchy

In practical environments, including those in the health care sector, there are several characteristics that lead to useful refinements of the model. For instance, if individual users create personal documents, the number of roles in a system may become quite large, yet many of them are similar. We assume that every object belongs to an owner, and thus an owner role is always required for each object: this can be initiated parametrically. As another characteristic, some roles should be predefined by the system, and at the same time, the model should provide subjects with the feature of customizing roles. The following features express facilities of our model in more detail:

Generic Role: This facility is to define a template for a set of possible roles. To derive an actual role from this template, a specific event acts as a trigger. For example, the *owner role* (indicated by black ovals in Figures 2 and 3) is a generic role, which is instantiated as soon as a subject creates an object; subject id and object id are the parameters of the instantiation. Based on this generic role, every subject who creates an object is assigned to a concrete owner role in which all methods on the object are permitted with grant option. Figure 2a illustrates this facility, where subjects S1 and S2 are assigned to the owner roles when they create objects d1 and d2, respectively. There is no administrative superiority in this feature since neither S1 nor S2 can disrupt each other's actions.

Predefined Role: There exist some primitive roles in the system. For example, to reduce the number of roles, our model provides a *public role* to which every subject is automatically assigned and which imports all permission from any role above it in the hierarchy. If owners want their objects to be accessible by everyone, they can connect their owner role as a super-role of the public role and export exactly those permissions they wish to grant on their objects. In this way, all users inherit the designated access rights via the role hierarchy. In Figure 2b, S1 and S2 will put the licenses for their public objects in the *public role*, and thereby make them accessible to all subjects, by connecting their owner role to the public role but only exporting a subset of the methods on objects d1 or d2, respectively, as desired. Thereafter, S1 or S2 can remove access to their objects from the *public role* or change the permissions on their objects whenever needed by changing what is exported or by severing the connection completely. Hence, neither S1 nor S2 has superiority over the other; and once the system has been initiated, there is no centralized control.

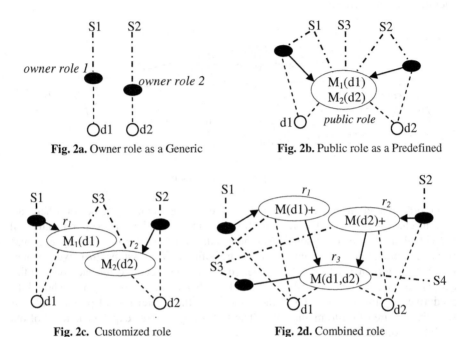

Fig. 2a. Owner role as a Generic   **Fig. 2b.** Public role as a Predefined

Fig. 2c. Customized role   **Fig. 2d.** Combined role

Customized Role: Besides the generic and predefined roles, all subjects are able to create their own customized roles. Every subject can choose an arbitrary subset of the permissions in its owner role to create a customized role, and then assign arbitrary subjects to this role. More generally, any subject assigned to a fertile role, i.e., one in which some permissions have grant option, may create a new sub-role with a subset of the fertile permissions and assign other subjects to that new role. Customized roles thus form the role hierarchy, in which owner roles are the roots. For instance, any physician may customize the privileges assigned to the physicians group to create a particular role for nurses. In Figure 2c, owners S1 and S2 have created roles r_1 and r_2 to access objects d1 and d2, respectively. They both have assigned user S3 to these roles. Therefore, S3 has access to both d1 and d2. S1 or S2 can remove S3's access at any time, independently. Again, neither S1 nor S2 has superiority over the other, and there is no centralized control.

Combined Role: Subjects can create a combined role if they have inheritable permissions in more than one role. In other words, a combined role is a role, which has more than one immediate senior role. In health care systems, an accountant may combine several roles to make several medical objects accessible to an insurance representative. In Figure 2d, owners S1 and S2 have created fertile roles (i.e. with delegation permissions) r_1 and r_2 to access objects d1 and d2, respectively; both S1 and S2 are willing to export permissions on their documents. They have also assigned subject S3 to their roles. Therefore, S3 can create r_3 and inherit (import) access permissions on both d1 and d2. Moreover, S3 can assign other subjects (e.g. S4) to r_3. Both S1 and S2 can remove access privileges for S3 and its dependents (e.g. S4) from their objects by severing the inheritance chain without disrupting one another. For example, S1 (the owner of r_1) can remove access for S3 and S4, from d1 simply by removing both edges S3$\rightarrow$ r_1 and $r_1\rightarrow$ r_3. Therefore, r_3 no longer inherits anything from r_1.

We have created an XML schema to represent roles and assignments, and we have developed the principal update algorithms needed for our proposed model. (These are omitted from this paper because of insufficient space.)

4 Use Case

In this section, we illustrate our model through a use case focused on a typical medical record database. This application has been mainly inspired from the XACML use cases [6, 18]; however, we have adapted it to reflect a more decentralized application environment.

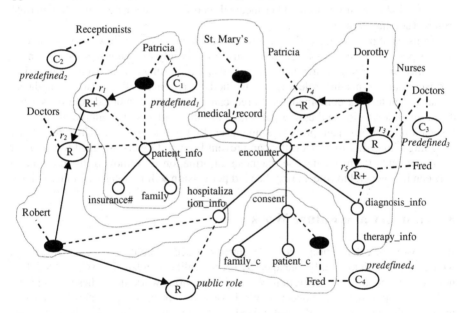

Fig. 3. UMAC for Health Care Systems

Figure 3 illustrates how features explained in Figure 2 are applied in this application. For readability, we omit the subject hierarchy from the illustration. Dotted boundaries highlight the ownership domains within which each subject creates and controls a part of the health record database.

We assume that St. Mary's Hospital is the owner of medical records; however, elements of a medical record may belong to different owners such as patients or doctors. Patricia is a patient in our example. She, similar to any other user, has been initially assigned to role *predefined$_1$* so that she can copy (create) her personal information in the system as a new patient. When she needs to see a doctor, she creates her personal information together with role r_1, and assigns receptionists of St. Mary's Hospital to this role. Then, by exploiting role *predefined$_2$*, receptionist Robert serves Patricia's request and creates her hospitalization information (such as room number and arrival date) and, using the grant permission in role r_1, also creates role r_2 for doctors to read her request; besides, he exports read permission on Patricia's hospitalization information to the public role, which is accessible to all subjects. Then, doctor Dorothy attends to Patricia, and creates her diagnosis information using role *predefined$_3$*. As the doctor in charge, Dorothy creates role r_3 for other doctors and nurses to read Patricia's diagnosis information. Dorothy also creates role r_4 to prevent Patricia from reading it herself. Notice that if Patricia is a doctor or a nurse, conflict resolution should ensure that she will be prevented from reading this record. The consent section is used for granting informed consent, which should not be modified once it has been written. According to hospital policy, a member of Patricia's family, namely Fred, can read her medical records if he signs (creates) an informed consent. Upon creating the informed consent (using role *predefined$_4$*), Fred will be able to read Patricia's medical record by being assigned to role r_5. Fred is also able to allow others, including Patricia, to read her medical records by creating a new role inherited from r_5 (not diagrammed).

In this example, we have shown how corporate policy can allow various subjects such as patients, receptionists, doctors, and patient family to administer access control over different parts of a medical record. Every time an item of data is created, a corresponding ownership role with all methods is automatically created or updated. As an example of a combined role, Fred can create one combined role on several diagnoses information and assign Patricia to see them all. As an example of selective revocation, Dorothy can prevent some user U from seeing Patricia's record by assigning him or her to r_4. Dorothy can prevent Fred and others assigned to role r_5 or its descendents from reading the diagnosis information by removing the connection between the ownership role and r_5; the read permission will no longer be inherited.

5 Summary and Future Work

In this work, we have proposed a decentralized access control system, UMAC, in which access to data is fully managed by users. Unlike standard RBAC, UMAC does not require a central administration. We enrich previous work along these lines [3] by including object database concepts. We have also introduced four classes of roles, namely generic, predefined, customized, and combined, through which UMAC provides suitable capabilities for very large systems. To support our model, we have developed primary access control algorithms, as well as an XML schema representing the roles hierarchy. We have also applied our model to enforce access control policies in a medical records application. As a further part of our research, we developed a simulator by which we can generate and evaluate various instances of the UMAC model and a variety of implementation structures. Using our simulator, we are performing some tests on real data.

We propose several directions for continuing this research. The first is to develop an efficient (space) data structure, flexibly managed by users. Designing corresponding efficient (speed) access control algorithms will be the major contribution of this work. A second direction is conflict resolution and rule reorganization as major issues in establishing access rules.The next contribution would be developing a delegation framework for efficient controls and flexible revocation. This is particularly important when the access administration is not central; since without centralization it is hard to maintain adequate safety and accountability properties.

Acknowledgement. We gratefully acknowledge the Natural Science and Engineering Research Council of Canada, Communications and Information Technology Ontario, Open Text Corporation, and the University of Waterloo for their financial support.

Bibliography

1. M. A. Al_Kahtani and R. Sandhu. Induced Role Hierarchies with Attribute-Based RBAC. In *Proc. of the 8th ACM Symposium on Access Control Models and Technologies*, pp. 12-20, June 2003.
2. D. Bell and L. LaPadula. *Secure Computer System: Unified Exposition and Multics Interpretation*. Technical Report, ESD-TR-75-306, The MITRE Corp, March 1976.
3. E. Bertino, S. Jajodia, and P. Samarati. A Flexible Authorization for Relational Data Management Systems. *ACM Transactions on Information Systems*, vol. 17, no. 2, pp. 101-140, April 1999.
4. K. J. Biba. *Integrity Considerations for Secure Computer Systems*. Technical Report, ESD-TR-76-372, USAF Electronic Systems Division, April 1977.
5. R. A. Botha and J. H. P. Eloff. Separation of Duties for Access Control Enforcement in Workflow Environments. *IBM Systems Journal*, vol. 40, no. 3, pp. 666-682, 2001.
6. S. Damodaran and C. Adams. XACML- Summary of Use Cases. http://xml.coverpages.org/RLTC-XACML-Reqs200207.pdf. 2001.
7. D. F. Ferraiolo, G. J. Ahn, R. Chandramouli, and S. I. Gavrila. The Role Control Center: Features and Case Studies. In *Proc. of the 8th ACM Symposium on Access Control Models and Technologies*, pp. 12-20, June 2003.
8. D.F. Ferraiolo and D.R. Kuhn. Role Based Access Control. In *Proc. of the 15th NIST-NCST National Computer Security Conference*, pp. 554-563, October 1992.
9. R. Focardi and R. Gorrieri. Non Interference: Past, Present and Future. In *Proc. of DARPA Workshop on Foundations for Secure Mobile Code*, 1997.
10. J. Goguen and J. Meseguer. Security Policy and Security Models. In *Proc. of the 1982 IEEE Symposium on Security and Privacy*, pp. 11-20, IEEE Computer Society Press, April 1982.
11. G. S. Graham and P. J. Denning. Protection - Principles and Practice. In *Proc. of AFIPS Spring Joint Computr Conference, vol. 40,* 1972.
12. P. P. Griffith and B. W. Wade, An Authorization Mechanism for a Relational Database System, *ACM Transactions on Database Systems*, vol. 1, no. 3, pp. 242-255, 1976.
13. M. A. Harrison, W. L. Ruzzo, and J. D. Ullman. Protection in Operating Systems. *Communications of ACM*. vol. 19, no. 8, August 1976.
14. W.A. Jansen. Inheritance Properties of Role Hierarchies. In *Proc. of the 21st NIST-NCSC National Information Systems Security Conference*, October 1998.

15. A. K. Jones, R. J. Lipton, and L. Snyder. A Linear Time Algorithm for Deciding Security. In *Proc. of Foundations of Computer Science '76*, pp. 33-41, IEEE, 1976.
16. V. E. Jones. *Access Control for Client Server Object Databases*. Ph.D. Thesis, Department of Computer Science, University of Illinois at Urbana-Champaign, 1997.
17. J. B. D. Joshi, and B. Shafigh. Dependencies and Separation of Duty Constraints in GTRBAC. In *Proc. of the 8th ACM Symposium on Access Control Models and Technologies*, pp. 51-64, June 2003.
18. M. Kudo. Use Cases for Access Control on XML Resources. http://www.oasis-open.org/committees/xacml/docs /UseCase.doc. 2001.
19. D.R. Kuhn. Mutual Exclusion of Roles as a Means of Implementing Separation of Duty in Role-Based Access Control Systems. Second ACM Workshop on Role-Based Access Control, pp. 23-30, November 1997.
20. B. W. Lampson. Protection. In *Proc. of the 5th Annual Princeton Conference on Information Sciences and Systems*, pp. 437-443, March 1971.
21. J. S. Park, and J. Hwang. Role-based Access Control for Collaborative Enterprise in Peer-to-Peer Computing Environments. In *Proc. of the 8th ACM Symposium on Access Control Models and Technologies*, pp. 93-99, June 2003.
22. R. Sandhu. Lattice-Based Access Control Models. *IEEE Computer*. vol. 26, no. 11, pp. 9-19, November 1993.
23. R. Sandhu. The Typed Access Matrix Model. In *Proc. of the IEEE Symposium on Security and Privacy*, pp. 122-136, 1992.
24. H. F. Wedde, and M. Lischka. Cooperative Role-Based Administration. In *Proc. of the 8th ACM Symposium on Access Control Models and Technologies*, pp. 21-32, June 2003.
25. T. Yu, D. Srivastava, L. V. S. Lakshmanan, and H. V. Jagadish. Compressed Accessibility Map: Efficient Access Control for XML. In *Proc. of Very Large Data Bases*, pp. 478-489, August 2002.
26. D. Zhuo. *On Fine-Grained Access Control for XML*. Master's Thesis, School of Computer Science, University of Waterloo, 2003.

Specifying an Access Control Model for Ontologies for the Semantic Web*

Cecilia M. Ionita and Sylvia L. Osborn

Dept. Of Computer Science,
The University of Western Ontario,
London, Ontario, Canada
cionita@uwo.ca/sylvia@uwo.ca

Abstract. Security and privacy are important components of the Semantic Web; the need for research in this area is widely recognized. In this paper we propose a model that regulates access control on ontologies developed for the Semantic Web. Based on the Role Graph Model, our work models the ontology resources as directed, acyclic graphs, incorporating the basic features of the OWL Lite language. We also show how the privileges are propagated and how we can use constraints to deny access to resources in the Semantic Web, an environment where information can be easily accessed through logic inferences.

1 Introduction

The World Wide Web has grown dramatically over the last few years. By 2002 there were around a billion Web users and a higher number of available documents [9]. This growth makes it difficult to find, access and maintain information to be available for users. The content of the World Wide Web today is mostly processed by humans via natural language. To overcome problems related to accessing and processing the information, Tim Berners-Lee introduced the Semantic Web concept, envisioned as an extension to the current web, where information is represented in a way so that it can be easily understood and manipulated by machines on a global scale. The Semantic Web is described as an environment in which the "web of links" is transformed into the "web of meaning". It is meant to be accessible and comprehensible to automated software agents without human intervention. In order to achieve its goal, the Semantic Web lays its foundation on some already well-known technologies like XML, as well as several new ones like ontologies, RDF (Resource Description Language), etc.

The increasing need to protect data on the web, especially personal information, has raised the issue of security and privacy for the Semantic Web, an environment based on extensive data interconnection and information retrieval tools. Research is concentrating on developing a well-understood model and language for expressing access control. The semantic web is based on XML technologies,

---

* This research was supported by the Natural Sciences and Engineering Research Council of Canada.

W. Jonker and M. Petković (Eds.): SDM 2005, LNCS 3674, pp. 73–85, 2005.

therefore it is only natural to find access control models also based on the ones developed for XML documents. However, specifying access control requirements for subjects and objects based only on predicates and identifiers is not enough because we have to consider also the metadata defined in the ontologies that describes them.

In this paper we propose an access control model that defines authorizations on the elements of ontologies that are used to describe information about subjects and objects in the Semantic Web environment. We will begin in Section 2 by making a summary of the related work that investigates security within the Semantic Web. Section 3 describes basic concepts relevant to this research area as well as to this paper. In Section 4 we describe our access control model and define the authorization propagation rules. Section 5 summarizes the paper and presents future research.

2 Related Work

We will start by mentioning papers regarding XML access control, since the most important Semantic Web security models are based on XML technology. There are several authorization-based access control models. In [19], an authorization model is built for distributed hypertext systems. Here the authorization can be specified at different granularity levels, based on data types and their relationships. In [4], Damiani et al. proposed another access control model for XML documents and DTDs using a special authorization sheet attached to them. Their model is extended in [5] where an access control system is introduced to specify access restrictions to Web documents. Bertino et. al. in [2] proposed an XML-based language, X-Sec, for defining subject credentials and security policies needed for Web document protection. In [1], a content-based authorization model is defined in the context of Digital Libraries to describe specific access control requirements for this environment.

Some of these authors extended their research in the Semantic Web security area. There are some attempts to adopt XML-based data exchange formats and protocols from distributed systems by the Semantic Web. Some examples are XML digital signatures [8], XML encryption [7] and X.509 Public Key certificates [11]. In the area of authorization specification in the Semantic Web environment, we mention some important papers from the last few years. In [10] the authors proposed a language for describing security policies and trust information based on ontology languages. Denker et al. focus the work in [6] on DAML web services. They introduced a framework for annotating web services with security information and also developed security-based ontologies to describe and exchange security requirements for these services. In [17] an access control model is proposed based on the concepts described in ontologies and the relationship between them. The authors also introduced a Semantic Access Control Language based on OWL for specifying security policies. Kagal et al., in [13], introduced a security framework based on a semantic policy language and also a distributed policy management system for authentication and access control. An XML based security engine is proposed in [21] to identify undesirable disclosed data due to ontology-based inference attacks. In [14], Kim et al. argues the need for a privacy ontology and stresses that trust and security must be built into the Semantic Web to protect personal information.

3 Basic Concepts

3.1 The Role Graph Model

The Role Graph Model [15] is an access control model whose basic functionality is similar to the one described in the RBAC model developed by Sandhu et al. [20]. The entities used in this model are users, roles and privileges. They are grouped into three planes: the user/group plane contains the Group Graph [16] in which one can model users, groups and the relationships between them, the role plane where roles and role-role relationships are defined, and the privilege plane which allows one to model implications among privileges. A privilege is considered the basic unit of authorization. It is defined as a pair (object, access mode) where the object is defined according to the context in which the security model is being applied. For example, in an object-oriented environment an object would be a class or a set of instances. An access mode is any valid operator or method on the object, such as read or write. The role plane contains the Role Graph which defines the relationships between roles. The nodes of this graph represent the roles defined as a set of privileges. A role is represented by a pair (name, pset) giving the name of the role and its set of privileges respectively. There are two types of privileges assigned to a role: the direct privileges are the ones that are not inherited from any other role in the graph and the effective privileges are the union of all the direct and inherited privileges of a role. The edges in the graph represent the is-junior relationship. Role r_i *is-junior* to r_j iff r_i.pset $\subset r_j$.pset.

The Role Graph has the following properties: it is acyclic, directed, there is a single MaxRole that contains all privileges from all the roles and there is a single MinRole which contains the minimum set of privileged assigned to any user. There is always a path between every role and MaxRole and MinRole. There is a path from role r_i to r_j iff r_i.pset $\subset r_j$.pset. Role graph design is managed through a set of algorithms defined in [15]. Algorithms are given for role and edge addition/deletion and privilege addition/deletion to/from a role. All of the algorithms run in time polynomial in the size of the role graphs and the privilege sets.

Role Models are ivery useful because it is easy to manage the assignments of users to privileges by grouping the latter into roles, therefore allocating a large number of privileges in one step. Another advantage of RBAC is that when a user ceases to need the privileges in a role, they can all be deleted at once by removing the user from the role.

3.2   Ontologies

Ontologies, one of the Semantic Web's important components, help embed common meanings and relationships of terms across different structures making possible semantic interoperability. Their use brings to search engines numerous improvements in retrieving precise information as well as computing results based on related data and specific inferences. Ontologies are meant to be used by people and applications in order to share domain specific vocabularies in domains such as medicine, finance, etc.

The OWL Web Ontology language is probably the most complex tool developed so far to define ontologies. OWL is a language that helps design Web-based ontologies for an easier integration of information between communities. It is developed to be understood by computer applications and not by humans. OWL is based on RDF Schema [22] but it is has a stronger syntax for defining properties and classes. As part of its vocabulary we mention a few examples: class equivalence (owl.equivalentClass), cardinality (owl:minCardinality), transitivity (owl:TransitiveProperty), etc.

4   An Access Control Model

In this section we define an access control model that applies to the ontology elements in a Semantic Web environment. As part of building this new technology, incorporating security is very important. In the Web of today or in any relational database management system, we have to deal with a large number of resources and information related in a syntactic way and not semantically. This is why all the inferences are made manually at the user level. On the contrary, the Semantic Web will contain the resources semantically linked so that a software agent will be able to easily obtain information making use of logic inferences and knowledge management. In such an environment the need to integrate security as soon as possible becomes obvious.

In order to create a model that controls the access to the resources, we use the concepts from the Role Graph model and OWL features and apply them to the ontology structures created with this ontology language. In this paper we will use the Lite version of OWL in order to incorporate the basic functionalities of the language. We plan to extend our work as future research by taking into consideration the more advanced features of OWL DL and Full.

We start by briefly introducing the characteristics of the OWL Lite language that will be integrated into our model. The two basic terms are classes and properties which are both considered resources. A class denotes a group of individuals grouped together on the basis of some common properties. Classes can be organized into hierarchies using rdfs:subClassOf . Two classes can be defined to be equivalent using equivalentClass. There is one special class called Thing which is the superclass of all OWL classes and another one called Nothing which is the subclass of all OWL classes.

Properties are used to define relationships between individuals or between individuals and data types. They can also be organized into hierarchies using rdfs:subPropertyOf and they can also be defined to be equivalent using equivalentProperty. The property characteristics that we are taking into consideration are: inverse of a property, transitive property, symmetric property, functional property and inverse functional property.

The reasons why we chose the Role Graph Model as the best alternative for an access control model in the Semantic Web environment are:

- Both the Role Graph Model and the OWL language structure their elements in similar ways. In the context of the Role Graph Model, it is very natural to add additional hierarchies represented by directed acyclic graphs.
- The Role Graph Model performs well in environments with large number of users and privileges, which is the case with the Semantic Web.
- The management of the assignment of privileges to users is very easy because of the use of roles that facilitates the allocation of an arbitrary number of privileges in only one step.

Let us start defining the basic concepts of our access control model.

4.1 Authorization Users

The Semantic Web content will be mostly accessed and processed by machines and software agents that are also called reasoners. Their capabilities of inference are the biggest security concern. The users of today's Web will also access the information on the Semantic Web. Both agents and human users should be considered to be authorization users, based on their identities and location, as described in [5].

4.2 Roles

A role is composed a pair consisting of the role name and the set of privileges assigned to that role. Figure 1 contains an example of a role graph in a company environment containing roles like HR Manager, Engineer, Project Leader, etc.

4.3 Access Modes

As we have stated in Section 2, a privilege is defined as a pair consisting of the authorization object that is being accessed and the access mode or operation. The types of access modes for XML documents are very restrictive. Some papers consider only reading and authoring [3] as access modes while others also include update and extend operations [23]. Some of these access modes are also suitable for OWL documents since OWL's language syntax is based on XML. In our paper we consider read and extend as valid operations. Their meaning is reading elements of an ontology and extending an ontology with classes or properties. In addition we add a new operation specific to the Semantic Web context, called reason. Assigning this access mode gives the user permission to access elements that are inferred through a reasoning operation. The access modes are organized

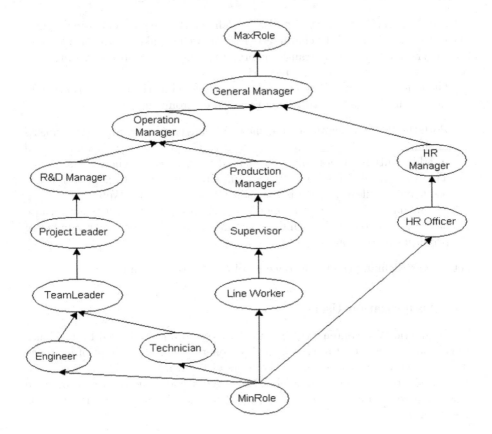

Fig. 1. Example Role Graph

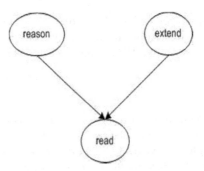

Fig. 2. Access Mode Graph

into a graph (called the authorization type graph in [23]), where an edge from the extend operation to the read operation means that holding the privilege to extend a given object *o* implies also having the privilege to read the same object *o*. The graph containing the operations for this paper is given in Figure 2.

4.4   Authorization Objects

The resources, namely classes and properties, are the authorization objects in OWL ontologies. Following the model of the Role Graph, we structure the resources into graphs. In this case we have to build two graphs, one for the ontology classes called the Class Graph and one for the ontology properties called the Property Graph. The characteristics of these structures are:

- both graphs are directed and acyclic
- there is a Thing resource as a superclass to all the OWL resources
- there is a Nothing resource as a subclass to all the OWL resources
- an edge in the Class Graph going from class c_1 to class c_2 has the meaning that c_1 is a subclass of c_2 and c_2 is a superclass of c_1.
- an edge in the Property Graph going from property p_1 to property p_2 has the meaning that p_1 is subproperty of p_2 and p_2 is superproperty of p_1.

The last two characteristics come as a natural modeling of the rdfs:subClassOf and rdfs:subPropertyOf features from the OWL Lite language that represent the basic relationship between two classes and properties, respectively.

The nodes of the Class Graph can contain more than one class when these classes are related through the equivalentClass feature. For example, we can model the Car and Vehicle classes as equivalent and put them both in the same node of the Class Graph. The same principle applies to the Property Graph using the equivalentProperty feature. As an example we and have hasMarks and hasGrades as two equivalent properties in the same node.

In the beginning of this section we introduced briefly the property characteristics that we will include in our model. Here is a more detailed description of them and some examples:

inverseOf defines a property p_1 as the inverse of another property p_2. For example, trains and isTrainedBy are the examples of two inverse properties.

TransitiveProperty defines transitive properties. For example, supervises can be defined as transitive, because if John supervises Laura and Laura supervises Peter, then a reasoner can infer that John supervises Peter, too.

SymmetricProperty defines two properties as symmetric. For example, colleague is a symmetric property because if John is the colleague of Laura, then it can be deduced that Laura is the colleague of John.

FunctionalProperty defines properties that have a unique value for each individual. For example, hasStudentNo is a functional property.

InverseFunctionalProperty defines a property as an inverse of a functional property. Considering the above example, we can say that isStudentNo is an inverse functional property of hasStudentNo property.

Our objective is to incorporate these features into our model, more precisely into the Property Graph. In order to do this we have to extend the definition of this graph by adding to each property node an indicator that holds the type or types of that property. Its value corresponds to one of the five characteristics defined above.

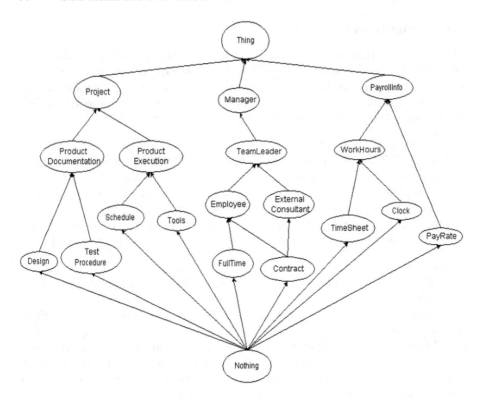

Fig. 3. Example Class Graph

Using the above definitions, we can specify a privilege as a pair of authorization object and access mode, where the authorization object is made of one or both of the resources (classes and properties) depending on the degree of the security restriction we want to enforce.

Figures 3 and 4 contain examples of a Class Graph and a Property Graph respectively, representing a part of an ontology defined for a company structure and the activities of the company.

We can see that the class graph in Figure 3 shows the isSubclassOf information about several kinds of objects which might be part of the description of the security requirements of the company. It deals with company employee classes as well as company artifacts like project schedules, project documentation and payroll administration data.

As we can see in Figure 4, some properties have attached a special indicator specifying one or more types. The properties situated in one node, with no indicator, are defined as equivalent. An example of this is entersDataIn and inputDataIn. Properties contained in a node with an IP indicator mean that they are the inverse of each another; in the example, reportsTo and supervises are inverse properties. The property worksWith is symmetric and isPartOf is an example of a transitive property.

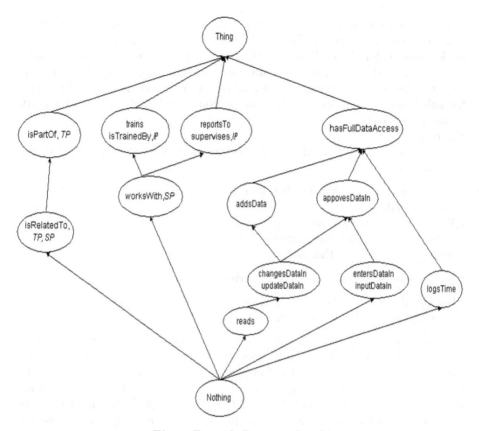

Fig. 4. Example Property Graph

As we said before, these properties represent the relationships between classes. For example we can have statements like: "Manager hasFullDataAccess on PayrollInfo", "TeamLeader trains Employee", "Design isPartOf Product Documentation", "Employee reportsTo TeamLeader", etc. Using the access modes defined in Figure 2, examples of privileges are: (Manager, Read), ((Manager, hasFullDataAccess), Read), ((Product Documentation, isRelatedTo), Reason), (supervises, Read), etc. When we assign the privilege (Manager, Read) to a user through a role, it means that the user is allowed to read any information about the Manager class. If the privilege is ((Manager, trains), read), then a user who has this privilege can read information about the training carried out by Managers. If the privilege ((Product Documentation, isRelatedTo), Reason) is assigned to a role, then any user or software agent assigned to this role can reason about how objects of type Product Documentation are related to each other.

4.5   Propagation of Privileges

The propagation policies are very similar to the ones defined for the Role Graph Model. Users assigned to a role have, within their effective privileges, two kinds of privileges associated. One kind deals with access modes and how they relate to classes. The other kind deals with the properties of the classes, and the access modes allowed for these. These are the explicit authorizations associated with a user. In addition to these, there are two sets of implicit authorizations that can be deduced by the system. This kind of authorization is computed through the subclass and subproperty relationships from the Class Graph and Property Graph respectively.

Example 1:

Let us assume we have the following example privileges set assigned to the Supervisor role:

{ ((TeamLeader, approvesDataIn), Read),
(Design, Read),
((Workhours, isPartOf), Reason),
((Contract, changeDataIn), Extend),
(ProductionExecution, Extend) }

Also assume our ontology has the following statements:

"TeamLeader approvesDataIn Timesheet" and
"TeamLeader addsData Workhours"

Is a person assigned to the Supervisor role allowed to see both statements in the ontology about the TeamLeader? From the set of privileges in the Supervisor role, we can see that a Supervisor has a Read access mode on the TeamLeader class and the approvesDataIn property, and a Reason access mode on the WorkHours class. From the Class Graph we see that TimeSheet is a subclass of WorkHours, meaning that the Reason access mode propagates to the TimeSheet class as well. From the Access Modes Graph we know that the Reason access mode implies a Read access mode. Therefore, we can easily deduce that the Supervisor role also has a Read access mode on the TimeSheet class. That means that a Supervisor can see the first statement in our example.

For the second statement above, the Supervisor has a Read access mode on the TeamLeader and WorkHours class but no authorization on the addsdataIn property. That means that Supervisors cannot see the information from the second statement.

Example 2:

As another example, let us suppose we have the same privileges in the Supervisor role and the following statements in our ontology:

"TeamLeader approvesDataIn Workhours"
"Timesheet isPartOf WorkHours"
"WorkHours isPartOf Payrolll"

It can be easily seen that the Supervisor can see the first statement. For the second statement, we know from the set of privileges that our role has the Reason access mode on the Workhours class and the isPartOf property. As we have shown above, from the Class Graph we can infer that the Supervisor also can Reason on the TimeSheet. Therefore, the second statement can also be seen by the Supervisor.

In the third statement our role has an authorization on WorkHours and isPartOf but we cannot infer any authorization on the Payroll. Therefore, the Supervisor cannot see the information from this statement.

Example 3:

As a final example, let us suppose that our ontology has the following information:

"Contract reads Schedule"
"Contract reads Design"

From the role's set of privileges we can see that the Supervisor has an Extend access mode on the Contract and ProductionExecution classes and the changeDataIn property. From the Class Graph and the Property Graph we can deduce that this role can also see the first statement because of the subclass relation between ProductExecution and Schedule and the subproperty relation between reads and changeDataIn. For the second statement, Supervisors have no authorization on the Design class, therefore they cannot see it.

The denial of access to resources is specified explicitly in the form of constraints explained in the next section.

4.6   Constraints

Constraints are used in our model to express the denial of access to resources; they take precedence over all explicit or propagated privileges. In some papers, the constraints are modeled as negative permissions [18,17]. Here, all the constraints defined for the Role Graph Model in [12] can be applied to our architecture of graphs. The possibility of logical inference creates the need for more complex restrictions. In the Semantic Web environment we have to consider new ways of reaching the information; sometimes the relationships between resources expressed in ontologies gives new possibilities for finding out private information. As a way of preventing this, we define here constraints on these resources that will prevent the regular user or the software agent to reason about unwanted data. One way of doing this is by expressing constraints based on the indicators of the property nodes in the Property Graph or by using other basic property and classes restrictions defined in the OWL Lite language. This is meant to be a significant extension to the Role Graph constraint-management model to deal with the increased power of possible intruders using reasoning engines instead of regular technologies from today. The foundation of our model will have an artificial intelligence core capable of computing the extended information offered by the ontology (like property and class characteristics) along with a user's role in order to create dynamic constraints. These will act as a firewall for malicious users trying to get access beyond their privileges through information gained by reasoning.

5   Conclusions and Future Work

In this paper we have proposed an access control model for the ontologies used in the Semantic Web. Based on the Role Graph Model, we modeled resources, classes and properties with directed, acyclic graphs, incorporating the basic features of the OWL Lite language. A noticeable advantage of our work over similar models like [17] is that we take into consideration the properties that define relationships between classes, by specifying authorizations and propagation rules based on them. Combining the two separate authorization graphs for classes and properties and their propagation policies, we captured the semantic relationships from ontologies, the main idea behind the Semantic Web.

As future research, we want to integrate other important features of the OWL language, as it is the most comprehensive tool for developing ontologies. As an immediate approach, we want to extend our model to be able to model union and intersection of classes and cardinality restrictions. We also want to further explore the interaction between the classes and properties by taking into consideration *rdfs:domain* and *rdfs:range* features of OWL.

References

1. N. R. Adam, V. Atluri, E. Bertino, and E. Ferrari. A content-based authorization model for digital libraries. *IEEE Transactions Knowledge and Data Engineering*, 14(2):296–315, 2002.
2. E. Bertino, S. Castano, and E. Ferrari. On specifying security policies for web documents with an XML-based language. In *6th ACM Symposium on Access Control Models and Technologies (SACMAT 2001)*, pages 57–65, 2001.
3. E. Bertino and E. Ferrari. Secure and selective dissemination of XML documents. *ACM TISSEC*, 5(3):290–331, 2002.
4. E. Damiani, S. De Capitani Di Vimercati, S. Paraboschi, and P. Samarati. Design and implementation of an access control processor for XML documents. *Computer Networks*, 33(6):59–75, 2000.
5. E. Damiani, S. De Capitani di Vimercati, S. Paraboschi, and P. Samarati. Fine-grained access control system for XML documents. *ACM Trans. on Information and System Security*, 5(2):169–202, 2002.
6. G. Denker, L. Kagal, T. Finin, M. Paolucci, and K. Sycara. Security for DAML web services: Annotation and matchmaking. In *Proc. of the 2nd International Semantic Web Conference (ISWC2003)*, Sanibel Island, Florida, USA, October 2003.
7. D. Eastlake and J. Reagle. XML encryption syntax and processing. W3C Candidate Recommendation, August 2002.
8. D. Eastlake, J. Reagle, and D. Solo. XML-signature syntax and processing. RFC 3275, March 2002.
9. D. Fensel, J. Hendler, H. Lieberman, and W. Wahlster. *Spinning the Semantic Web: Bringing the World Wide Web to Its Full Potential.* The MIT Press, 2003.
10. T. Finin and A. Joshi. Agents, trust, and information access on the semantic web. *SIGMOD Record*, 31(4):30–35, December 2002.
11. R. Housley, W. Polk, W. Ford, and D. Solo. Internet x.509 public key infrastructure certificate and certificate revocation list. RFC 3280, April 2002.
12. Cecilia M. Ionita and Sylvia L. Osborn. Privilege administration for the role graph model. In *Research Directions in Data and Applications Security, Proc. IFIP WG11.3 Working Conference on Database Security*, pages 15–25. Kluwer Academic Publishers, 2003.

13. L. Kagal, T. Finin, and A. Joshi. A policy based approach to security for the semantic web. In *Proc. of the Second International Semantic Web Conference (ISWC2003)*, Sanibel Island FL, October 2003.

14. A. Kim, L.J. Hoffman, and C.D. Martin. Building privacy into the semantic web: An ontology needed now. In *Proc. of the International Workshop on the Semantic Web*, Honolulu, Hawaii, May 2002.

15. M. Nyanchama and S. L. Osborn. The role graph model and conflict of interest. *ACM TISSEC*, 2(1):3–33, 1999.

16. S. Osborn and Y. Guo. Modeling users in role-based access control. In *Fifth ACM Workshop on Role-Based Access Control*, pages 31–38, Berlin, Germany, July 2000.

17. L. Qin and V. Atluri. Concept-level access control for the semantic web. In *Proc. of the ACM Workshop on XML Security*, October 2003.

18. F. Rabitti, E. Bertino, W. Kim, and D. Woelk. A model of authorization for next-generation database systems. *ACM Trans Database Syst*, 16(1):88–131, 1991.

19. P. Samarati, E. Bertino, and S. Jajodia. An authorization model for a distributed hypertext system. *IEEE Trans. on Knowledge and Data Engineering*, 8(4):555–562, 1996.

20. R. Sandhu, E.J. Coyne, H.L. Feinstein, and C.E. Youman. Role-based access control models. *IEEE Computer*, 29:38–47, Feb. 1996.

21. A. Stoica and C. Farkas. Ontology guided security engine. *Journal of Intelligent Information Systems*, 2004.

22. w3.org. Resource description framework. http://www.w3.org/TR/rdf-schema/.

23. Jingzhu Wang and Sylvia L. Osborn. A role-based approach to access control for XML databases. In *Proc. ACM SACMAT*, 2004.

A Formal Access Control Model for XML Databases*

Alban Gabillon

Université de Pau et des Pays de l'Adour, IUT de Mont de Marsan,
LIUPPA/CSySEC, 40 000 Mont de Marsan, France
alban.gabillon@univ-pau.fr

Abstract. In this paper, we first define a logical theory representing an XML database supporting XPath as query language and XUpdate as modification language. We then extend our theory with predicates allowing us to specify the security policy protecting the database. The security policy includes rules addressing the read and write privileges. We propose axioms to derive the database view each user is permitted to see. We also propose axioms to derive the new database content after an update.

1 Introduction

Several discretionary access control models for eXtensible Markup Language (XML) documents [2] have been proposed [1][7][13][11] [14][10]. In [10], we first reviewed most of the existing access control models for XML and discussed their weaknesses. Based on our study, we then defined a new model suggesting a solution to cope with the problems that our study revealed. The model in [10] has the following characteristics:

- The model is an interpretation for XML of the SQL security model (with some additional features).
- Each user is provided with a view of the source database he or she is permitted to see.
- The model includes a new position privilege that allows knowing about the existence of an XML node but not about its label. Nodes on which users hold a position privilege are shown with a RESTRICTED label in users' views. Thus, sensitive labels are hidden while the structure of the XML document is preserved.
- The model includes various write privileges and defines the access controls for the write operations.

However, the model in [10] has two drawbacks:

- It is defined in an informal way.
- Like the security model of SQL, it ignores interactions between the read privilege and the write privilege. In other words, write operations are evaluated on the source database and not on the user's view. As a consequence, users can build some covert channels to learn about the data they are not permitted to see.

---

* This work was supported by funding from the French ministry for research under "ACI Sécurité Informatique 2003-2006. Projet CASC".

W. Jonker and M. Petković (Eds.): SDM 2005, LNCS 3674, pp. 86–103, 2005.

The purpose of this paper is to formally define a new security model which does not have the negative aspects of the model in [10]:

- We use mathematical logic to define our model. With logic, we can homogeneously define the database, the query language, the security policy and the access controls. This approach enables an easy and precise way of computing the facts that users are authorized to see/update.
- The model we define in this paper is partly based on the model in [10]. In particular, it includes the `position` privilege we introduced in [10]. However, interactions between the read privilege and the write privilege are now investigated in details and, as a major consequence, write operations are now evaluated on views and not on the source database.

We have implemented a Prolog-based prototype simulating a secure XML database. Logical formulae given in this paper are Horn clauses and have been implemented as such in the prototype. This prototype can be downloaded from the following address: `http://www.univ-pau.fr/~gabillon/xmlsecu`.

In section 2, we make an informal overview of our model and we underline the main limitations of existing security models for XML. In section 3, we define the logical theory representing an XML database. Since we use XPath [4] as a query language and xUpdate [15] as a modification language, we give their logical interpretation. In section 4, we extend our theory with predicates allowing us to define the security policy protecting the database. The security policy includes rules addressing read and write privileges. We define the logical formulae allowing us to derive the database view each user is permitted to see. We also give the logical formulae allowing us to derive the new database after an update. Finally, section 5 concludes this paper.

2 Informal Overview of Our Model

Most of the existing security models for XML define a view-based access control strategy for handling the `read` privilege. However, these models suffer from problems that were pointed out in [18]:

- Regarding the model in [11], if access to a node is denied then the user is not allowed to access the entire sub-tree under that node even if access to part of the sub-tree is permitted, therefore limiting the availability of data.
- Regarding the model in [7], in order to preserve the structure of the document, the authors allow elements with negative authorizations (i.e. access denied) to be released if the element has a descendant with a positive authorization (access permitted), thus making the semantics of the negative authorization unclear.

Some of the existing security models for XML consider the `write` privilege but,

- they do not clearly indicate in which framework the different update operations for XML are supported,
- the access control strategy that they use for handling the `write` privilege is not clearly described,

– interactions between read access controls and write access controls are not investigated.

In fact, these security models were designed to be implemented as extensions to existing web servers.

2.1 View Access Control

In order to solve the problems mentioned in [18], we introduced in [10] a special privilege protecting the *existence* of nodes. Therefore, our model includes two kinds of read privileges: one privilege which allows knowing about the existence of a node (we call it the `position` privilege) and another privilege which allows knowing both the existence and the label (we call it simply the `read` privilege). The security designer has now two options:

– if user `s` is forbidden to know about the existence of node n then the security designer denies both `position` and `read` privileges on node n to user `s`. In that case node n and possible descendant nodes (even those for which the user has permission to read) are not shown in the view user `s` is permitted to see.
– if only the label of node n is sensitive then the security designer grants to user `s` the `position` privilege on node n (without granting the `read` privilege). Node n is shown in the view with RESTRICTED label and descendant nodes for which the user has permission to see are also shown in the view. Label RESTRICTED was first used by Sandhu and Jajodia in the context of multilevel databases [19]. Its semantics is "the label exists but you are not allowed to see it".

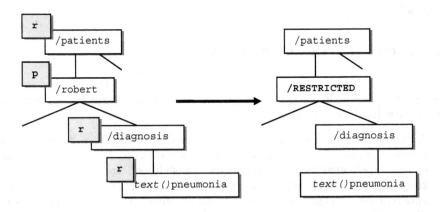

Fig. 1. View Access Control

Left tree in figure 1 shows a sample medical files database. Let `s` be a user. Tag `r` (respectively `p`) attached to a node represents the fact that user `s` holds the `read` (respectively `position`) privilege on that node. Right tree represents the view user `s` is permitted to see. User `s` is permitted to read illnesses (most probably for statistical purpose) but she is forbidden to see patients' names.

2.2 Write Access Controls

SQL ignores interactions between the read privilege and the write privilege. Indeed, if a user submits a write operation (via one of the standard SQL commands: INSERT, UPDATE or DELETE) then this operation is evaluated on the source database and not on the data the user is permitted to read. As a consequence, users can easily learn about the data they are not permitted to see. For example, consider user_A who is the owner of the employee table and who has granted to user_B the sole update privilege on employee.

user_B is not permitted to see user_A's employee table,

```
SQL> SELECT * FROM user_A.employee;
ERROR ORA-01031: insufficient privilege
```

but user_B is permitted to update user_A's employee table:

```
SQL> UPDATE user_A.employee SET salary=salary+100 WHERE salary > 3000;
2 rows updated
```

Although user_B is not permitted to see user_A's employee table, she has been able to learn, through an update command, that there are two employees with a salary greater than 3000. The UPDATE command was evaluated on data user_B was not permitted to see. Note, in particular, that the WHERE clause performed a read operation on the employee table. We could show various examples exploiting this vulnerability. The model in [10] has the same vulnerability since it is an interpretation for XML of the SQL security model. In [10], an operation updating XML data is evaluated on the source database regardless of the read privileges held by the user submitting the operation.

In this paper, our approach is different. Since a write operation is a process running on behalf of a user we consider that it should have the privileges and the limitations of the user. In particular the write operation should not be able to read the data the user is not permitted to see. This means that the write operation has to be evaluated on the user's view and not on the source database.

Our model supports three kinds of write privileges (insert, delete and update). We give the exact semantics for each of these privileges. We state the privileges that each XUpdate operation requires for completion and we formally define the access controls for each of the XUpdate operations.

3 XML Database

Mathematical logic has been used to formalize databases in two main directions. These directions are usually called the proof theoretic approach and the model theoretic approach. The former represents a database as a logical theory; the latter represents a database as an interpretation of a logical theory [16]. In this paper, we adopt the proof theoretic approach, that is, each database is associated with its logical theory db. We also make the *closed world assumption*. The closed world assumption holds that anything that we cannot show to be true is false.

3.1 XML Documents Modeled as Trees

For the sake of simplicity, we shall not consider the type of XML nodes. An XML document is a *tree* of *nodes*. Each node is the parent of zero or more *child* nodes.

Each node has one and only one parent except one fundamental node which has no parent and which is called the *document* node. We state that each node is associated with a *unique identifier* and a *label*:

- Node identifiers are obtained by applying a *numbering scheme*. Several numbering schemes have been proposed [21][6][24][8]. They all support the representation of ancestor and sibling relationships between nodes i.e. one can derive the relationship between any two given nodes by looking at their unique numbers. In this paper we assume the numbering scheme does not require renumbering after an update i.e. numbers assigned to existing nodes remain the same even after an update modifying the tree structure. Such a numbering scheme could be the LSDX numbering scheme [8] or our own persistent numbering scheme [12].
- Labels are the data. Labels are small for nodes of type element (in the XML terminology they are referred to as names) and they can be very large for nodes of type text (in the XML terminology they are referred to as values or PCDATA).

Figure 2 shows an XML document which we shall use throughout the remainder of this paper. Strings patients, franck, service, otolarynology ... are labels. n_1, n_2, n_3, ... denote numbers identifying nodes. We state that the document node has identifier / and position /. The document node has only one child node which is called the *root element* node. Identifier of the root element is n_1 and label is patients.

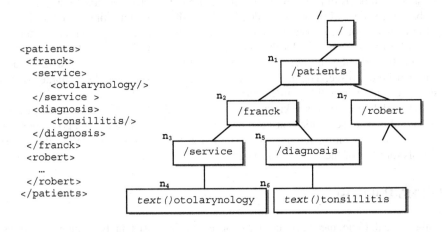

```
<patients>
 <franck>
  <service>
     <otolarynology/>
  </service >
  <diagnosis>
     <tonsillitis/>
  </diagnosis>
 </franck>
 <robert>
    ...
 </robert>
</patients>
```

Fig. 2. XML document

3.2 Language

Language L of theory db is based on first-order logic with equality. For the sake of simplifying our logical formulae, we shall consider that the database may contain only one document. We shall use the following two-place predicate to represent the database content:

- node(n, v) reads "there is a node with label v identified by number n"

We shall also use the following predicates to learn about the database tree geometry:

- $\text{child}(x, y)$, reads "node[1] x is a child of node y"
- $\text{child\_or\_self}(x, y)$, reads "node x is a child of node y or, x and y are the same"

There are also other tree geometry predicates like parent, descendant, descendant_or_self, ancestor, following_sibling …

3.3 Axioms

Set of axioms A of theory db includes the classical axiom schemata of first order logic with equality plus some proper axioms. We divide these proper axioms into the following two sets:

- the set F of atomic facts recorded in the database.
- the set of formulae allowing us to derive facts belonging to the tree geometry predicates.

The sample database we shall use throughout this paper includes the document in figure 2:

$$F = \begin{Bmatrix} \text{node}(/,/), \text{node}(n_1, \text{patients}), \text{node}(n_2, \text{franck}), \text{node}(n_3, \text{service}), \\ \text{node}(n_4, \text{otolarynology}), \text{node}(n_5, \text{diagnosis}), \text{node}(n_6, \text{tonsillitis}), \text{node}(n_7, \text{robert}), ... \end{Bmatrix} \quad (1)$$

Axioms allowing us to derive tree geometry facts depend on the numbering scheme and are not given in this paper. However, these axioms can be found in our prototype. For example, we can derive the following child relation from these axioms:

$$\{\text{child}(n_1, /), \text{child}(n_2, n_1), \text{child}(n_3, n_2), \text{child}(n_5, n_2), \text{child}(n_4, n_3), \text{child}(n_6, n_5), \text{child}(n_7, n_1), ...\}$$

3.4 XPath and XUpdate

We use the following three place xpath predicate to logically interpret XPath expressions:

- $\text{xpath}(p, n, v)$, reads "node with label v identified by number n is addressed by path p"

Since semantics of XPath is well known, we do not give axioms interpreting the xpath predicate. However, these axioms can be found in our prototype.

Updating XML data is still a research issue (e.g. see [22][20][3]). Today, XUpdate is a solution to update XML data. The reader may refer to [15] for a complete description of XUpdate. Throughout this section, we shall use the following notations:

- From the logical point of view, whenever we update the database we obtain a new logical theory representing the updated database. Let db_{new} be the new logical theory representing the updated database.

---

[1] More precisely, it should read, "node identified by number x is a child of node identified by number y".

- Let predicate$_{db}$ representing the predicate predicate in the theory db. Let predicate$_{db_{new}}$ representing the same predicate in the theory db$_{new}$.

For each xUpdate operation, we shall give the logical formulae that allow us to derive the theory db$_{new}$ from the theory db.

3.4.1 Updating Node Operations

There are two xUpdate instructions for updating XML nodes: xupdate:update and xupdate:rename. xupdate:update can be used to update the content of existing element nodes. xupdate:rename allows attribute or element nodes to be renamed. Both operations need two parameters: the path **PATH** selecting the nodes to update and the new label v$_{NEW}$.

xupdate:rename: The following two formulae allow us to derive facts belonging to the new set F after an xupdate:rename operation.

$$\forall n \forall v, node_{db}(n, v) \wedge \neg xpath_{db}(\mathbf{PATH}, n, v) \rightarrow node_{db_{new}}(n, v) \tag{2}$$

Label of nodes which are not addressed by **PATH** are not updated.

$$\forall n \forall v, xpath_{db}(\mathbf{PATH}, n, v) \rightarrow node_{db_{new}}(n, \mathbf{V_{NEW}}) \tag{3}$$

Label of nodes which are addressed by **PATH** are updated to v$_{NEW}$.

Example:

Let us consider the operation xupdate:rename which *renames* all nodes service in department:

-   **PATH** = //service
-   **V**$_{NEW}$ = department

From formulae 2 and 3, we can derive the new set F:

$$F = \begin{cases} node(/,/), node(n_1, patients), node(n_2, franck), node(n_3, \mathbf{department}), \\ node(n_4, otolaryngology), node(n_5, diagnosis), node(n_6, tonsillitis), node(n_7, robert), ... \end{cases}$$

xupdate:update: The following two formulae allow us to derive facts belonging to the new set F after an xupdate:update operation.

$$\forall n \forall v, node_{db}(n, v) \wedge \neg \exists n' \exists v', \left(xpath_{db}(\mathbf{PATH}, n', v') \wedge child_{db}(n, n')\right) \rightarrow node_{db_{new}}(n, v) \tag{4}$$

Children of nodes which are not addressed by **PATH** are not updated.

$$\forall n \forall n' \forall v', xpath_{db}(\mathbf{PATH}, n', v') \wedge child_{db}(n, n') \rightarrow node_{db_{new}}(n, \mathbf{V_{NEW}}) \tag{5}$$

Children of nodes which are addressed by **PATH** are updated to v$_{NEW}$.

Example:

Let us consider the operation xupdate:update which *updates* diagnosis of franck in pharyngitis:

-   **PATH** = /patients/franck/diagnosis
-   **V**$_{NEW}$ = pharyngitis

From formulae 2 and 3, we can derive the new set F:

$$F = \begin{cases} \text{node}(/,/), \text{node}(n_1,\text{patients}), \text{node}(n_2,\text{franck}), \text{node}(n_3,\text{service}), \\ \text{node}(n_4,\text{otolarynology}), \text{node}(n_5,\text{diagnosis}), \text{node}(n_6,\textbf{pharyngitis}), \text{node}(n_7,\text{robert}),\ldots \end{cases}$$

3.4.2   Creating Node Operations

There are three xupdate instructions for creating XML fragments: xupdate:insert-before, xupdate:insert-after and xupdate:append. xupdate:insert-before can be used to insert a new tree as the *immediate* preceding sibling of existing nodes. xupdate:insert-after can be used to insert a new tree as the *immediate* following sibling of existing nodes. xupdate:append can be used to insert a new tree as the last child of existing nodes. All these operations need two parameters: a path **PATH** selecting some nodes and the tree **TREE** to insert. Let us assume **node**$_{\text{TREE}}$ be the two-place predicate used to represent the tree to insert.

$$\forall n \forall v, \text{node}_{\text{db}}(n, v) \rightarrow \text{node}_{\text{db}_{\text{new}}}(n, v) \tag{6}$$

If a node belongs to the original document then it belongs to the final document.

$$\forall n \forall v \forall n' \forall v' \forall n'' \forall o, \textbf{node}_{\textbf{TREE}}(n', v') \wedge \text{xpath}_{\text{db}}(\textbf{PATH}, n, v) \wedge \text{create\_number}(n, n', o, n'')$$
$$\rightarrow \text{node}_{\text{db}_{\text{new}}}(n'', v') \tag{7}$$

The tree to insert shall be inserted as the last subtree of *each* node selected by **PATH** (append), or as a new preceding-sibling tree of each node selected by **PATH** (insert-before), or as a new following-sibling tree of each node selected by **PATH** (insert-after). Therefore, each node **n'** belonging to the tree to insert is inserted at as many places as nodes addressed by **PATH**. Created numbers n'' assigned to inserted nodes are given by the create_number predicate.

- create_number(n,n',o,n''), reads "node n' is inserted with number n'' by operation o on node n". o can be append, insert-before or insert-after.

We do not give axioms for deriving facts belonging to the create_number predicate since they depend on the numbering scheme. Axioms implementing our own numbering scheme [12] can be found in our prototype.

Example:
Let us consider the operation xupdate:append which inserts a new medical record:
- **PATH** = /patients
- The tree **TREE** to insert is the following:

$$\{\text{node}(n_1',\text{albert}), \text{node}(n_2',\text{service}), \text{node}(n_3',\text{cardiology}), \text{node}(n_4',\text{diagnosis}),\}$$

From formulae 6 and 7, we can derive the new set F:

$$F = \begin{cases} \text{node}(/,/), \text{node}(n_1,\text{patients}), \text{node}(n_2,\text{franck}), \text{node}(n_3,\text{service}), \\ \text{node}(n_4,\text{otolarynology}), \text{node}(n_5,\text{diagnosis}), \text{node}(n_6,\text{tonsillitis}), \text{node}(n_7,\text{robert}),\ldots \\ \text{node}(n_1'',\text{albert}), \text{node}(n_2'',\text{service}), \text{node}(n_3'',\text{cardiology}), \text{node}(n_4'',\text{diagnosis}) \end{cases}$$

From the tree geometry axioms we can derive:

$$\left[\begin{array}{l} \text{preceding}\_\text{sibling}(n_7, n_1''), \text{preceding}\_\text{sibling}(n_2'', n_4''), \\ \text{child}\left(n_1'', n_1\right), \text{child}\left(n_2'', n_1''\right), \text{child}\left(n_3'', n_2''\right), \text{child}\left(n_4'', n_1''\right) \end{array}\right]$$

3.4.3 Deleting Node Operations

There is one XUpdate instruction for deleting XML nodes: xupdate:remove. xupdate:remove can be used to delete existing subtrees. It requires one parameter: the path PATH selecting subtrees to delete.

The following formula allows us to derive facts belonging to the new set F after an xupdate:remove operation.

$$\forall n \forall v, \text{node}_{db}(n, v) \wedge \text{undeleted}(n) \rightarrow \text{node}_{db_{new}}(n, v) \tag{8}$$

If a node belongs to the original document and if it does not belong to a deleted subtree then it belongs to the final document.

— undeleted(n), reads "node n does not belong to a deleted subtree"

We can derive facts belonging to the undeleted predicate from the following formulae:

$$\forall n \forall v, \text{node}_{db}(n, v) \wedge \neg \exists n' \exists v', \left(\begin{array}{l} \text{descendant}\_\text{or}\_\text{self}_{db}(n, n') \\ \wedge \text{xpath}_{db}(\textbf{PATH}, n', v') \end{array}\right) \rightarrow \text{undeleted}(n) \tag{9}$$

This formula says that nodes which are not deleted are the nodes which do not belong to a subtree whose root node is addressed by path PATH.

Example:

Let us consider the xupdate:remove operation which *removes* element diagnosis from franck's medical file:

— **PATH** = /patients/franck/diagnosis

From formula 8 and 9, we can derive the new set F:

$$F = \left\{\begin{array}{l} \text{node}\left(/,/\right), \text{node}\left(n_1, \text{patients}\right), \text{node}\left(n_2, \text{franck}\right), \text{node}\left(n_3, \text{service}\right), \text{node}\left(n_4, \text{otolarynology}\right), \\ \text{node}\left(n_7, \text{robert}\right), \dots \end{array}\right\}$$

4 Secure XML Database

We extend the logical theory db to represent a secure XML database.

4.1 Extended Theory

We extend the language with predicates subject and isa for representing the subject hierarchy,

— subject(s), reads "s is a subject"
— isa(s, s'), reads "subject s is a subject s'"

We also introduce the predicate `rule` for writing the security policy:

- `rule(accept,r,p,s,t)`, reads "subject s is granted privilege `r` on nodes addressed by path `p`". `t` is the priority of the rule.
- `rule(deny,r,p,s,t)`, reads "subject s is denied privilege `r` on nodes addressed by path `p`". `t` is the priority of the rule.

Since accept and deny rules may conflict with each other, we define predicate `perm` to represent the actual privileges held by subjects:

- `perm(s,r,n)`, reads "subject s is (definitely) granted privilege `r` on node n"

We extend our theory with the following sets:

- the set s of formulae representing the subjects recorded in the database,
- the set R_s of formulae allowing us to derive the subject hierarchy
- the set P of atomic formulae representing the security policy,
- the set R_P of formulae allowing us to solve conflicts between security rules,

4.2 Subjects

Let us consider the subjects hierarchy at figure 3. In each tree, internal nodes are *roles* [17] and external nodes are *users*.

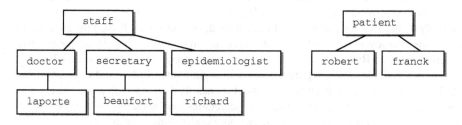

Fig. 3. Subject Hierarchy

The following set s represents this hierarchy:

$$S = \begin{cases} \text{subject (staff), subject (secretary), subject (doctor), subject (epidemiologist),} \\ \text{subject (patient), subject (beaufort), subject (laporte), subject(richard),} \\ \text{subject(robert), subject(franck), isa(secretary, staff), isa(doctor, staff),} \\ \text{isa (epidemiologist, staff), isa(laporte, doctor), isa(beaufort, secretary),} \\ \text{isa (richard,epidemiologist), isa(robert, patient), isa(franck, patient)} \end{cases} \quad (10)$$

Set R_s includes the two following axioms allowing us to derive the reflexive and transitive closure of the `isa` relation:

$$\forall s, \ subject(s) \rightarrow isa(s,s) \quad (11)$$

$$\forall s \forall s' \forall s'', \ isa(s,s') \land isa(s',s'') \rightarrow isa(s,s'') \quad (12)$$

4.3 Security Policy

The security policy may refer to the following privileges:
`{position, read, delete, insert, update}`

- if user s holds the `position` privilege on node n then user s has the right to know the existence of n.
- if user s holds the `read` privilege on node n then user s has the right to see node n.
- if user s holds the `insert` privilege on node n then user s has the right to add a new sub-tree to node n.
- if user s holds the `update` privilege on node n then user s has the right to update node n (i.e. change its label).
- if user s holds the `delete` privilege on node n then user s has the right to delete the sub-tree of which node n is the root.

Privileges should not be confused with *operations*. Operations need privileges to complete. For example, both `xupdate:append` and `xupdate:insert-before` need the `insert` privilege to complete.

Due to space limitation, we cannot represent the *security administration model*. In particular, we cannot state the policy constraining the management of users, roles and security rules. We cannot also represent any kind of delegation mechanism, whereas in [10] we included the privilege to transfer privileges. This privilege is referred to as the *grant option* in SQL.

Let us now consider the example of security policy defined by axiom 13. First rule states that staff members have the privilege to `read` the whole document. Second rule partially denies that right from secretaries. Indeed, secretaries are denied the right to see diagnosis. However, rule 3 states that secretaries may know whether the patient was diagnosed or not. Rule 4 and rule 5 state that patients may access their own medical file ($USER is a variable containing the session user login name). Rule 6 and rule 7 state that epidemiologists are forbidden to see patient names. Rule 8 states that secretaries may insert new medical files. Rule 9 states that secretaries may update patient names. Rules 10, rule 11 and rule 12 state that doctors can pose/update/delete a diagnosis.

$$P = \begin{cases}
1.\ \text{rule(accept,read,//*,staff,10),} \\
2.\ \text{rule(deny,read,//diagnosis/*,secretary,11),} \\
3.\ \text{rule(accept,position,//diagnosis/*,secretary,12),} \\
4.\ \text{rule(accept,read,/patients,patient,13),} \\
5.\ \text{rule(accept,read,/patients/descendant-or-self::*[\$USER],patient,14)} \\
6.\ \text{rule(deny,read,/patients/*,epidemiologist,15)} \\
7.\ \text{rule(accept,position,/patients/*,epidemiologist,16)} \\
8.\ \text{rule(accept,insert,/patients,secretary,17),} \\
9.\ \text{rule(accept,update,/patients/*,secretary,18),} \\
10.\ \text{rule(accept,insert,//diagnosis,doctor,19),} \\
11.\ \text{rule(accept,update,//diagnosis/*,doctor,20),} \\
12.\ \text{rule(accept,delete,//diagnosis/*,doctor,21)}
\end{cases} \tag{13}$$

From practical point of view, we assume that the security administrator inserts these rules one by one. The last issued command has the *priority* over the previous ones and possibly cancels them. The timestamp indicating when the command was issued plays the priority role. For example, rule 1 which says that staff members have the permission to see the whole document is partially cancelled by rule 2 which partially denies that right to some staff members (secretaries).

Set R_P includes the following axiom allowing us to solve the conflicts between the rules and to derive the *actual privileges* held by each subject:

$$\forall s \forall s' \forall r \forall p \forall t \forall n \forall v, \text{isa}(s, s') \land \text{rule}(\text{accept}, r, p, s', t) \land \text{xpath}(p, n, v)$$

$$\land \neg \exists s'' \exists p' \exists t', \begin{pmatrix} \text{isa}(s, s'') \land \text{rule}(\text{deny}, r, p', s'', t') \\ \land \text{xpath}(p', n, v) \land (t' > t) \end{pmatrix} \rightarrow \text{perm}(s, n, r) \tag{14}$$

This axiom says that if there is an accept rule applying to privilege r, subject s and node n and if there is no subsequent deny rule applying to privilege r, subject s and node n then subject s holds privilege r on node n.

4.4 Access Controls

4.4.1 Read Access Controls

The purpose of this section is to define link axioms allowing us to derive the view of the source document that subjects are permitted to see. Each view is represented by a logical theory. Let us denote by s the current session user. Let us denote by view the theory representing the view that user s is permitted to see. The view access control strategy of our model can be informally described as follows:

- A node n is selected by the view access control mechanism if user s holds either a read or a position privilege on node n and the parent of node n is itself a selected node. Axioms 15, 16 and 17 implement that principle. The fact that a node requires its parent to be selected, in order for it to be selected, shows that the view is a *pruned* version of the source document.
- A selected node for which user s holds only the position privilege is shown with the RESTRICTED label. Axiom 17 implements that principle.

Note that *selected nodes are not renumbered in the view*. This cannot lead to inference channels since numbers are for internal processing only and are not visible to users.

The following formula allows us to derive facts belonging to the view user s is permitted to see:

$$\text{node}_{\text{view}}(/, /) \tag{15}$$

This formula says that $\text{node}_{\text{view}}(/, /)$ always belong to the view regardless of user privileges.

$$\forall n \forall v \forall n' \forall v' \forall s, \text{node}_{\text{db}}(n, v) \land \text{logged}(s) \land \text{perm}(s, n, \text{read}) \land \text{child}_{\text{db}}(n, n') \land \text{node}_{\text{view}}(n', v')$$

$$\rightarrow \text{node}_{\text{view}}(n, v) \tag{16}$$

This formula says that if the current session user has the permission to *read* node n with label v and if the parent of node n is itself a selected node then the access control mechanism selects node n with label v.

$$\forall n \forall v \forall n' \forall v' \forall s, node_{db}(n,v) \wedge logged(s) \wedge perm(s,n,position)$$
$$\wedge \neg perm(s,n,read) \wedge child_{db}(n,n') \wedge node_{view}(n',v') \rightarrow node_{view}(n,RESTRICTED) \quad (17)$$

This formula says that if current session user has the permission to *know the existence* of node n and if the parent of node n is itself a selected node then the access control mechanism selects node n with label RESTRICTED. If the session user also holds the read privilege then this axiom does not apply.

− logged(s), reads "s is the current session user"

Axioms 15, 16 and 17 can, of course, be implemented by a tree traversal algorithm. In [10], we give such an algorithm.

We can now derive the view of the sample source database (see axiom 1) each subject is permitted to see.

View for secretaries is the following:

$$\left[\begin{array}{l} node(/,/), node(n_1,patients), node(n_2,franck), node(n_3,service), node(n_4,otolarynology), \\ node(n_5,diagnosis), node(n_6,RESTRICTED), node(n_7,robert), ... \end{array} \right]$$

Secretaries can see everything except the content of diagnosis elements. If the diagnosis is posed, then they are provided with the RESTRICTED label.

View for patient Robert is the following:

$$\left[\begin{array}{l} node(/,/), node(n_1,patients), node(n_7,robert), node(n_8,service), node(n_9,pneumology), \\ node(n_{10},diagnosis), node(n_{11},penumonia) \end{array} \right]$$

Robert is the current session user. As a patient he has access to its medical file only. View for epidemiologists is the following:

$$\left[\begin{array}{l} node(/,/), node(n_1,patients), node(n_2,RESTRICTED), node(n_3,service), \\ node(n_4,otolarynology), node(n_5,diagnosis), node(n_6,tonsillitis), node(n_7,RESTRICTED)... \end{array} \right]$$

Epidemiologists can see everything except patient names.

Doctors can see everything without restriction. Therefore, view for doctors includes the whole database represented by axiom 1.

4.4.2 Write Access Controls

The purpose of this section is to define the link axioms allowing us to derive the new database content after an update. The link axioms must take into account the privileges of the user performing the update.

Each xUpdate operation requires the path **PATH** parameter to select nodes to update. In order to avoid the vulnerability we described in section 2.2, *we require nodes to update to be selected on the view the user is permitted to see*. This has the following implications:

- Users cannot perform write operations on nodes they cannot see.
- Since users express xUpdate operations by looking at their view, **PATH** parameter might include some node tests equal to RESTRICTED.

Note that only the "selecting nodes" step is performed on the view. Thanks to their numbers, corresponding database nodes are then retrieved and updated.

Let s be the current session user submitting the xUpdate operation. Let n be one of the nodes selected by **PATH**.

- xupdate:rename: user s needs the update privilege on node n.
- xupdate:update: user s needs the update privilege on the child node of node n.
- xupdate:append: user s needs the insert privilege on node n.
- xupdate:insert-before: user s needs the insert privilege on the parent of node n.
- xupdate:insert-after: user s needs the insert privilege on the parent of node n.
- xupdate:remove: user s needs the delete privilege on node n.

Before defining the link axioms allowing us to derive the new database after an update, we need to consider the following issues:

- Each xUpdate operation may address several nodes via the **PATH** parameter. Depending on the privileges held by the user submitting the operation, the xUpdate operation may succeed for some nodes and fail for others.
- Let us consider an xupdate:rename operation addressing a node n. Let us assume node n is shown in the user's view with a RESTRICTED label. Since renaming node n would update the original label that the user is not permitted to see, we enforce that nodes which are shown with RESTRICTED label cannot be updated.
- Let us consider the xupdate:update operation. This operation requires that the user holds the update privilege on the child of each selected node n. In fact, the xupdate:update operation on node n is equivalent to the xupdate:rename operation on the child of node n. Therefore, the child of node n has to belong to the user's view with its original label, that is, the user needs to hold the read privilege on node n.
- Let us consider an xupdate:remove operation addressing a node n. If the user removes node n then he actually deletes the subtree of which node n is the root. Some of the nodes which belong to that subtree may not be visible (i.e. may not belong to the user's view). Shall we reject the operation if some nodes of the deleted subtree do not belong to the user's view? On one hand, it would preserve the integrity of data the user is not permitted to see. On the other hand, it would reveal to the user the existence of data she is not permitted to see. In fact there is no definite answer to this question. This is typically a case of conflict between confidentiality and integrity. In this paper, we prefer to emphasize the confidentiality that is the remove operation is accepted (see axiom 25).

Link axioms allowing us to derive the new database after an update are given below. Note that for each axiom we use the $xpath_{view}$ predicate for selecting nodes to update from the view:

xupdate:rename: We need to adapt axioms 2 and 3 as follows:

$$\forall n \forall v \forall s, \mathrm{node}_{db}(n,v) \wedge \neg \begin{pmatrix} \mathrm{xpath}_{\mathrm{view}}(\mathbf{PATH},n,v) \wedge \mathrm{logged}(s) \\ \wedge\, \mathrm{perm}(s,n,\mathrm{update}) \end{pmatrix} \rightarrow \mathrm{node}_{db_{\mathrm{new}}}(n,v) \tag{18}$$

Label of nodes which are not addressed by **PATH** or for which the current session user does not hold the update privilege are not updated.

$$\forall n \forall v \forall s, \mathrm{xpath}_{\mathrm{view}}(\mathbf{PATH},n,v) \wedge \mathrm{logged}(s) \wedge \mathrm{perm}(s,n,\mathrm{update}) \rightarrow \mathrm{node}_{db_{\mathrm{new}}}(n,\mathbf{V_{NEW}}) \tag{19}$$

Label of nodes which are addressed by **PATH** and for which the current session user holds the update privilege are updated to $\mathbf{v_{NEW}}$.

xupdate:update: We need to adapt axioms 4 and 5 as follows:

$$\forall n \forall v \forall s, \mathrm{node}_{db}(n,v) \wedge \neg \exists n' \exists v', \begin{pmatrix} \mathrm{xpath}_{\mathrm{view}}(\mathbf{PATH},n',v') \wedge \mathrm{child}_{\mathrm{view}}(n,n') \\ \wedge \mathrm{logged}(s) \wedge \mathrm{perm}(s,n,\mathrm{update}) \wedge \mathrm{perm}(s,n,\mathrm{read}) \end{pmatrix}$$
$$\rightarrow \mathrm{node}_{db_{\mathrm{new}}}(n,v) \tag{20}$$

Label of nodes whose parent is not addressed by **PATH** or for which the current session user does not hold both the update privilege and the read privilege are not updated.

$$\forall n \forall v \forall n' \forall v' \forall s, \mathrm{xpath}_{\mathrm{view}}(\mathbf{PATH},n',v') \wedge \mathrm{child}_{\mathrm{view}}(n,n') \wedge \mathrm{logged}(s)$$
$$\wedge \mathrm{perm}(s,n,\mathrm{update}) \wedge \mathrm{perm}(s,n,\mathrm{read}) \rightarrow \mathrm{node}_{db_{\mathrm{new}}}(n,\mathbf{V_{NEW}}) \tag{21}$$

Label of nodes whose parent is addressed by **PATH** and for which the current session user holds both the update and the read privilege are updated to $\mathbf{v_{NEW}}$.

xupdate:append: We only need to adapt axioms 7:

$$\forall n \forall v \forall n' \forall v' \forall n'' \forall s, \mathbf{node_{TREE}}(n',v') \wedge \mathrm{xpath}_{\mathrm{view}}(\mathbf{PATH},n,v) \wedge \mathrm{logged}(s) \wedge \mathrm{perm}(s,n,\mathrm{insert})$$
$$\mathrm{create}\_\mathrm{number}(n,n',\mathrm{append},n'') \rightarrow \mathrm{node}_{db_{\mathrm{new}}}(n'',v') \tag{22}$$

The tree to insert shall appear as the last subtree of each node selected by **PATH** for which the current session user holds the insert privilege.

xupdate:insert-before: We need to adapt axiom 7 as follows:

$$\forall n \forall v \forall n' \forall v' \forall n'' \forall f \forall s, \mathbf{node_{TREE}}(n',v') \wedge \mathrm{xpath}_{\mathrm{view}}(\mathbf{PATH},n,v) \wedge \mathrm{child}_{\mathrm{view}}(n,f)$$
$$\wedge \mathrm{logged}(s) \wedge \mathrm{perm}(s,f,\mathrm{insert}) \wedge \mathrm{create}\_\mathrm{number}(n,n',\mathrm{insert\text{-}before},n'') \tag{23}$$
$$\rightarrow \mathrm{node}_{db_{\mathrm{new}}}(n'',v')$$

The tree to insert shall appear as the preceding sibling subtree of each node n selected by **PATH** provided the current session user holds the insert privilege on the parent node of n.

xupdate:insert-after: We need to adapt axiom 7 as follows:

$$\forall n \forall v \forall n' \forall v' \forall n'' \forall f \forall s, \mathbf{node_{TREE}} \left(n', v'\right) \wedge \mathrm{xpath_{view}} \left(\mathbf{PATH}, n, v\right) \wedge \mathrm{child_{view}} \left(n, f\right)$$

$$\wedge \mathrm{logged}(s) \wedge \mathrm{perm}\left(s, f, \mathrm{insert}\right) \wedge \mathrm{create\_number}(n, n', \mathrm{insert\text{-}after}, n'') \tag{24}$$

$$\rightarrow \mathrm{node_{db_{new}}} \left(n'', v'\right)$$

The tree to insert shall appear as the following sibling subtree of each node n selected by **PATH** provided the current session user holds the insert privilege on the parent node of n.

xupdate:remove: We only need to adapt axiom 9:

$$\forall n \forall v \forall s, \mathrm{node_{db}}\left(n, v\right) \wedge \neg \exists n' \exists v', \begin{pmatrix} \mathrm{descendant\_or\_self_{db}}\left(n, n'\right) \\ \wedge \mathrm{xpath_{view}}\left(\mathbf{PATH}, n', v'\right) \\ \wedge \mathrm{logged}(s) \wedge \mathrm{perm}\left(s, n', \mathrm{delete}\right) \end{pmatrix} \rightarrow \mathrm{undeleted_{db}}\left(n, v\right) \tag{25}$$

This formula says that nodes which are not deleted are the nodes which do not belong to a subtree that the current session user has the permission to delete and whose root is addressed by **PATH**.

5 Conclusion

In this paper, we gave the formal definition of a secure XML database. We represented the database content, the query language, the modification language, the subject hierarchy, the security policy and the access controls.

All the logical formulae given in this paper are Horn clauses. Based on these clauses, we wrote a prototype in Prolog simulating a secure XML database. The prototype includes a small database, an XPath and XUpdate interpreter, a sample subject hierarchy, a sample security policy and the access control formulae. It can be downloaded from http://www.univ-pau.fr/~gabillon/xmlsecu. The purpose of this prototype was simply to validate the correctness of the axioms given in this paper. The prototype uses our own numbering scheme [12] which does not require renumbering nodes after an update.

We are also currently implementing an XSLT-based [5] security processor based on our model, on top of a native XML database (Xindice [23]).

In [9], the authors suggest applying filters reflecting the user privileges on the queries and then evaluating the queries on the source document. We are also investigating the possibility of using this approach. However, before applying this solution, we have to make sure that we can express query filters providing us with answers compatible with the authorized views. In particular, we have to investigate how answers to filtered queries could include RESTRICTED labels. This is further work related to implementation that remains to be done.

Acknowledgment

The author would like to thank Emmanuel Bruno and the anonymous referees for fruitful comments about the paper.

References

[1] E. Bertino, S. Castano, E. Ferrari and M. Mesiti. "Specifying and Enforcing Access Control Policies for XML Document Sources". World Wide Web Journal, vol. 3, n. 3, Baltzer Science Publishers. 2000.

[2] T. Bray et al. "Extensible Markup Language (XML) 1.0". World Wide Web Consortium (W3C). http://www.w3c.org/TR/REC-xml (October 2000).

[3] E. Bruno, J. Le Maitre and E. Murisasco, "Extending XQuery with Transformation Operators", Proceedings of the 2003 ACM Symposium on Document Engineering (DocEng 2003), ACM Press, Grenoble, France, November 20-22 2003, pp. 1-8. [Réf. F75].

[4] J. Clark and Steve DeRose . "XML Path Language (XPath) Version 1.0". World Wide Web Consortium (W3C). http://www.w3c.org/TR/xpath (November 1999).

[5] J. Clark. "XSL Transformations (XSLT) Version 1.0". World Wide Web Consortium (W3C). http://www.w3c.org/TR/xslt (November 1999).

[6] Cohen, E., Kaplan, H. and Milo, T. (2002): Labelling dynamic XML trees, in Proceedings of *PODS* 2002.

[7] E. Damiani, S. De Capitani di Vimercati, S. Paraboschi, P. Samarati, "Securing XML Documents," in Proc. of the 2000 International Conference on Extending Database Technology (EDBT2000), Konstanz, Germany, March 27-31, 2000.

[8] Maggie Duong and Yanchun Zhang. LSDX: A New Labelling Scheme for Dynamically Updating XML Data. In proc of ACSW2005 – 16th Australasian Database Conference. Newcastle, Australia.

[9] I. Fundulaki and M. Marx. "Specifying Acces Control Policies for XML Documents with XPath". In ACM Symp. on Access Control Models and Technologies (SACMAT), 2004.

[10] Alban Gabillon. "An Authorization model for XML databases". Proc. of the 11th ACM Conference on Computer Security (Workshop Secure Web Services). George Mason University, Fairfax, VA, USA. October 2004.

[11] Alban Gabillon and Emmanuel Bruno. "Regulating Access to XML documents". Fifteenth Annual IFIP WG 11.3 Working Conference on Database Security. Niagara on the Lake, Ontario, Canada July 15-18, 2001.

[12] Alban Gabillon and Majirus Fansi. "A Persistent Labelling Scheme for XML and tree Database". Submitted to the IEEE International Conference on Signal-Image Technology & Internet- Based Systems 2005.

[13] M. Kudo and S. Hada. "XML Document Security based on Provisional Authorisation". Proceedings of the 7th ACM conference on Computer and communications security. November, 2000, Athens Greece.

[14] C. Lim, S. Park, and S. H. Son, "Access Control of XML Documents considering Update Operations" ACM Workshop on XML Security, Fairfax, VA, Oct. 2003

[15] A. Laux et L. Martin. XML Update (XUpdate) language. XML:DB working draft, http://www.xmldb.org/xupdate. September 14, 2000

[16] R. Reiter. "Toward a logical reconstruction of relational database theory". In On Conceptual Modelling: Perspectives from Artificial Intelligence, Databases and Programming Languages. Springer Verlag, 1983

[17] R. Sandhu. "Role-Based Access Control". Advances in Computers. Vol 48. Academic Press. 1998.

[18] A. Stoica and C. Farkas, "Secure XML Views," In Proc. 16th IFIP WG11.3 Working Conference on Database and Application Security, 2002.

[19] R. Sandhu and S. Jajodia. Polyinstantiation for cover stories. In European Symposium on Research in Computer Security. Toulouse, France.1992. Springer Verlag.

[20] Gargi M. Sur, Joachim Hammer, and Jerome Simeon, "UpdateX - An XQuery-Based Language for Processing Updates in XML." International Workshop on Programming Language Technologies for XML (PLAN-X 2004), Venice, Italy, January 2004.

[21] Tatarinov, I., Viglas, S., Beyer, K., Shanmugasundaram, J., Shekita, E. and Zhang: Storing and Querying Ordered XML Using a Relational Database System, in Proceedings of SIGMOD 2002.

[22] I. Tatarinov, Zachary G. Yves, Alon Y. Halevy, Daniel S. Weld. "Updating XML". In ACM SIGMOD 2001 May 21-24, Santa Barbara, California, USA.

[23] Apache software foundation. Xindice, http://xml.apache.org/xindice.

[24] Yu, X. J., Luo, D., Meng, X. and Lu, H.: Dynamically Updating XML Data: Numbering Scheme Revisited, in World Wide Web: Internet and Web Information System, 7, 2004.

Can Attackers Learn from Samples?

Ganesh Ramesh

Department of Computer Science,
University of British Columbia,
201-2366 Main Mall, Vancouver, B.C. V6T 1Z4
ramesh@cs.ubc.ca

Abstract. Sampling is often used to achieve disclosure limitation for categorical and microarray datasets. The motivation is that while the public gets a snapshot of what is in the data, the entire data is not revealed and hence complete disclosure is prevented. However, the presence of prior knowledge is often overlooked in risk assessment. A sample plays an important role in risk analysis and can be used by a malicious user to construct prior knowledge of the domain. In this paper, we focus on formalizing the various kinds of prior knowledge an attacker can develop using samples and make the following contributions. We abstract various types of prior knowledge and define measures of quality which enables us to quantify how good the prior knowledge is with respect to the true knowledge given by the database. We propose a lightweight general purpose sampling framework with which a data owner can assess the impact of various sampling methods on the quality of prior knowledge. Finally, through a systematic set of experiments using real benchmark datasets, we study the effect of various sampling parameters on the quality of prior knowledge that is obtained from these samples. Such an analysis can help the data owner in making informed decisions about releasing samples to achieve disclosure limitation.

1   Introduction

Data owners often face situations where sharing their data is either a necessity or will yield some kind of benefit. The problem with sharing is the breach of privacy caused by revealing sensitive information in the data. Various methods have been proposed to deal with this problem. Techniques like transformations, random data perturbations and k-anonymization, modify the data in such a way that sensitive information is either suppressed or modified to prevent being disclosed (or inferred). One of the techniques that is used as an alternative to sharing the entire database, is to release a small sample of the database: the main motivation being that while the public gets a snapshot of the kind of data that exists in the actual database, it is unlikely that a user can create accurate models of the original data using a small sample of the database. Moreover, in many practical domains, it is not very difficult for a casual observer to obtain a sample of data. For example, an observer of a market basket can casually note down the contents of a basket and later relate them with the barcodes of the product to

W. Jonker and M. Petković (Eds.): SDM 2005, LNCS 3674, pp. 104–123, 2005.

construct a sample of market basket data. Similarly, a casual observer can note down the contents of an online shopper and note down the contents of an online store's transaction database. While this may be unethical in an ideal situation, malicious users will go to any extent to obtain knowledge of the domain they intend to attack. Hence, a sample plays an important role in the analysis of risk in information sharing. While similar analysis exists for other transformation techniques, this paper focusses on sampling. Typically, the sample is used by malicious users to construct statistical knowledge of the domain, also called as *prior knowledge*, with which the attacker can try to identify sensitive information in the actual database. In this work, we focus on formalizing what kinds of prior knowledge the attacker can develop, using the information in the sample and how good such knowledge is based on the parameters of the sample. Such an analysis can help the data owner in making a self assessment of the risk involved in releasing a sample of the database to the public or in sharing a sample of the database.

More specifically, we make the following contributions. We abstract various types of *prior knowledge* a malicious user can construct from a sample and formalize them (section 3.1). These include knowledge of the actual frequency of the items in the database, knowledge about the interval in which the frequency of an item can lie in, knowledge about how the frequency of an item relates to the frequency of other items and so on. We define various *measures of quality* which enables one to quantify how good the prior knowledge is with respect to the actual true knowledge in the database (section 3.2). We propose a general purpose lightweight sampling framework with which a data owner can assess the impact of various sampling parameters on the quality of prior knowledge (section 4). We study various types of sampling: Single sample with and without replacement and bootstrap sampling where the master sample may be drawn with or without replacement. We also propose methods with which attackers or data owners (for self assessment) can construct prior knowledge from these samples. Finally, through a rigorous experimental analysis using real benchmark datasets, we present the effect of various sampling parameters on the quality of prior knowledge that is obtained from the samples (section 5).

1.1 Research Questions

An informal list of problem statements addressed in this paper is given below. 1. Suppose that a sample of the database is released, what are the various types of knowledge an attacker can construct from this sample? 2. How close is the knowledge constructed from the sample to the true knowledge that is present in the database? 3. Does it matter how the sample is drawn from the database? 4. How do the parameters like sample size affect the knowledge that is constructed from the sample?

2 Related Work

A predominant amount of work in *disclosure limitation* like [15,11,10] focus on applying statistical disclosure limitation methods for categorical and microarray datasets. A number of techniques like *cell suppression, data swapping, rounding, sampling, anonymization* and *synthetic data generation* are used for achieving *statistical disclosure control.* Many of these methods perturb the characteristics of the data in the process of limiting disclosure.

Privacy has been studied in the context of association rule mining. In [9], Evfimievski et al. propose a framework for mining association rules in which the data items in transactions are randomized to preserve privacy of individual transactions. They analyze the nature of privacy breaches caused by using the association rules discovered from this database and propose randomization operators to limit such breaches. The problem of hiding association rules by transforming the input database is studied by Verykios et al. in [19]. The authors are interested in modifying the input database such that a given set of associations is hidden in the transformed database. They assume that the associations to be hidden are pre-marked and use heuristics to transform the database in order to hide the marked associations. All these studies, however, do not deal with prior knowledge that can be constructed by an attacker.

In [4], Agrawal and Srikant propose an approach for privacy preserving classification that is based on mining on perturbed data, with the perturbed distribution closely matching the real distribution. Furthermore, Agrawal and Aggarwal in [5] discuss an expectation maximization algorithm which provides robust estimates of the original distribution based on perturbation and provides some interesting results on the relative effectiveness of different perturbing distributions in terms of privacy. In [12], Iyengar uses the approaches of suppression and generalizations to satisfy privacy constraints. In [2], Aggarwal and Yu use an approach based on *condensation groups* to model indistinguishability of data records and use it to create anonymized data which has similar characteristics to the original multidimensional dataset and apply it to the classification problem. Cryptographic techniques for privacy preserving data mining have been explored in [13]. Finally, the *k*-anonymity model studied in [17,18,3,16] uses domain generalization hierarchies in order to transform and replace each record value with a corresponding generalized value. In sum, all these studies focus on perturbing the data so that the results of data mining the perturbed data remain similar to the original data. Privacy has also been studied in the context of statistical databases. The security problem in statistical databases deals with protecting a database from returning information about an individual or answering a sequence of queries from which individual information can be deduced, where the statistical databases allow only queries that retrieve statistical information. These methods are characterized in the survey [1].

Laks et al. [14] consider the problem of assessing the risk in disclosing anonymized data in the presence of prior knowledge. They model prior knowledge through belief functions and depending on how much the attacker knows about the domain, the belief functions are categorized as ignorant, point-valued and interval belief functions. They also use a notion of compliancy to model how accurately the frequency of an item can be guessed by an attacker and use the analysis to come up with a recipe based on which data owners can decide whether to release their anonymized data or not. While [14] considers prior knowledge obtained through samples, this work differs from them in two ways. First, the types of prior knowledge we consider are different. Second, the focus of this work is to see how accurate prior knowledge obtained from samples are as opposed to helping a data owner resolve the dilemma of disclosure. Also, we evaluate the impact of various sampling methods on the accuracy of prior knowledge. The main motivation for this study was however derived from their work. Finally, Clifton [7] argues that releasing a small sample poses no threat to the data owner as little information can be revealed. We discuss the implications of our work on this statement later on in the paper.

3 Preliminaries

We consider a universal set $\mathcal{I}$ of n items. A subset $X \subseteq \mathcal{I}$ is called an *itemset*. A transaction t is a nonempty itemset. A database $\mathcal{D} = \langle t_1, \ldots, t_m \rangle$ is a nonempty sequence of transactions. Each transaction is identified by a *unique* identifier called the *transaction identifier* or *tid*. For the rest of this paper, we use nonnegative integers to represent items and tids. The tid for transaction t_i will be i and $\mathcal{I}$ will be identified with the set $\{1, 2, \ldots, n\}$. The size of an itemset $X \subseteq \mathcal{I}$ is the cardinality of the itemset $|X|$. An itemset of size k will be referred to as a k-*itemset*. The size of a database $\mathcal{D}$ denoted $|\mathcal{D}|$, is the number of transactions in $\mathcal{D}$.

A transaction t *contains* an itemset X, whenever $X \subseteq t$. The **support** of itemset X in $\mathcal{D}$, denoted $\pi(X, \mathcal{D})$, is the *number* of transactions in $\mathcal{D}$ that contain X, i.e $|\{t \in \mathcal{D} \mid X \subseteq t\}|$. The **frequency** of an itemset X in the database $\mathcal{D}$, denoted $\mathcal{F}(X, \mathcal{D})$ is the fraction of transactions in $\mathcal{D}$ that contain X. More formally, $\mathcal{F}(X, \mathcal{D}) = \frac{|\{t \in \mathcal{D} \mid X \subseteq t\}|}{|\mathcal{D}|} = \frac{\pi(X, \mathcal{D})}{|\mathcal{D}|}$.

Often in practice, many situations do not attach the same degree of importance to every item in the universe $\mathcal{I}$. To model this case, we define a *weight function* $w : \mathcal{I} \to \mathbb{R}$, that associates a real number with each item in $\mathcal{I}$. For consistency, we assume that the weights are assigned in such a way that the higher the value, the more important the item is. The other cases can be handled analogously.

A random sample $\mathcal{S}$ of the database is a set of transactions drawn from the database $\mathcal{D}$ uniformly at random. For the purposes of our discussion, it is enough to keep in mind that a sample is usually smaller than the size of the database. The size of the sample is denoted as $|\mathcal{S}|$ and is the number of transactions in the sample. A $k\%$-sample is a sample $\mathcal{S}$ such that $|\mathcal{S}| = \frac{k}{100} \cdot |\mathcal{D}|$, i.e. the number of transactions in the sample is $k\%$ of the number of transactions in the database.

3.1 Prior Knowledge

When samples are released, an attacker can use the information in the sample to gather domain knowledge. As the attacker builds such knowledge *prior* to using them for inferring more about sensitive data, we refer to such knowledge as *prior knowledge*. For the rest of the paper, by prior knowledge, we refer to the information gained by the attacker, by analyzing a sample of data that is released by any data owner. While it is always likely that an attacker can build and use prior knowledge in arbitrary ways, for the purposes of this work, we are interested in the following types of prior knowledge.

Definition 1 (Frequency Knowledge). *The first type of knowledge is that of frequency of individual items. Depending on the type of knowledge constructed by the attacker, we classify the frequency knowledge into two types:* exact *and* interval, *which we define below.*

1. *We say that the attacker has* exact frequency knowledge, *denoted $\mathcal{K}^\circ$, when the prior knowledge associates every item $x \in \mathcal{I}$ with a frequency value in $[0, 1]$. More formally, $\mathcal{K}^\circ$ is a function that maps every item $x \in \mathcal{I}$ to a real number in the interval $[0, 1]$. Thus, when the attacker has exact frequency knowledge $\mathcal{K}^\circ$, then it is the attacker's belief that $\mathcal{K}^\circ(x)$ is the frequency of item $x \in \mathcal{I}$ in the database.*

2. *We say that the attacker has* interval frequency knowledge, *denoted $\mathcal{K}^{[\,]}$, whenever the prior knowledge associates every item $x \in \mathcal{I}$ with an interval $[l_x, r_x]$, where $0 \leq l_x \leq r_x \leq 1$. Thus, when the attacker has interval frequency knowledge $\mathcal{K}^{[\,]}$ as prior knowledge, then it is the attacker's belief that the frequency of the item $x \in \mathcal{I}$ in the database lies in the range given by $\mathcal{K}^{[\,]}(x)$.*

The notion of *exact* and *interval* frequency knowledge can be used to model the confidence an attacker has in the frequency of items. For an item whose frequency is precisely known, an attacker may associate a single value of frequency to its prior knowledge. However, for an item whose frequency is unknown, the attacker may wish to associate the most general interval in which the frequency can lie, namely $[0, 1]$. The *interval* frequency knowledge can be used to model such precision, as exact knowledge is precisely the interval $[l, l]$ (if l is the attacker's knowledge of the frequency of an item x).

Example 1. Let us consider the case when $\mathcal{I} = \{1, 2, 3, 4, 5\}$. An example of $\mathcal{K}^\circ$ is given by the function $\mathcal{K}^\circ(1) = 0.2, \mathcal{K}^\circ(2) = 0.3, \mathcal{K}^\circ(3) = 1, \mathcal{K}^\circ(4) = 0, \mathcal{K}^\circ(5) = 0.7$. This models the case where the attacker believes that the frequency of item 1 in the database is 0.2 or 20%, the item 4 does not occur in the database, item 3 occurs in every transaction in the database and so on. An example of $\mathcal{K}^{[\,]}$ is given by $\mathcal{K}^{[\,]}(1) = [0.1, 0.5], \mathcal{K}^{[\,]}(2) = [0.35, 0.45], \mathcal{K}^{[\,]}(3) = [0.5, 0.5], \mathcal{K}^{[\,]}(4) = [0, 1], \mathcal{K}^{[\,]}(5) = [0.6, 0.6]$.

Apart from frequency, the attacker can also use the relative order of the frequency of items. We model the prior knowledge of the order of frequency of items as follows.

Definition 2 (Frequency Order Knowledge). *The frequency order knowledge of an attacker, denoted $\mathcal{K}^\prec$, is an ordered partition $(P_\mathcal{I}, <)$ defined as follows. $P_\mathcal{I} = \{P_1, \ldots, P_k\}$ is a partition of the set of items $\mathcal{I}$. Thus, $\bigcup_{i=1}^{k} P_i = \mathcal{I}$*

and $P_i \cap P_j = \emptyset$ for $1 \leq i < j \leq k$. The partitions contain items whose frequencies are believed to be identical by the attacker. There is an additional ordering of these partitions defined by the ordering $<$. The ordering $P_i < P_j$ models the attacker's belief that the frequency of items in partition P_i is less than the frequency of items in partition P_j. This is assumed to be a partial order and hence, if two partitions are incomparable according to $<$, this models the user's lack of knowledge about how to compare the frequency of items in partitions P_i and P_j. We can also think of $\mathcal{K}^{\prec}$ as an edge labelled graph $G_{\mathcal{K}^{\prec}} = (\mathcal{I}, E)$ with two types of labels $\{=, <\}$. There is an edge labelled $" ="$ between $x \in \mathcal{I}$ and $y \in \mathcal{I}$, whenever x and y belong to the same partition $P_i \in P_{\mathcal{I}}$. There is an edge labelled $" <"$ between $x \in \mathcal{I}$ and $y \in \mathcal{I}$ whenever there exists two partitions P_i and P_j such that $x \in P_i$, $y \in P_j$ and $P_i < P_j$.

Definition 3 (Rank of an Item and Rank Knowledge). *Let $\mathcal{I}$ be a universe of items and let $\mathcal{F}(x, D)$ be the frequency of item x in database D. Let F be the set of distinct frequency values of the items in D. The* rank *of an item x is the number of frequency values in F that is greater than orq equal to x's frequency in the database. More formally, $F = \{f \mid \exists x \in \mathcal{I} : \mathcal{F}(x, D) = f\}$. The rank of item $x \in \mathcal{I}$, denoted $rank(x, D) = |\{f \mid (f \in F) \wedge (f \geq \mathcal{F}(x, D))\}|$.*

We say that an attacker has Rank Knowledge, *denoted $\mathcal{K}^{pos}$, when the prior knowledge associates an item $x \in \mathcal{I}$ with a positive integer in the range $\{1, 2, \ldots, |\mathcal{I}|\}$. This models the fact that the attacker believes the rank of item $x \in \mathcal{I}$ in the database to be $\mathcal{K}^{pos}(x)$.*

From definition 3, it is easy to see that the most frequent items in a database are assigned a rank of 1, the next most frequent items are assigned a rank of 2 and so on. In practice, the attacker can determine the rank of items from a sample of the dataset and use it as prior knowledge. Unlike the Frequency Order Knowledge, the *Rank Knowledge* need not necessarily associate every item with a rank. It may map a subset $\mathcal{I}' \subset \mathcal{I}$ of items to a rank value (hence a *partial function*). Note that we can also generalize the Rank Knowledge to a *range* of rank values instead of a single value. This is a natural generalization to the belief that the rank of an item lies between l and r, where l and r are valid rank values (between 1 and $|\mathcal{I}|$). It should be noted that the actual ranks of items in the original database may be entirely different from those assigned to them by an attacker. This is understandable, as the attacker bases prior knowledge on a sample of data. As an example, the frequencies of items may be distributed in such a way that there are two partitions of the items in groups of two frequencies and hence have ranks 1 and 2 respectively. However, the attacker's prior knowledge may be that every item has a distinct frequency and hence a distinct rank value in the range $\{1, 2, \ldots, |\mathcal{I}|\}$.

Example 2. Figure 1(a) gives an example of *Frequency Order Knowledge* for a set of 5 items $\mathcal{I} = \{1, 2, 3, 4, 5\}$. The knowledge is shown pictorially and contains 4 partitions. $P_2 = \{3, 5\}$ is the only partition containing more than 1 item, while $P_1 = \{1\}$, $P_3 = \{2\}$ and $P_4 = \{4\}$ are the other partitions. The partitions model the attacker's belief that items 3 and 5 have the same frequency and the other

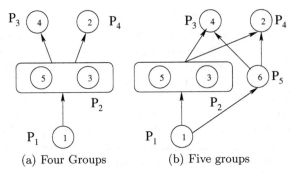

(a) Four Groups   (b) Five groups

Fig. 1. Example of Frequency Order Knowledge

items have distinct frequencies in the database. The ordering of frequencies is represented by directed edges between the various partitions. Thus, the attacker believes that the frequency of item 1 is less than those of items 3 and 5, the frequency of items 3 and 5 are less than those of 2 and 4, respectively. Note that the attacker has no idea how to compare the frequencies of 2 and 4 and hence they are incomparable. The frequency of item 1 is less than that of items 2 and 4 respectively, by transitivity. Figure 1(b) gives another example of frequency order knowledge. It is the same as the one in figure 1(a), except for the fact that there is an additional item, numbered 6 whose frequency is believed to be less than those of items 2 and 4, greater than item 1 but for which the attacker has no idea how the frequency relates to those of items 3 and 5.

All the types of prior knowledge we have discusses thus far, associate statistical knowledge to items. The following type of prior knowledge captures the belief an attacker has about what the most frequently occurring items are.

Definition 4 (TOP-K Knowledge). *Given a value of $k \leq |\mathcal{I}|$, the TOP-K Knowledge, denoted* topK *is a subset $\mathcal{I}' \subseteq \mathcal{I}$, such that $|\mathcal{I}'| = k$. This models the attacker's prior belief that the top k most frequent items in the database is given by the set $\mathcal{I}'$. Alternately, the value of k can be specified as a percentage. In this case, the Top-K knowledge, denoted* topK$^{\%}$*, deals with a fraction $\frac{k}{100}$ of items.*

Example 3. The Top-K knowledge topK $= \{2, 5\}$, for $k = 2$, over $\mathcal{I} = \{1, 2, 3, 4, 5\}$, models the fact that the attacker believes that items 2 and 5 are the two most frequently occurring items in the database. This is also the same as topK$^{\%}$(40) as 40% of $\mathcal{I}$ is 2.

Note that when two items have the same frequency and the value of k is such that only one of them can be in the set of top k items, then the ties can be broken arbitrarily. However, for correctness, each of these top k sets are considered correct.

3.2 Measuring Quality of Prior Knowledge

Let us assume that the attacker has access to a sample $\mathcal{S}$ of the original database $\mathcal{D}$. The attacker can use the sample to construct any (or all) of the types of knowledge that were defined in section 3.1. How close is the attacker's knowledge to the original facts in the database? To quantify this, we define measures of *quality* of the prior knowledge. As an example, if the attacker believes that the frequency of item x is 0.5 and the actual frequency of item x is 0.55 in the database, then the attacker has a better knowledge of the frequency of x than if the attacker believes that the frequency of item x is 0.3. The measure of *quality* allows us to determine which types of knowledge are close to the actual knowledge (and hence bad for the owner of the data but good for the attacker). We define and formalize measures of quality with the various types of prior knowledge that were defined earlier.

Definition 5 (Mean Frequency Difference). *Let $\mathcal{K}^\circ$ be the exact frequency knowledge of an attacker over the set $\mathcal{I}$ of items. Let $\mathcal{F}(x, \mathcal{D})$ be the frequency of item $x \in \mathcal{I}$ in the database and let $w : \mathcal{I} \to \mathbb{R}$ be a weight function associated with $\mathcal{I}$. Then, the (weighted) mean frequency difference, denoted Δ, measures the average absolute difference in frequencies of the prior knowledge and the actual frequency of items in $\mathcal{I}$. More formally,*

$$\Delta = \frac{1}{|\mathcal{I}|} \cdot \sum_{x \in \mathcal{I}} \frac{|\mathcal{K}^\circ(x) - \mathcal{F}(x, \mathcal{D})|}{w(x)} \tag{1}$$

The weighted mean frequency difference Δ, measures how far the frequency of items are from their original frequency values in the database. The higher the value of Δ, the poorer the quality of prior knowledge.

Definition 6 (Compliancy and Mean Compliant Interval Width). *Let $\mathcal{K}^{[\,]}$ be the interval frequency knowledge of an attacker. An item x is said to be compliant whenever $\mathcal{F}(x, \mathcal{D}) \in \mathcal{K}^{[\,]}(x)$. Thus, Compliant items are those items whose frequency intervals modelling prior knowledge, contain the actual frequency in the database. Let $\mathcal{C}(\mathcal{I}, \mathcal{K}^{[\,]}, \mathcal{D})$ be the set of compliant items defined as $\mathcal{C}(\mathcal{I}, \mathcal{K}^{[\,]}, \mathcal{D}) = \{x | \mathcal{F}(x, \mathcal{D}) \in \mathcal{K}^{[\,]}(x)\}$. The mean compliant interval width measures the average width of the attacker's belief for each compliant item and is defined as*

$$\mathsf{MCIW} = \frac{1}{|\mathcal{C}(\mathcal{I}, \mathcal{K}^{[\,]}, \mathcal{D})|} \cdot \sum_{x \in \mathcal{C}(\mathcal{I}, \mathcal{K}^{[\,]}, \mathcal{D})} |\mathcal{K}^{[\,]}(x)| \tag{2}$$

Let w be the weight function on $\mathcal{I}$. Then, we define the weighted interval compliancy measure as

$$\mathsf{WIC} = \sum_{x \in \mathcal{C}(\mathcal{I}, \mathcal{K}^{[\,]}, \mathcal{D})} \frac{w(x)}{|\mathcal{K}^{[\,]}(x)|} \tag{3}$$

Note that MCIW by itself, may not be appropriate to say that the interval frequency knowledge of an attacker is of good quality. We need to consider it along with the number of compliant items in order to measure quality. For example, in the first case, there may be 1 compliant item whose interval is of width 0.3 and in the second case, there may be 2 compliant items whose average width is 0.35. The interval width in the first case may be smaller but the number of items on which the attacker has reasonably good knowledge is only 1 in the first case, while it is 2 in the second case. Hence, we need to take these two kinds of knowledge together to determine the quality. This is done using the *weighted interval compliancy* measure, which accounts the importance of the item and the confidence with which the attacker can know the frequency of this item. The higher this measure, the greater the quality of knowledge of the attacker.

Definition 7 (Order Compliancy). *Let $\mathcal{K}^{\prec}$ be the* frequency order knowledge *of an attacker and let $G_{\mathcal{K}^{\prec}}$ be the corresponding graph. We say that an edge $e(x,y) \in E(G_{\mathcal{K}^{\prec}})$ is* order compliant, *whenever any of the following conditions are satisfied:*

- *$e(x,y)$ is labelled " $=$ " and $\mathcal{F}(x,\mathcal{D}) = \mathcal{F}(y,\mathcal{D})$*
- *$e(x,y)$ is labelled " $<$ " and $\mathcal{F}(x,\mathcal{D}) < \mathcal{F}(y,\mathcal{D})$*

More formally, the set of order compliant *edges are defined as: $EC = \{e(x,y) \in E(G_{\mathcal{K}^{\prec}}) \mid ((l(e) = "=") \wedge (\mathcal{F}(x,\mathcal{D}) = \mathcal{F}(y,\mathcal{D}))) \vee ((l(e) = "<") \wedge (\mathcal{F}(x,\mathcal{D}) < \mathcal{F}(y,\mathcal{D})))\}$ The* Order Compliancy Measure, *denoted* OCM *is defined as*

$$OCM = \frac{|EC|}{|E(G_{\mathcal{D}})|} \tag{4}$$

where, $E(G_{\mathcal{D}})$ is the set of edges in the graph representing the order in the actual database.

Note that the set EC is the set of all edges for which the order knowledge of the attacker is consistent with the order of the frequency of items found in the actual database. The *order compliancy measure* is thus a normalized measure of the pairs of items for which the order knowledge is consistent with those in the actual database.

Definition 8 (Rank Measure). *Let $\mathcal{K}^{pos}$ be the* rank knowledge *of an attacker. For each item $x \in \mathcal{I}$, $|\mathcal{K}^{pos}(x) - rank(x,\mathcal{D})|$ gives how far the attacker's knowledge of the rank of x is compared with the actual rank of item x in the database. The* rank measure, *denoted* RM, *measures the average absolute difference between the actual rank and the one given by the rank knowledge, over all the items in $\mathcal{I}$ and is defined as*

$$RM = \frac{i}{|\mathcal{I}|} \sum_{x \in \mathcal{I}} |\mathcal{K}^{pos}(x) - rank(x,\mathcal{D})| \tag{5}$$

A second measure that is used in this work is the number of items whose actual rank exactly coincides with the rank knowledge of the attacker. The set $R = \{x \in \mathcal{I} | \mathcal{K}^{pos}(x) = rank(x,\mathcal{D})\}$ is the set of those items whose rank knowledge is equal to the actual rank in the database. The fraction of such items is given by $\frac{|R|}{|\mathcal{I}|}$ and this is also used to measure the quality of $\mathcal{K}^{pos}$. The higher this value, the better the rank knowledge.

Definition 9 (Top-K Measure). *Given a fixed integer k, let I_k be the k most frequent items in the database. This includes all the items that have the highest frequency, those of second highest frequency and so on, upto the kth highest frequency value. Let* topK *be the* top-k knowledge *of the attacker and let w be the* weight function *on $\mathcal{I}$. The* Top-K Measure *is defined as*

$$\mathsf{TKM} = \frac{|\mathsf{topK} \cap I_k|}{|\mathsf{topK}|} \tag{6}$$

The weighted Top-K Measure *is defined as*

$$\mathsf{WTKM} = \mathsf{TKM}. \sum_{x \in \mathsf{topK} \cap I_k} w(x) \tag{7}$$

4 Extracting Prior Knowledge Using Sampling

Once a sample is released to the public, an attacker can extract different kinds of knowledge from the samples. There are two different perspectives for analyzing samples. The first perspective is from the point of view of the attacker. As an attacker, the prior knowledge obtained from the samples should be reliable and of good quality. The second perspective is from the point of view of the data owner. To protect the privacy of the sensitive information, releasing a sample is not good if the attacker can construct prior knowledge of high quality from the sample. So, an analysis of samples can help the data owner in identifying the risks involved in releasing samples to the public. On the other hand, part of this analysis can be used by the attacker to determine which types of knowledge and of what quality can be derived from the sample.

Figure 2 shows the general framework for analysis of samples, whose main components are:

1. The Sample Generating Procedure: This is used to generate one or more random samples of a given size from a database, based on the type of sampling method (section 4.1).
2. Constructing Prior Knowledge: Once one or more samples are available, how do we use the samples to construct prior knowledge? This component, though not explicitly shown in the figure, is the one that takes us from a collection of samples to obtaining prior knowledge from the samples (section 4.2).
3. Comparison Procedure: This component is responsible for determining the measures of quality of prior knowledge by comparing the prior knowledge from the samples with the actual knowledge in the database (section 4.2).

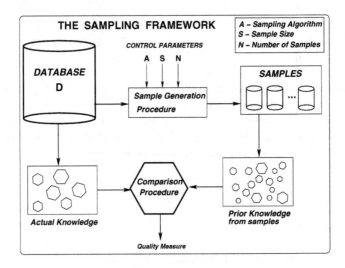

Fig. 2. The Sampling Framework

4.1   The Sample Generation Procedure

This procedure takes a database $\mathcal{D}$, the number of samples (N) and sample size (S) as input parameters and produces as output N samples, each consisting of S transactions, generated by a sampling method. We consider the following sampling methods for this work.

1. Sampling with/without replacement: A random sample of S tids is generated from the set $\{1, 2, \ldots, M\}$ of transaction ids with/without replacement. If more than 1 sample is generated, then each time a random sample of S tids is drawn with/without replacement from the set $\{1, 2, \ldots, M\}$ of the database tids. The transactions that correspond to the tids selected in S are used for the sample. When the sampling is done with replacement, a transaction may be read multiple times as the tids may repeat.
2. Bootstrap Sampling: An initial sample of size S is generated from the database either with or without replacement. This becomes the seed set and let the tids of this sample S be $\{1, 2, \ldots, S\}$. Each of the N samples are constructed by generating S tids with replacement from the seed set $\{1, 2, \ldots, S\}$ of tids. We refer to each sample generated in this manner as a *bootstrap sample*.

4.2   Constructing Prior Knowledge from the Sample(s) and the Comparison Procedure

For this section, let us assume that $S_1, \ldots, S_N$ are N samples, each of size S. For an item $x \in \mathcal{I}$, let $\mathcal{F}(x, S_i)$ denote the frequency of item x in sample S_i, for $1 \leq i \leq N$. Using these frequencies, we now describe how they can be used to compute the various types of prior knowledge described in section 3.1.

Exact Frequency Knowledge $\mathcal{K}^\circ$: The exact frequency knowledge for an item is computed by taking the average of the frequency of the item in all the N samples. More formally, $\mathcal{K}^\circ(x) = \frac{1}{N} \cdot \sum_{i=1}^{n} \mathcal{F}(x, S_i)$.

Interval Frequency Knowledge $\mathcal{K}^{[\ ]}$: Various methods can be used to construct the interval frequency knowledge for an item $x \in \mathcal{I}$. Let $\mathcal{K}^\circ(x) = \frac{1}{N} \cdot \sum_{i=1}^{n} \mathcal{F}(x, S_i)$ denote the average frequency of item x in all the samples. The interval is constructed around this frequency for an item x. We consider the following two methods and denote the interval frequency knowledge $\mathcal{K}^{[M]}$ and $\mathcal{K}^{[\delta]}$ respectively: 1. Let $m_x = min\{\mathcal{F}(x, S_1), \ldots, \mathcal{F}(x, S_N)\}$ and let $M_x = max\{\mathcal{F}(x, S_1), \ldots, \mathcal{F}(x, S_N)\}$. Then, $\mathcal{K}^{[M]}(x) = [m_x, M_x]$. 2. Let δ_i denote the mean (or median) frequency gap between the frequencies of various items in sample S_i and let $\delta = \frac{1}{N} \cdot \sum_{i=1}^{N} \delta_i$ be the average of all the mean/median frequency gaps across all the samples. The interval knowledge $\mathcal{K}^{[\delta]}$, associated with item x is $\mathcal{K}^{[\delta]}(x) = [\mathcal{K}^\circ(x) - \delta, \mathcal{K}^\circ(x) + \delta]$.

Note that the interval $[m_x, M_x]$ is a single point when the number of samples is 1. Hence, for the single sample case, we only consider the interval frequency knowledge $\mathcal{K}^{[\delta]}$.

Frequency Order Knowledge $\mathcal{K}^\prec$: To compute the frequency order knowledge $\mathcal{K}^\prec$, we first model the relationship between the frequencies of pairs of items as *predicates*. Instead of modelling $\mathcal{K}^\prec$ as an ordered partition, we convert the order information into a numeric measure. Let $\mathcal{F}(x, S)$ denote the average frequency of item x in all the samples and let $\mathcal{F}(x, \mathcal{D})$ denote the frequency of x in $\mathcal{D}$. We say that $=_S (x, y)$ (or $=_\mathcal{D} (x, y)$) whenever $\mathcal{F}(x, S) = \mathcal{F}(y, S)$ (respectively $\mathcal{F}(x, \mathcal{D}) = \mathcal{F}(y, \mathcal{D})$). Predicates $<_S (x, y)$, $>_S (x, y)$, $<_\mathcal{D} (x, y)$ and $>_\mathcal{D} (x, y)$ are defined analogously. For $x \in \mathcal{I}, y \in \mathcal{I}$, define $P(x, y)$ as follows.

$$P(x, y) = \{(x, y) : (x \neq y) \wedge ((=_S (x, y)\wedge =_\mathcal{D} (x, y))$$
$$\vee (<_S (x, y)\wedge <_\mathcal{D} (x, y)) \vee (>_S (x, y)\wedge >_\mathcal{D} (x, y)))\}$$

Thus, $P(x, y)$ is the set of all pairs of items which have the same order of frequencies in both the sample and the database. The frequency order knowledge is then defined to be the fraction of pairs between which the frequency order obtained from the sample is consistent with that in the database. This is given by

$$\mathcal{K}^\prec = \frac{|\{P(x, y)\}|}{\binom{|\mathcal{I}|}{2}} \tag{8}$$

Rank Knowledge $\mathcal{K}^{pos}$: To compute rank knowledge from the samples, we compute the rank of each item based on their frequency in the database (denoted $rank(x, \mathcal{D})$ for item x) and their average frequency in the samples (denoted $rank(x, S)$ for item x). The rank knowledge is the computed as the average absolute difference between the ranks in the samples and those in the database. This is formally defined as

$$\mathcal{K}^{pos} = \frac{\sum_{x \in \mathcal{I}} |rank(x, S) - rank(x, \mathcal{D})|}{|\mathcal{I}|} \tag{9}$$

Note that many items can have the same frequency and hence this measure may be too pessimistic in computing the quality of rank knowledge. We handle this when computing the Top-K knowledge, which accounts for groups of frequencies.

Top-K Knowledge topK$^\%$: For measuring the $Top - K$ knowledge, we first compute the set of frequency groups in which the $k\%$ of items with the highest frequency in the database lie in. We then compute the Top-K items to be the union of all items in these frequency groups, which *may* be more than $k\%$ of the number of items. We compute the corresponding set of items using the average frequency of the items in the samples. These groups are then compared to obtain the topK$^\%$ measure.

Table 1. Tabular Summary of Prior Knowledge

Prior Knowledge	Notation	Computed From Samples
Exact Frequency	$\mathcal{K}^\circ$	$\mathcal{K}^\circ(x) = \frac{1}{N} \cdot \sum_{i=1}^{n} \mathcal{F}(x, S_i)$
Interval Frequency	$\mathcal{K}^{[\,]}$	1. $\mathcal{K}^{[M]}(x) = [m_x, M_x]$ (For multiple samples)
		2. $\mathcal{K}^{[\delta]}(x) = [\mathcal{K}^\circ(x) - \delta, \mathcal{K}^\circ(x) + \delta]$
Frequency Order	$\mathcal{K}^\prec$	$\mathcal{K}^\prec = \frac{|\{P(x,y)\}|}{\binom{|\mathcal{I}|}{2}}$
Rank Knowledge	$\mathcal{K}^{pos}$	$\mathcal{K}^{pos} = \frac{\sum_{x \in \mathcal{I}} |rank(x,S) - rank(x,\mathcal{D})|}{|\mathcal{I}|}$

5   Experimental Results

5.1   Experimental Setup and Implementation

We used real benchmark datasets obtained from the UCI repository [1] and the FIMI repository [2]. Table 5.1 shows the characteristics of the datasets. The domain varies from 76 to 41271 items, and the number of transactions varies from 3196 to 990003. The number of frequency groups and the number of singleton frequency groups are given. In many cases, the latter number is high in relation to the total number of items. Although we performed our experiments on all the datasets that are listed in the table, we present our results only on ACCIDENTS, KOSARAK and RETAIL due to space limitations. Note that for all the datasets the median frequency gap is much smaller than the average frequency gap and for all the datasets except CHESS and CONNECT, this is smaller by a few orders of magnitude. We expect this to impact the compliancy measurements which will be addressed in a later section.

All procedures to extract samples from the benchmark datasets were implemented in $C++$. The procedure first collects the sampling parameters: sample

---

[1] $http://kdd.ics.uci.edu$
[2] $http://fimi.cs.helsinki.fi/fimi03/$

Table 2. Tabular Summary of Datasets and Their Parameters

Dataset	# Transactions	# Items	# Freq. Gps	Mean Gap	Median Gap
ACCIDENTS	340184	469	310	0.003236	0.000179
RETAIL	88163	16470	582	0.00099	0.0000113
KOSARAK	990003	41271	1886	0.00032225	0.000001
CHESS	3196	76	73	0.01389	0.00657
MUSHROOM	8124	120	90	0.01124	0.00394
CONNECT	67557	130	125	0.0081	0.0029
PUMSB	49046	2113	650	0.00154	0.000041

size, number of samples, type of sampling (with or without replacement). We used the random number generators provided as part of the *GNU Scientific Library* to generate random samples. The procedure has the option to choose from the 15 random number generators available in the library. To generate a single sample, we first create an array to store the tids that are to be in the sample. We then read the dataset parameters from a configuration file and use the number of tids in the dataset to generate a sample (with or without replacement) of tids. We then sort the array and in one pass count the frequency of items in the sample and the dataset simultaneously. In case of bootstrapping, it is unreasonable to assume that there will be enough main memory space to allocate a number of arrays (one for each sample for say 25 samples) especially for a large sample size, say a 95% sample, of tids from the dataset. Hence, in this case, the master sample is written out to a temporary file which is then used for subsequent computation.

5.2   Effect of Sample Parameters on Frequency Difference

Figure 3 presents the average frequency difference of items as the sample size is varied for the three datasets ACCIDENTS, KOSARAK and RETAIL. Figure 3(a) shows the variation of the average frequency difference and median frequency difference with varying sample size when a *single* sample is chosen with and without replacement. The first observation is that even for a 10%-sample, the average/median frequency difference between the sample frequency and actual frequency in the datasets is very small. For ACCIDENTS and RETAIL, this means that on the average, using a 10%-sample, an attacker can construct the frequency of an item that is only 0.0001 off from the actual frequency (a little higher is the attacker uses average frequency difference instead of median). For KOSARAK, the difference is even smaller - 0.00001. With increasing sample size, this difference decreases which means that the frequency knowledge constructed from samples of higher size gets more and more accurate with increasing sample size. This decrease is more pronounced when the sample is drawn without replacement.

Figures 3(b) and 3(c) show the impact of bootstrapping on the average frequency difference measurements. The two cases are when the original master sample (from which the bootstrap samples are drawn) is taken with replacement

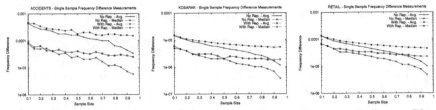

(a) ACCIDENTS, KOSARAK, RETAIL - Single Sample Frequency Difference Plots

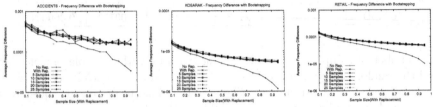

(b) ACCIDENTS,KOSARAK,RETAIL - Average Frequency Difference for Bootstrapping with Replacement

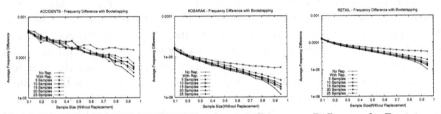

(c) ACCIDENTS,KOSARAK,RETAIL - Average Frequency Difference for Bootstrapping without Replacement

Fig. 3. Frequency Difference Measurements

and without replacement. From figure 3(b), it is evident that bootstrapping does not make a big difference over single samples, when the master sample is drawn with replacement. However, when the master sample is drawn without replacement, as shown in Figure 3(c), the effect of drawing more and more bootstrap samples causes the average frequency difference to decrease (and hence the knowledge becomes better as the number of samples increase), especially when the sample size is large. For small sample sizes, the variation in the average frequency difference measurements is not notable with either the sampling method or the number of bootstrap samples that are drawn. The effect is only when the sample size is large - say 0.5 or above, when the master sample is taken without replacement (figure 3(c)).

5.3   Effect of Sample Parameters on Rank Difference

Figure 4 shows the variation in the average rank difference of items for the three datasets ACCIDENTS, KOSARAK and RETAIL when the sample size is varied from 10% to 95%. The behaviour of average rank difference measurements were pretty similar to those of the average frequency difference measurements. A single sample taken without replacement yielded the smallest average rank difference and was consistently better than sampling with replacement and bootstrap samples. The difference was very pronounced for large sample sizes. We do not present the bootstrap samples where the master sample was drawn with replacement. This is because the average rank difference measurements for these samples were pretty much close to the single sample drawn with replacement. The variation in the average rank difference measurements were not too noticeable even for large sample sizes. However, it is definitely noteworthy that when the number of bootstrap samples are increased (when the master sample is taken without replacement), there is a decrease in the average rank difference among items, even though this decrease is very small. In all cases, it can also be observed that the single sample without replacement has the best possible quality for the average rank difference measure.

The average rank difference measurement is taken over all the items and this difference may not be uniform for all the items. To better study the rank difference measure, it is important to consider whether the frequency of an item in the database has anything to do with how good one can determine its rank from a sample. To study this aspect, we plot the average rank difference as a function of the frequency of items in the database for the smallest (10%) and the largest (95%) sample sizes for all the three datasets and these plots are shown in Figure 4(b). As seen from these plots, it can be concluded that even for the smallest sample size of 10%, for the items which appear in the database with very high frequency, it is possible to estimate the rank of these items better than the low frequency items. The estimates for the low frequency items become significantly better as the sample size becomes 95%. Note that

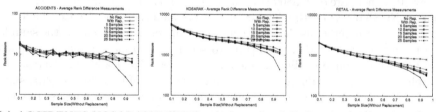

(a) ACCIDENTS,KOSARAK,RETAIL - Average Rank Difference for Bootstrapping without Replacement

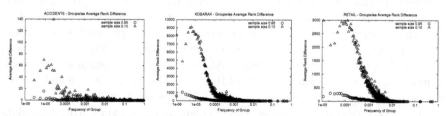

(b) ACCIDENTS,KOSARAK,RETAIL - Frequency Groupwise Average Rank Difference for 10% and 95% samples

Fig. 4. Rank Difference Measurements

ACCIDENTS contain roughly 470 items, KOSARAK contains roughly 41000 items and RETAIL contains roughly 16500 items. This means that for a 95% sample, the margin of error in ranks for the low frequency items is only a small fraction of the size of the items and hence the rank of the low frequency items are not too far from their actual ranks.

5.4   Effect of Sample Size on Compliancy and Top-K Measures

Figure 5 shows the compliancy and top K measurement plots for the three datasets. Let us first consider the compliancy and order compliancy plots shown in figure 5(a). The variation of compliancy and order compliancy measures with the sample size are shown for the three datasets ACCIDENTS, KOSARAK and RETAIL, for a single sample drawn with or without replacement. The interval compliancy is measured with the median frequency gap used to construct the intervals.

For the ACCIDENTS dataset, the fraction of items that are compliant increases with increase in sample size. The increase is substantial when the sample is drawn without replacement with around 70% of items compliant when the sample size is 10%, reaching around 95% compliancy for a sample size of 95%. The difference in compliancy between the sampling procedures is also substantial, reaching around 12%, for large sample sizes. However, for RETAIL and KOSARAK, the compliancy first starts decreasing with increasing sample size, when the sample is drawn without replacement and then starts to increase reaching a high value for the largest sample size of 95%. This behavior is attributed to the property of the datasets. Note that the ratio of the number of transactions to the number of items is not as high as for the other datasets. For a small sample of say 10%, there are only 8800 transactions in RETAIL and only 99000 transactions in KOSARAK but the domain of items remain the same. Hence, the items tend to cluster together as their frequencies are under-determined. As the sample size increases, some of the items start to separate into more frequency groups and hence the sample median frequency gap drops. This leads to a decrease in compliancy. As the sample size increases, the number of frequency groups start to stabilize, causing the normal trend to kick in and we see an increase in compliancy. However, for sampling with replacement, the compliancy continues to decrease all the way in both RETAIL and KOSARAK.

For all the three datasets, it can be observed from figure 5(a) that the order compliancy remains roughly the same or increases with increasing sample size, when the sample is drawn with or without replacement. For higher sample sizes, the order compliancy measure is better when the sample is drawn without replacement reaching close to 100% for a 95% sample. Another observation which is worthwhile to note is that even for a small sample of 10%, it is possible to obtain a high degree of compliancy and order compliancy (around 70% for all three datasets).

Let us now consider the top-k measurement plots in figure 5(b). The plots show the measurements for the top 10% of items in terms of their frequency, as the sample size is varied, for the three datasets. For the ACCIDENTS dataset, all the sampling procedures identify the top 10% of the most frequent items

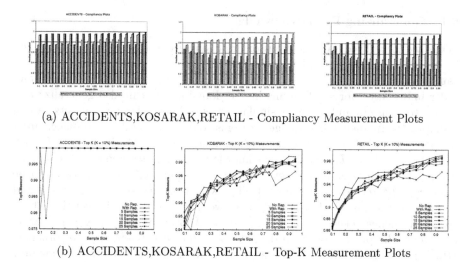

(a) ACCIDENTS,KOSARAK,RETAIL - Compliancy Measurement Plots

(b) ACCIDENTS,KOSARAK,RETAIL - Top-K Measurement Plots

Fig. 5. Compliancy and Top-K Measurement Plots

almost accurately for all the sample sizes. Note that even for a small sample size of 10%, all the methods except one, give 100% accuracy and the lowest accuracy value is close to 98%. For the KOSARAK and RETAIL datasets, the top-k accuracy measurement increases with increase in sample size. A single sample drawn without replacement enjoyed higher accuracies over the other methods, varying from an accuracy of around 95% for a 10% sample to around 99% for a 95% sample in KOSARAK and from around 91% accuracy for a 10% sample to around 99% accuracy for a 95% sample in RETAIL. As the number of bootstrap samples increase, the accuracy of top-k measurements increases, tending towards the value obtained by a single sample without replacement. For small sample sizes, the number of bootstrap samples did not affect the quality of the top-k measure over that obtained from a single sample with replacement.

6   Discussion

Once can conclude from the experimental study that for the real datasets considered, even small samples can be used by outsiders to learn reasonably accurate prior knowledge. In some cases, the accuracy is almost close or as good as the actual knowledge in the database. If sampling is considered as a method to limit disclosure, as argued in [7], then an additional point to consider is the kind of prior knowledge that can be built from these samples. For the cases of prior knowledge considered, we can conclude that sampling is not good for the sample sizes considered in our experiments. Either lower sample sizes have to be considered or other suppression techniques need to be used to prevent disclosure. The scope of this work does not stop here. We can further consider generalizations of prior knowledge as described below.

6.1   Generalizing Prior Knowledge

While we formalized various types of prior knowledge that can be constructed by an attacker using samples, these are not the only kinds of knowledge one can consider. For the purposes of this work, we only focus on frequency and order information for single items in the domain. One can also generalize this notion to itemsets and consider similar types of knowledge for itemsets. As an example, the frequency knowledge for items could be generalized to *higher order* frequency knowledge by associating a frequency value in the interval $[0, 1]$ with each itemset $X \subseteq \mathcal{I}$. The interval knowledge and order knowledge could be defined in an analogous manner. We expect the analysis of such cases to be more complicated as we are now dealing with a lattice space of itemsets and quantifying the quality of prior knowledge would require analysis over this lattice space and hence take more time and space. Another important generalization is to relax the prior knowledge defined to *partial prior knowledge*. In practice, attackers may have knowledge for a subset of items in the domain and they may have NO information about certain other items in the domain. In many cases, even the domain is not completely available to the attacker in which case, only a subset of the universe is known. This leads to a refinement in the definition of prior knowledge from functions to partial functions. The hope is that our current analysis can be restricted to the subset of items on which prior knowledge exists to derive measurements.

6.2   Summary and Ongoing Work

Samples form an important ingredient in sharing data and are often employed in real situations. An important concept for risk assessment is what malicious users can learn from these samples. Prior knowledge, which is an important consideration for analysis is an often overlooked issue while analyzing risk and security [14]. In this paper, we formalized various types of prior knowledge that can be constructed by an attacker using samples. We gave precise formalization of the quality of such knowledge. Through a lightweight sampling framework and a systematically designed set of experiments on real benchmark datasets, we present empirical analysis of how effective such prior knowledge is in practice. We observe that even for small sample sizes, it is possible to obtain good quality prior knowledge that is reasonably accurate. Our ongoing work is addressing the various manifestations of prior knowledge especially in the context of data mining tasks and how one can use the analysis using samples to make informed decisions about risk and security.

References

1. Adam N.R. and Wortmann J.C.   Security-Control Methods for Statistical Databases: A Comparative Study. *ACM Computing Surveys*, 21(4), 1989.
2. Aggarwal C.C and Yu P.S. A Condensation Approach to Privacy Preserving Data Mining. *EDBT*, 2004.

3. Aggarwal.G et. al. Anonymizing Tables. *ICDT Conference*, 2005.
4. Agrawal R. and Srikant R. Privacy Preserving Data Mining. *ACM SIGMOD Conference*, 2000.
5. Agrawal D. and Aggarwal C.C. On the Design and Quantification of Privacy Preserving Data Mining Algorithms. *ACM PODS Conference*, 2001.
6. Agrawal R., Imielinksi T., Swami A. Mining Association Rules between Sets of Items in Large Databases. *ACM SIGMOD Conference*, 1993.
7. Clifton C. Using Sample Size to Limit Exposure to Data Mining. *Journal of Computer Security*, 8(4), 2000.
8. Dinur I., Nissim K. Revealing Information while Preserving Privacy. *ACM PODS Conference*, 2003.
9. Evfimievski A. et. al. Privacy Preserving Mining of Association Rules. *Information Systems*, 29(4) 2004.
10. Domingo-Ferrer J. et. al. Information-Theoretic Disclosure Risk Measures in Statistical Disclosure Control of Tabular Data. *IEEE SSDBM Conference*, 2002.
11. Fienberg S.E. et. al. Disclosure Limitation using perturbation and related methods for Categorical Data. *Journal of Office Statistics*, 14, 1998.
12. Iyengar V. S. Transforming Data to Satisfy Privacy Constraints. *ACM KDD Conference*, 2002.
13. Y. Lindell and B. Pinkas. Privacy Preserving Data Mining. *Advances in Cryptology LNCS 1880*, Aug 2000.
14. Laks V.S. Lakshmanan and Raymond T. Ng and Ganesh Ramesh. To Do or Not To Do: The Dilemma of Disclosing Anonymized Data. *ACM SIGMOD Conference*, 2005.
15. Moore Jr. R. A. Controlled Data-Swapping Techniques for Masking Public Use Microdata Sets. *Statistical Research Division Report Series, RR 96-04, US Bureau of Census, Washington D.C.*, 1996.
16. Meyerson A. and Williams R. On the Complexity of Optimal k-Anonymity *ACM PODS Conference*, 2004.
17. Samarati P. and Sweeney L. Protecting Privacy when Disclosing Information: *k*-anonymity and its Enforcement through Generalization and Suppression. *IEEE Symposium on Research in Security and Privacy*, 1998.
18. L.Sweeney. k-anonymity: a model for protecting privacy. *International Journal on Uncertainty, Fuzziness and Knowledge-based Systems*, 10(5), 2002.
19. Verykios V. et. al. Association Rule Hiding. *IEEE TKDE*, 16(4) 2004.

Dynamic Disclosure Monitor (D^2Mon): An Improved Query Processing Solution[*]

Tyrone S. Toland[1], Csilla Farkas[2], and Caroline M. Eastman[2]

[1] Department of Informatics, University of South Carolina Upstate,
800 University Way, Spartanburg, SC 29303, USA
ttoland@uscupstate.edu

[2] Department of Computer Science and Engineering, University of South Carolina,
Columbia, SC 29208, USA
{farkas, eastman}@cse.sc.edu

Abstract. The Dynamic Disclosure Monitor (D²Mon) is a security mechanism that executes during query processing time to prevent sensitive data from being inferred. A limitation of D²Mon is that it unnecessarily examines the entire history database in computing inferences. In this paper, we present a process that can be used to reduce the number of tuples that must be examined in computing inferences during query processing time. In particular, we show how *a priori* knowledge of a database dependency can be used to reduce the search space of a relation when applying database dependencies. Using the database dependencies, we develop a process that forms an index table into the database that identifies those tuples that can be used in satisfying database dependencies. We show how this process can be used to extend D²Mon to reduce the number of tuples that must be examined in the history database when computing inferences. We further show that inferences that are computed by D²Mon using our extension are *sound* and *complete*.

1 Introduction

Providing a balance between security requirements and data availability is an ongoing challenge in data management. Current security access models, such as Mandatory Access Control, Discretionary Access Control, and Role-Based Access Control do not prevent the discovery of sensitive information through inference channels. An inference channel discloses data that is classified at a higher level by using data that is classified at a lower level. Detecting and preventing the disclosure of sensitive data via inference channels is referred to as the *inference problem* [9]. Solutions to the *inference problem* can be categorized as either a *database design* [2,3,7,8,11,14,15,17,18,21] or a *query processing* [4,10,12,13,16,19] solution.

A database design solution involves identifying and removing inference channels at design time. This solution can result in over-classifying data items. The

---

[*] This work was partially supported by the National Science Foundation under grants numbers IIS-0237782 and P200A000308-02.

W. Jonker and M. Petković (Eds.): SDM 2005, LNCS 3674, pp. 124–142, 2005.

procedure for preventing sensitive data from being inferred during query processing time involves examining query results to determine if the user can use the results along with some database constraints to infer some sensitive data. In this approach, current query results are released if the results cannot be combined with previously released query results and the metadata to determine some sensitive data; otherwise, query results are not released to the user.

Consider the following example using a query processing security mechanism called Dynamic Disclosure Monitor (D^2Mon) [6]. The architecture is shown in Figure 1. The algorithm is shown in Algorithm 1. For this example we use the *Employee* relation in Table 1, which contains information about employee Name, Rank, Salary, and Department. The relation satisfies the functional dependency (FD) $Rank \rightarrow Salary$. The security requirement is that the employees' salaries should be kept confidential for which partial tuples over attributes *Name* and *Salary* can only be accessed by authorized users. However, to increase data availability unauthorized users are allowed to access *Name* and *Salary* separately.

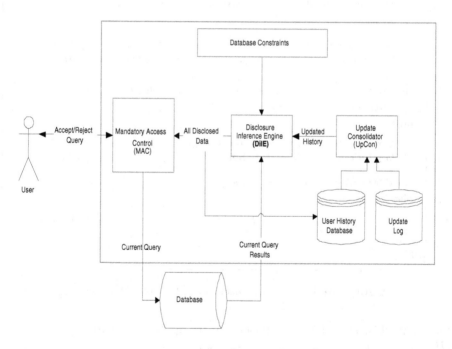

Fig. 1. Dynamic Disclosure Monitor (D^2Mon)

Suppose an unauthorized user requests the following two queries:
Query 1: "List the name and rank of the employees working in the Toy department." ($\Pi_{Name,Rank}\sigma_{Department='Toy'}$)

Input:
   1 User's query (object) Q_i
   2 User's id U
   3 Security classification $< \mathcal{O}, \mathcal{U}, \lambda >$
   4 User's history database $U_{history}$ (i.e., data which were previously retrieved by the user)
   5 $\mathcal{D}$, a set of database constraints
Output: Answer to Q_i and update of the user's history database or refusal of Q_i

1 Mandatory Access Control (MAC) evaluates direct security violations

if *direct security violation is detected* **then**
   | Q_i is rejected (i.e., D^{2}Mon functions as the basic MAC mechanism)
else
   | (no direct security violation was detected)
   | **begin**

2 | | Use **Update Consolidator** (UpCon) to modify $U_{history}$ according to the relevant updates to create $U_{updated-history}$
   | | Let $U_{all-disclosed} = U_{updated-history} \cup Q_i(answers)$
   | | **repeat**

3 | | | Use **Disclosure Inference Engine** (DiIE) to generate all data that can be disclosed from the $U_{all-disclosed}$ and the *database constraints* $\mathcal{D}$
4 | | | $U_{all-disclosed} = U_{all-disclosed} \cup U_{newly-disclosed}$
   | | **until** *no change occurs*
   | **end**

   | MAC reevaluates security violations in $U_{all-disclosed}$:
5 | if *Illegal disclosure is detected* **then**
6 | | Reject Q_i and $U_{history} = U_{updated-history}$
   | else
7 | | Accept Q_i and $U_{history} = U_{all-disclosed}$ (i.e., security is not violated)
   | **end**
end

Algorithm 1: Dynamic Disclosure Monitor (D^2Mon)

Query 2: "List the salaries of all clerks in the appliance department."
$(\Pi_{Salary}\sigma_{RANK='Clerk' \wedge Department='Appliance'})$.

In Table 1, we show the user history database that is used by D^{2}Mon to store released query results. Delta values represent values that were not released to the user. Since the *Employee* relation satisfies the FD *Rank* $\rightarrow$ *Salary* and both Query 1 and Query 2 have *Rank* $= 'Clerk'$ in the respective result sets, a user

Table 1. Employee relation

ID	NAME	RANK	SALARY	DEPT.
1	John	Clerk	38,000	Toy
2	Mary	Secretary	28,000	Toy
3	Chris	Secretary	28,000	Marketing
4	Joe	Manager	45,000	Appliance
5	Sam	Clerk	38,000	Appliance
6	Eve	Manager	45,000	Marketing

can join the two queries via the *Rank* value to reveal the fact that John's salary is \$38,000 (i.e., $\delta_1 = \$38,000$). D^2Mon is capable of detecting such indirect data disclosures.

To satisfy the FD *Rank* → *Salary*, we need to identify those tuples that have the same value for *RANK*. The tuples with ID's 1 and 5, respectively, are the only tuples that can satisfy the FD and therefore need to be used in the inference processing. It follows trivially from the definition of FD's, that the FD *Rank* → *Salary* means that only those tuples that have the same attribute value for *Rank* should be retrieved. In this paper, we present an approach that shows "how" to apply database dependencies represented as a Horn-clause in an efficient manner. We propose a concept called *Useful Common Attribute*, that defines a list of attributes from the prerequisite of the dependency which must contain the same values. We use this concept to develop an index table from the database dependencies prerequisite onto the tuples in the history database that satisfies the database dependency. The index table will reduce the search space to a constant operation. This will in turn provide a means by which we can retrieve the tuples in the history database in an efficient manner and hence reduce the overall inference processing time.

In this paper, we deal with generalized dependencies, which cover equality generating (e.g., functional) and tuple generating (e.g., multivalued and join) dependencies, respectively (see Ullman [20]). Our examples, for simplicity, show a simple functional dependency application.

We are not proposing a new concept with respect to a history database. We are proposing a "prediction" on which attributes are needed to apply dependencies. We use this prediction to index the history database to improve performance.

Table 2. History Database

Query #	ID	NAME	RANK	SALARY	DEPARTMENT
1	1	John	Clerk	δ_1	Toy
1	2	Mary	Secretary	δ_2	Toy
2	5	δ_3	Clerk	\$38,000	Appliance

This paper is organized as follows. In Section 2 we give an overview of the Dynamic Disclosure Monitor (D^2Mon) security architecture. This section also provides some preliminary notation and concepts. In Section 4 we develop our proposed solution. In Section 5 we discuss the complexity of our solution. Section 6 presents some related work. In Section 7 we conclude this paper and discuss some future work.

2   Preliminaries

2.1   Dynamic Disclosure Monitor (D^2Mon)

D^2Mon is a security architecture that runs during query processing time to prevent disclosure of sensitive data. The D^2Mon architecture is shown in Figure 1.

D^2Mon first uses the Mandatory Access Control (MAC) module to examine the user's query to determine if the user has the proper authority to submit the query. If the user does not have the proper authority, then the query is rejected; otherwise, the query is submitted to the Database Management System (DBMS) for execution. Once the query results are returned from the DBMS, then D^2Mon executes a module called Update Consolidator (UpCon). This module retrieves the updates from the Update Log that have occurred since the last query was processed.[1] UpCon retrieves the updates and performs a process called "stamping". That is, UpCon marks the data items in the history database that have been updated in the base relation with the updated data value from the Update Log. The motivation behind stamping the history database is to identify attributes that produce outdated inferences that do not lead to a security violation because the values do not produce values that are current in the history database.

D^2Mon will then add the current query results to the user's history database. D^2Mon uses a separate history database for each user which allows the system to manage the query results and inference processing of an individual user in a central location. Then, the Disclosure Inference Engine (DiIE) is applied to the history database to compute newly disclosed data. After which, MAC inspects the history database to determine if sensitive data has been revealed. If a security violation exists, then the current query is rejected and the history database is reset to the state before DiIE was ran; otherwise, if not sensitive data is revealed, then the current query results are returned to the user.

3   Preliminary Notation

In this paper we follow the notation defined in our earlier work [6]. We assume, as in [1,11,20,21] the existence of a *universal* relation as defined in [20], which states that a single relation can be constructed from the relations in a database

---

[1] We assume that the updates are executed by users with the appropriate access authority and that these updates are stored in an Update Log.

by taking the cross-product of those relations. Let $R = \{A_1, \ldots, A_k\}$ denote the schema of a *universal* relation and r the actual database instance over R. We shall denote by $dom(A_i)$ $(1 \leq i \leq k)$ the domain of attribute A_i and $t = (\ldots, A_i = c, \ldots) \in r$ a sub-tuple of r, where the value of attribute A_i is c. We also use the notation $t[A_i] = c$ to represent the value c of attribute A_i in tuple t.

Definition 1 (Stamped Attribute). *Let r be a relation over schema R. Let A be an attribute name from a schema R and $dom(A) = a_1, \ldots, a_l$ the domain of A. A stamped attribute SA is an attribute such that its value sa is of the form $a_i{}^{a_j}$ $(i, j = 1, \ldots, l)$, where $a_i \in dom(A) \cup \{-\}$ and $a_j \in dom(A) \cup \{-\}$. We call a_i the value of sa and a_j is the stamp or updated value of sa. We assign a_j the value that the attribute A has been updated to in the relation r. If the attribute A has been deleted, then we assign a_j the symbol $\{-\}$. We call this process stamping.*

For example, assume at some time t_1 that the user has received the tuple $< Clerk, \$38,000 >$ over the attributes $RANK$ and $SALARY$ from the *Employee* relation. Since the tuple was released, it is also stored in the user's history database.

If at some time $t_2(t_1 < t_2)$ the salaries of the clerks are modified, e.g, increased to \$39,520, the corresponding tuple in the history database is stamped as follows $< Clerk, \$38,000^{\$39,520} >$. We are able to determine from this tuple: (1) The attribute values *Clerk* and *\$38,000* have been released to the user and (2) The attribute value $RANK$ has not been modified; however, the attribute value of *Salary* has been modified to \$39,520. This modification is unknown to the user.

We recognize that previous *stamped* values can be overwritten by successive stamping procedures, but our proposed solution only requires that the most recent update to an attribute be stored.

Definition 2 (Projection Fact). *Let $\{A_1, \ldots, A_k\}$ and $\{SA_1, \ldots, SA_k\}$ be a set of attribute and stamped attribute, respectively, over schema R. A projection fact (PF) of type $A_1, \ldots, A_k$ is a mapping m from $\{A_1, \ldots, A_k\}$ to $\bigcup_{j=1}^{k} dom(A_j) \cup \bigcup_{j=1}^{k} dom(SA_j)$ such that $m(A_j) \in dom(A_j) \cup dom(SA_j)$ for all $j = 1, \ldots, k$. A projection fact is denoted by an expression of the form $R[A_1 = v_1, \ldots, A_k = v_k]$, where R is the schema name and $v_1, \ldots, v_k$ are values of attributes $A_1, \ldots, A_k$, respectively. A PF is classified as one of the following:*

1. *A stamped projection fact (SPF) is a projection fact $R[A_1 = v_1, \ldots, A_k = v_k]$, where at least one of v_j $(j = 1, \ldots, k)$ is a stamped attribute value.*
2. *A non-stamped projection fact is a projection fact $R[A_1 = v_1, \ldots, A_k = v_k]$, where all v_js are constants in $dom(A_j)$.*

For example, $Employee[NAME = John, Rank = Clerk]$ is a non-stamped projection fact, while $Employee[NAME = John, Rank = Clerk^{Manager}]$ is a stamped projection fact.

In the remainder of this paper the term *projection fact* may refer to either a stamped or a non-stamped projection fact. The type of *projection fact* (i.e., stamped or non-stamped) will be clear from its context.

Definition 3 (Query-answer pair). *An atomic query-answer pair (QA-pair) is an expression of the form $(P, \Pi_Y \sigma_C)$, where P is a projection fact over Y that satisfies C or P is a stamped projection fact, such that the un-stamped projection fact generated from P satisfies C. A query-answer pair is either an atomic QA-pair or an expression of the form $(\mathcal{P}, \Pi_Y \sigma_C)$, where $\mathcal{P}$ is a set of projection facts (stamped or non-stamped) $\{P_1, \ldots, P_l\}$ such that every P_i, $(i = 1, \ldots, l)$ is over Y and satisfies C.*

Similar to Brodsky et al. [1], the database dependencies will be defined by way of Horn-clauses, which can express tuple generating-dependencies and equality-generation dependencies [20]. The definition is as follows.

Definition 4 (Database Dependencies). *) Let r denote a relation with schema $R = \{A_1, \ldots, A_l\}$. Let $\mathcal{D} = \{d_1, \ldots, d_m\}$, where $m > 0$, be a set of dependencies for R. Each $d_i \in \mathcal{D}$ is of the following form: $\forall x_1, \ldots, x_l\ p_1 \wedge \ldots \wedge p_k \rightarrow q$, where $x_1, \ldots, x_l$ are the free variables in $p_1, \ldots, p_k$ $(k \geq 1)$. The p_i's are called the prerequisites and have the form $R[A_1 = a_1, \ldots, A_l = a_l]$, where a_i is either a constant or a variable that must appear in the prerequisite. The consequence q can have the following forms:*

1. *If the consequence q is either of the form $A_i = A_j$ $(A_i, A_j \in R)$ or $A_i = c$ $(c \in dom(A_i))$, then d_i is an equality generating dependency*
2. *If the consequence q has the form $R[A_1 = a_1, \ldots, A_l = a_l]$ where $A_1, \ldots, A_l$ are all of the attributes of the schema R (i.e., the constraint is full) and each a_i is either a constant or a variable that must appear in the prerequisite p_i $(i = 1, \ldots, k)$, then d_i is a tuple generating dependency.*

Generating dependencies are outside the scope of this paper. The interested reader is referred to [1,20]. We now show how we can represent an equality generating dependency (i.e., functional dependency).

As an example of functional dependency (FD) consider the *Employee* relation in Table 1 that satisfies the FD: *Rank $\rightarrow$ Salary*. Using Definition 4, this would be represented as follows. Due to space limitations, we use N, R, S, and D for Name, Rank, Salary, and Department, respectively:

$$Employee(N = a_1, R = b, S = c_1, D = d_1) \wedge Employee(N = a_2, R = b, S = c_2, D = d_2) \rightarrow c_1 = c_2.$$

We now define how the prerequisites (i.e., body) of the Horn-clauses are mapped to a tuple of a relation.

Definition 5 (Atom mapping of dependencies). *Given a Horn-clause constraint $p_1, \ldots, p_n \rightarrow q$ and a relation r over schema R, we define an atom mapping as a function $h : \{p_1, \ldots, p_n\} \rightarrow r$ such that*

1. *h preserves constants; i.e., if $h(R[\ldots, A_i = c, \ldots]) = (c_1, \ldots, c_i, \ldots, c_m) \in r$ and c is a constant (i.e., $c \in dom(A_j) \cup dom(SA_j)$), then $c = c_i$*
2. *h preserves equalities; i.e., if $p_i = R[\ldots, A_k = a, \ldots]$, $p_j = R[\ldots, A_l = a, \ldots]$ and $h(p_i) = (c_1, \ldots, c_k, \ldots, c_m)$, $h(p_j) = (c'_1, \ldots, c'_l, \ldots, c'_m)$, then $c_k = c'_l$.*

4   Useful Common Attribute

We proposed in our initial work a security mechanism called the Dynamic Disclosure Monitor (D^{2}Mon) [6]. We develop in this section a procedure that can be used to reduce the search space and ultimately the complexity of D^{2}Mon.

4.1   Problem Discussion and Motivation

The complexity of the inference algorithm used by D^{2}Mon is high, since it applies the database dependencies to the entire history database in a brute force manner. That is, D^{2}Mon does not use any *a priori* knowledge about the prerequisite tuple mapping into the history database to reduce the number of tuples that should be retrieved when performing inference processing. As discussed in the Introduction, we need to define a process such that only those tuples that satisfy the body of the database constraints are retrieved, which will reduce the number of tuples in the history database to be examined. Consider, the example from the Introduction that uses the *Employee* relation from Table 1 that satisfies the FD *Rank* → *Salary*. This database constraint is represented as a Horn-clause in the following manner:

Equation 1. $Employee(N = a_1, R = b_1, S = c_1, D = d_1) \land Employee(N = a_2, R = b_1, S = c_2, D = d_2) \rightarrow c_1 = c_2$.

Consider the history database in Table 1 in which we use Definition 5 to map $h(p_1) \rightarrow (N = John, R = Clerk, S = \delta_1, D = Toy)$ and $h(p_2) \rightarrow (N = \delta_3, R = Clerk, S = \$38,000, D = Appliance)$, respectively. It follows from the FD that John's salary is \$38,000.

Notice that the mapping of p_1 to a particular tuple restricts the mapping of p_2. That is, we know that both tuples that are mapped to by p_1 and p_2, respectively, must contain the same attribute value for Rank (i.e., Clerk). Therefore, once the mapping $h(p_1) \rightarrow (N = John, R = Clerk, S = \delta_1, D = Toy)$ is performed, then the tuples that p_2 maps to must be of the form $h(p_2) \rightarrow (N = a_2, R = Clerk, S = c_2, D = d_2)$, where a_2, c_2, d_2 are free-variables and $Rank = Clerk$. Instead of using this knowledge to map p_2 to $(N = \delta_3, R = Clerk, S = \$38,000, D = Appliances)$, D^{2}Mon would use an exhaustive search to check each tuple in the history database to determine the tuples that p_2 can be mapped to in order to satisfy the prerequisite of Equation 1. To process the entire history database in Table 1, D^{2}Mon would test $3^2 = 9$ mappings of the tuples in the history database. This comes from the fact that there are two prerequisites and three tuples in the history database. However, to satisfy the database constraint $Rank \rightarrow Salary$ in the history database, D^{2}Mon only needs to map $h(p_1) \rightarrow (N = John, R = Clerk, S = \delta_1, D = Toy)$ and $h(p_2) \rightarrow (N = \delta_3, R = Clerk, S = \$38,000, D = Appliance)$, respectively. Therefore, there are eight mappings that D^{2}Mon can omit from the inference process.

We use the aforementioned observation to construct an index file on the history database that will be used to retrieve only those tuples that satisfy the prerequisites of a database dependency. That is, given a database dependency $p_1 \wedge \ldots \wedge p_l \rightarrow c$, we use prerequisite p_i, the tuples to which p_i maps to, and p_{i+1} to construct a modified p'_{i+1} that can be used to form an index on the history database that contains only those tuples that satisfy the prerequisite, p_{i+1}. If we use this approach in the previous example, then we would construct $p'_2 = (N = a_2, R = Clerk, S = c_2, D = d_2)$, which will map $h(p'_2) \rightarrow (N = \delta_3, R = Clerk, S = \$38,000, D = Appliance)$ in the history database.

4.2   Our Solution

We define in this section a prerequisite index table that will be used to retrieve only those tuples that can be used to satisfy the prerequisites of a database dependency. This prerequisite index table requires some preliminary definitions which we now present.

Definition 6 (Set of Prerequisite Attributes). *Let r denote a relation with schema $R = \{A_1, \ldots, A_l\}$. Let $p_1 \wedge \ldots \wedge p_n \rightarrow q$ be a Horn-clause constraint as defined in Definition 4. We define the* set of prerequisite attributes *for a prerequisite p_j as the set of attributes $A_i \in p_j$. We denote the set by $A(p_j)$.*

As an example, suppose we have prerequisite $p_1 = Employee(N = a_1, R = b, S = c_1, D = d_1)$. Then, the set of prerequisite attributes $A(p_1) = \{N, R, S, D\}$.

Definition 7 (Useful Common Attributes). *Let r denote a relation with schema $R = \{A_1, \ldots, A_l\}$. Let $p_1 \wedge \ldots \wedge p_n \rightarrow q$ be a Horn-clause constraint on r. Let $p_i = R[A_{i_1} = a_{i_1}, \ldots, A_{i_l} = a_{i_l}]$ and $p_j = R[A_{j_1} = a_{j_1}, \ldots, A_{j_l} = a_{j_l}]$, where $(1 \le i < j \le l)$. Let $A(p_i)$ and $A(p_j)$ denote the set of prerequisite attributes in p_i and p_j, respectively. We define the* useful common attributes *of p_i and p_j as the set of attributes $A_k \in A(p_i) \cap A(p_j)$ such that for each $A_{i_k} = a_{i_k} \in p_i$ and each $A_{j_k} = a_{j_k} \in p_j$, either (1) One of the values a_{i_k} or a_{j_k} is a variable, or (2) Both a_{i_k} and a_{j_k} are the same variables (i.e., $a_{i_k} = a_{j_k}$). We shall denote the useful common attributes by $\mathcal{A}_{i-j} = A(p_i) \cap_{cu} A(p_j)$, where $(1 \le i < j \le l)$.*

Definition 7 is used to identify those attributes that must have the same attribute values in the tuples that are used in the mapping of the prerequisite of a database dependency. In Equation 1, $\mathcal{A}_{1-2} = A(p_1) \cap_{cu} A(p_2) = \{Rank\}$. It is the case that Name, Rank, Salary, and Department are all attributes that are in the intersection of p_1 and p_2; however, we must also apply that latter part of Definition 7. That is, we select attributes that appear in the intersection of p_1 and p_2 only if the value of one of the intersecting attributes in the prerequisite are a variable or if both prerequisite attribute values is the same, which is the case in the intersection of prerequisites p_1 and p_2.

Definition 8 (Modified Prerequisite). *Let r denote a relation with schema $R = \{A_1, \ldots, A_l\}$. Let d be a Horn-clause of the form $p_1 \wedge \ldots \wedge p_k \rightarrow q$. Let $p_i = R[A_1 = a_{i_1}, \ldots, A_l = a_{i_l}]$ and $p_j = R[A_1 = a_{j_1}, \ldots, A_l = a_{j_l}]$ be prerequisites in d $(1 \le i < j \le k)$ and $\mathcal{A}_{i-j} = A(p_i) \cap_{cu} A(p_j)$, the set of useful common attributes. Let $h(p_i) \rightarrow t$, where $t \in r$. We construct a modified p_j as follows:*

- If $A_m \in \mathcal{A}_{i-j}$ and $A_m = a_{i_m}$ $(1 \leq m \leq l)$ is in p_i, where a_{i_m} is a constant value, then replace the attribute value for A_m in p_j with $t[A_m]$ (i.e., the attribute value for A_m in t).

We denote a modified prerequisite p_j as $[p_j]^{modified}$.

Using Definition 8, if we have $p_1 = R(N = a_1, R = b_1, S = c_1, D = d_1)$, $p_2 = R(N = a_2, R = b_1, S = c_2, D = d_2)$, $\mathcal{A}_{1-2} = A(p_1) \cap_{cu} A(p_2) = \{Rank\}$, and $h(p_1) \rightarrow (N = John, R = Clerk, S = \delta_1, D = Toy)$, then $[p_2]^{modified} = R(N = a_2, R = Clerk, S = c_2, D = d_2)$. Then, the modified prerequisite could be mapped into the history database. That is, $h([p_2]^{modified}) \rightarrow (N = \delta_3, R = Clerk, S = \$38,000, D = Appliance)$.

Definition 9 (Prerequisite Index Mapping). *Let r denote a relation over schema $R = \{A_1, \ldots, A_l\}$ and let $p_1 \wedge \ldots \wedge p_l \rightarrow q$ be a Horn-clause constraints. Let S be the set of tuples mapped to in r by either $h(p_i)$ or $h([p_i]^{modified})$ $(1 \leq i \leq l)$. We define a prerequisite index mapping by the function $\nu : \{S\} \rightarrow r$, such that*

- *For each tuple $t \in S$, we form a 3-tuple of the form $(i, t[time], t[ID])$, where i is the subscript of the prerequisite (i.e., p_i) that mapped to tuple t, $t[time]$ is the time in which tuple t is inserted into r, and $t[ID]$ is the tuple ID, respectively.*

Definition 9 forms a 3-tuple relation consisting of the *time* and ID^2 of those tuples in the prerequisite mapping. We can use this definition to reduce the processing time of the dependency. That is, if we use Definition 9 to form a Prerequisite Index Mapping Table (PIM - Table) called Idx into the history database, then to determine if prerequisites p_i $(i = 1, \ldots, l)$ satisfy the dependency requires only a linear search of Idx. Because of the way the modified prerequisite is constructed, the entries in Idx must satisfy the prerequisites which can be determined in a linear time in the size of the Idx. We can use the tuple *time* and ID from the indexing table to retrieve the tuple(s) from the history database in one operation using the tuple *time* and ID. We shall use the notation $Idx[i]$ as the set of tuples in r that satisfies prerequisite p_i.

For example, in Figure 2 we show a history database with tuple time included. If a modified prerequisite $[p_2]^{modified} = R(N = a_2, R = Clerk, S = c_2, D = d_2)$ is constructed, then $\nu(h([p_2]^{modified})) = \{< 1, 1, 1 >, < 2, 3, 5 >\}$ from which we construct the PIM - Table in Figure 2. Again we need only search the index table to determine if entries in the mapping $\nu(h([p_2]^{modified}))$ satisfy database dependency in Equation 1. We discuss further complexity in Section 5.

Figure 3 shows the D^2Mon architecture that includes the PIM - Table. In Algorithms 2 and 3, we present the algorithms that compute the *set of useful common attributes* (Definition 7) and the *modified prerequisite* (Definition 8),

---

[2] Although we do not address tuple generating dependencies in this paper, we use the tuple time to distinguish those tuples that are generated via a tuple generation dependencies in D^2Mon which are assigned the same tuple ID (i.e., $ID = -999$).

Time	ID	NAME	RANK	SALARY	DEPARTMENT
1	1	John	Clerk	δ_1	Toy
2	2	Mary	Secretary	δ_2	Toy
3	5	δ_3	Clerk	\$38,000	Appliance

History Database

Prerequisite Number	Time	ID
1	1	1
2	3	5

Prerequisite Index Table

Fig. 2. Index table and history database with tuple time

respectively. We show in Algorithm 5 how Algorithms 2 and 3 can be used together to compute the consequence of a Horn-clause database constraint. That is, Algorithm 5 presents the *Apply Database Constraints algorithm*, which receives as input a set of Horn-clause dependencies and a history database. This algorithm returns a modified history database with the database dependencies applied as defined in Definition 4.

Input:
   1 Prerequisite, $p_i = R[A_1 = a_{i_1}, \ldots, A_l = a_{i_l}]$
   2 Prerequisite, $p_j = R[A_1 = a_{j_1}, \ldots, A_l = a_{j_l}]$
Output: S, a set of useful common attributes for $\mathcal{D}$
1 Let $S = \emptyset$
2 for $k = 1$ to $l - 1$ do
   Let $A_k \in A(p_i) \cap A(p_j)$
   if *(a_{i_k} or a_{j_k} is a variable) OR (a_{i_k} and a_{j_k} are the same variables)* then
      $S = S \cup A_k$
   end
end
return S

Algorithm 2: Set of Useful Common Attributes

As an example of Algorithm 5, suppose that the database constraint that is shown in Equation 1 is applied to the History Database in Figure 2. These steps are as follows:

1. Step 1, let $h_i(p_1) \rightarrow \{(Time = 1, ID = 1, N = John, R = Clerk, S = \delta_1, D = Toy), (Time = 2, ID = 2, N = Mary, R = Secretary, S = \delta_2, D = Toy), (Time = 3, ID = 5, N = \delta_3, R = Clerk, S = \$38,000, D = Appliance)\}$ in the history database and store these tuples in Q
2. In Step 2, $t = (Time = 1, ID = 1, N = John, R = Clerk, S = \delta_1, D = Toy)$
3. In Step 3, the PIM - Table, Idx is loaded with $\{< 1, 1, 1 >\}$, the index entry for tuple t
4. Step 4, we continue the prerequisite evaluation process.
5. The loop that states in Step 5 computes the useful common attributes between the current p_i and preceding p_j's ($1 \leq i < j \leq l$).

Dynamic Disclosure Monitor (D2Mon)

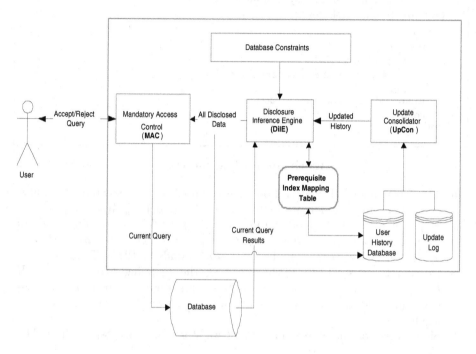

Fig. 3. D^2Mon with prerequisite index mapping table

Input:
    1 Prerequisite, $p_i = R[A_1 = a_{i_1}, \ldots, A_l = a_{i_l}]$
    2 Prerequisite, $p_j = R[A_1 = a_{j_1}, \ldots, A_l = a_{j_l}]$
    3 $\mathcal{A}_{i-j}$, useful common attributes between p_i and p_j
    4 Idx, a PIM - Table

Output: A modified prerequisite p_j if useful common attributes exist; otherwise, an unmodified prerequisite p_j

1 foreach $A_m \in \mathcal{A}_{i-j}$ **do**

2   **if** a_{i_m} *in* p_i *is a constant value* **then**
        Let $t \in Idx[i]$
        Let $p_j = R[\ldots, A_m = t[A_m], \ldots]$ {Replace the attribute value A_m in p_j with the attribute value $t[A_m]$}
    end

end
return p_j

Algorithm 3: Modified Prerequisite

Input:
    1 Set of Horn-clause constraints $\mathcal{D}$
    2 Relation r, which may contain null-values
Output: Updated relation r
begin
    repeat
        foreach $d_i \in \mathcal{D}$ **do**
            Apply Database Constraints(d_i, r)
        end
    until *No more changes to r occurs*
    return r
end

Algorithm 4: Chase process

6. The dependency in Equation 1 only has two prerequisites, so Step 6 computes only the useful common attribute set, $\mathcal{A}_{1-2} = A(p_1) \cap_{cu} A(p_2)$

7. Step 7, constructs the modified prerequisite $[p_2]^{modified}$ by calling *Modified Prerequisite* with $p_1 = R(N = a_1, R = b_1, S = c_1, D = d_1)$, $p_2 = R(N = a_2, R = b_1, S = c_2, D = d_2)$, $\mathcal{A}_{1-2} = \{Rank\}$, and the PIM - Table, Idx.

8. In Step 9 we store in X the result of the mapping $h([p_2]^{modified})$. If $h([p_2]^{modified})$ does not successfully map to an entry in r, then the prerequisite cannot be satisfied. We would then execute Step 12 to begin processing the next tuple.

9. Since X is not the empty, in Step 13 we store $\{< 2, 3, 5 >\}$ in the PIM - Table.

10. Since we have completed the evaluation of the prerequisite for database dependency using $t = (Time = 1, ID = 1, N = John, R = Clerk, S = \delta_1, D = Toy)$, we go to Step 14.

11. In Step 14, we can linearly traverse the PIM - Table to retrieve the tuples from r that satisfies the prerequisites of the database dependency. That is, we have reduced the number of tuples that need to be examined to successfully evaluate the prerequisite of the database dependency.

12. Step 14, Since all of the prerequisites have been satisfied, the consequence can be computed (i.e., $S = \{\delta_1 = \$38,000\}$) and applied to r.

13. In Step 15, we go back to Step 2 to process the next tuple.

Suppose in Step 2, that $h_i(p_1) \rightarrow (Time = 2, ID = 2, N = Mary, R = Secretary, S = \delta_2, D = Toy)$ occurs, then Algorithm 5 will correctly determines that this mapping will not lead to a successful evaluation of the body of the dependencies. This will be discovered when the algorithm processes the prerequisite p_2. That is, $\mathcal{A}_{1-2} = \{Secretary\}$ in Step 6. In Step 7, $[p_2]^{modified} = R(N = a_2, R = Secretary, S = c_2, D = d_2)$. Then, in Step 9 the mapping will fail. This in turn will cause Step 11 the condition will evaluate to false and we would execute Step 12 which will begin processing the next tuple.

As shown in Figure 1, the DiIE component of the D^2Mon architecture computes the inferences. Algorithm 1 shows the D^2Mon algorithm. Because of space

Input:

    1 $d = p_1 \wedge \ldots \wedge p_l \rightarrow q$, a Horn-clause dependency

    2 Relation r, which may contain null-values

Output: Updated r

map to in H

1 Let Q be the set, such that *atom mappings* $h_1, \ldots, h_k$ maps p_1 to $t_1, \ldots, t_k$ in r

2 **foreach** *mapping h_i in $h_1, \ldots, h_k$* **do**

3   Store an entry in the *Prerequisite Index Mapping Table, Idx*, consisting of the prerequisite number 1 (i.e., p_1), $t[time]$, $t[ID]$

4   **for** $j = 2$ *to* l **do**

       Let $[p_j]^{modified} = p_j$

5   **for** $i = 1$ *to* j **do**

6 $\mathcal{A}_{i-j} = A(p_i) \cap_{cu} A(p_j)$

7 $[p_j]^{modified} = $ Modified Prerequisite$(p_i, [p_j]^{modified}, \mathcal{A}_{i-j}, Idx)$

      end

8   **if** $[p_j]^{modified} \neq p_j$ **then**

9 $X = \nu(h_i([p_j]^{modified}))$ {Get the index values from tuples mapped to by the modified prerequisite, Definition 9 }

      else

10 $X = \nu(h_i(p_j))$ {Get the index values from tuples mapped to by the unmodified prerequisite p_j, Definition 9}

      end

11   **if** $X = \emptyset$ **then**

12   Go to Step 2 {Unable to satisfy dependency using initial tuple, t}

      else

13   Add X to Idx using prerequisite number, j

      end

   end

14   Using Idx, apply the dependency d to r as follows:

1. If d is an *equality-generating* dependency of the form $p_1, \ldots, p_l \rightarrow a = b$ then *equate* $h_i(a)$ and $h_i(b)$ as follows: (a) If both $h_i(a)$ and $h_i(b)$ are null-values then replace all occurrences of one of them in r with the other, (b) If one of them say $h_i(a)$, is not a null-value, then replace all occurrence of $h_i(b)$ in r with $h_i(a)$, (c) If both are not null-values (i.e., constants), do nothing. If $h_i(a) \neq h_i(b)$, we say that *inconsistency* occurred.

2. If d is a *tuple-generating dependency* of the form $p_1, \ldots, p_l \rightarrow R[A_1 = a_1, \ldots, A_n = a_n]$ and the tuple $(h_i(a_1), \ldots, h_i(a_n))$ is not in r, then add it to r.

15   Goto Step 2 {Begin processing next tuple.}

end

return r

Algorithm 5: Apply Database Constraints

limitations, the DiIE algorithm is not presented. We do, however, use the fact that the DiIE algorithm uses a variation of the *Chase* method from Ullman [20] to compute inferences. Algorithm 4 shows how we propose that our *Apply Database Constraints* algorithm should be used in the *Chase* algorithm.

We now present and prove some theoretical results.

Theorem 1. *Let $\mathcal{D}$ be a set of Horn-clause dependencies. The* Chase *algorithm is sound and complete when used with the* Apply Database Constraints *algorithm.*

We will use the following lemmas to prove Theorem 1.

Lemma 1 (Algorithm 3: Modified Prerequisite). *Let r be a relation and $d = p_1 \wedge \ldots \wedge p_k \rightarrow q$ a Horn-clause dependency. Let $T = h(p_i)$ (i.e., tuples to which p_i maps to in r) and $\mathcal{A}_{i-j} = A(p_i) \cap_{cu} A(p_j)$, a set of useful common attributes between p_i and p_j $(1 \leq i < j \leq k)$. Let $[p_j]^{modified}$ be the modified prerequisite returned from Algorithm 3 using $p_i, p_j,$ and $t \in T$. Then, $h([p_j]^{modified}) \subseteq h(p_j)$.*

Proof Sketch 1. Let $d = p_1 \wedge \ldots \wedge p_k \rightarrow q$ be a dependency. If $A(p_i) \cap_{cu} A(p_j) = \emptyset$, then $h([p_j]^{modified}) = \emptyset$. Therefore, $h([p_j]^{modified}) \subseteq h(p_j)$ is trivially true.

Suppose that $A(p_i) \cap_{cu} A(p_j) = \{A_i\}$. Assume by contradiction that $h([p_j]^{modified}) \not\subseteq h(p_j)$. Then there must exists some tuple $t = (\ldots, A_i = a_i, \ldots)$ in $h([p_j]^{modified})$, such that $t \notin h(p_j)$. It follows from Definition 8 that there exist some tuple $t' = (\ldots, A_i = a_i, \ldots)$ in $h(p_i)$, such that $t[A_i] = t'[A_i]$. But, for $h(p_j)$ to participate in the evaluation of dependency d, then there must be a tuple $t'' = (\ldots, A_j = a_j, \ldots)$ in $h(p_j)$, such that $A_j \in A(p_i) \cap_{cu} A(p_j)$. This asserts that, $A_j = A_i$ and $t''[A_j] = t'[A_i]$. Hence, t and t'' must be the same tuple. Therefore, $h([p_j]^{modified}) \subseteq h(p_j)$ and we have a contradiction to our original assumption. □

Lemma 2 (Algorithm 5: Apply Database Constraints). *Given a relation r over schema R, a set of Horn-clause database dependencies $\mathcal{D} = \{d_1, \ldots, d_m\}$ on r. Let $\mathcal{A} = \{\mathcal{A}_1, \ldots, \mathcal{A}_m\}$ be a set of useful common attributes computed with Algorithm 2. Then, the inferences computed by Algorithm 5 are valid.*

Proof Sketch 2. Assume by contradiction that q is an invalid consequence that was computed from a dependency $d_i \in D$. But, for this to happen, a $p_j \in d_i$ had to be incorrectly mapped to a tuple in r. Algorithm 5 has two steps in which prerequisite mapping occurs to tuples in r. We know by Definition 5 that if a mapping occurs in Step 10, it is performed correctly. In Step 9, we map to a tuple in relation r by using a modified prerequisite. By Definition 5, $h(p_j)$ are valid mappings. Then by Lemma 1, we know that $h([p_j]^{modified}) \subseteq h(p_j)$ and therefore $h([p_j]^{modified})$ is a valid mapping in Step 9 of the Algorithm 5. Since all of the tuples that are mapped to by the prerequisites of d_i are valid, then the consequence q must be a valid inference and we have a contradiction to our original assumption. □

We now use Lemma 1 and Lemma 2 to prove Theorem 1.

Proof Sketch 3. We know that D^2Mon is sound and complete without the use of Algorithm 5 [6]. To prove Theorem 1, we need to show that (1) All tuples disclosed by D^2Mon using Algorithm 5 are valid (i.e. soundness) and (2) D^2Mon discloses all valid inferences when used with Algorithm 5 (i.e., completeness).

The proof of soundness follows directly from Lemma 2. To prove completeness, assume that a tuple t is disclosed by D^2Mon using Algorithm 5, but is not disclosed by D^2Mon that does not use Algorithm 5. Recall, that Algorithm 5 only reorders the tuples in r to reduce the dependency processing time. For tuple t not to be disclosed by D^2Mon that uses Algorithm 5, then a dependency must have failed to be evaluated. We know that D^2Mon is sound when executed with Algorithm 5. So, if a tuple is not disclosed, then the PID-Table must be missing some tuple t', which causes the prerequisite of some dependency d to fail. But, for this to occur the mapping in either Step 9 or Step 10 must have failed, which would in turn execute Steps 11 and 12, respectively. We know that Step 9 and Step 10 could not fail since D^2Mon using Algorithm 5 is sound. Therefore, Step 13 will execute, which loads the PIM-Table with the index entries to evaluate the prerequisite of d. Since the prerequisites of d can be evaluate, we can generate t. Hence, we have a contradiction to our original assumption.   □

5   Complexity Analysis

The complexity analysis depends on the schema. We shall assume that there exist a schema $R = \{A_1, \ldots, A_k\}$. The complexity of Algorithm 2 depends on Step 2. The algorithm must check each of the k attribute values in the prerequisite. Therefore, this algorithm runs in $O(k)$, where k is the number of prerequisites in the body of the dependency. Algorithm 3 is bounded by Step 1. This step executes k times. So, the complexity of Algorithm 3 is also $O(k)$, where k is the number of prerequisites in the body of the dependency.

In computing the complexity of Algorithm 5, we need to compute the running time for Steps 2, 4, and 5, respectively. We shall assume that Steps 9 and 10 execute in one operation by a database management system. Steps 6 and 7 both execute in $O(k)$, where k is the number of prerequisites in the body of the dependency. Step 5 can execute l, where l is the number of prerequisites in a dependency. So, Step 5 can execute in $O(l \cdot k)$ time, where l is the number of prerequisites and k is the number of attribute values in the prerequisite. Step 4 also executes in $O(l)$. Step 2 can execute in $O(n)$, where n is the number of elements in the relation r. Therefore, the complexity of Algorithm 5 is $O(n \cdot l \cdot l \cdot k) = O(n \cdot k \cdot l^2)$, where n is the number of tuples in r, k is the number of attributes, and l is the number of prerequisites.

6   Related Work

For an overview of the inference problem, the reader is referred to Farkas et al. [5] and Jajodia et al. [9]. There are several query processing solutions to the inference problem.

The solution to the inference problem proposed by Marks [11] forms equivalence classes from the query results returned from the database. The equivalence classes are then used to construct a graph, which can be used to reveal inferences. The query results are referred to as views. The two types of views that are discussed are referred to as *total_disclosed* and *cover_by*, respectively. A *total_disclosed* view is one in which "tuples in one view can actually be created from those in another" [11]. A *cover_by* view is one in which the "release of even one tuple will disclose a tuple in . . ." another view [11]. The inference process is to convert a query to a view and insert it into the graph. Then, inspect the graph to see if it will introduce any inference channels that will lead to some sensitive data. If it does, then reject the query; otherwise, release the current query results. Because the approach presented by Marks examines inferences at the attribute level, preprocessing can be done by examining the query before execution to see if it contains attributes that will produce an inference channel that will reveal sensitive data. Obviously, in this approach, if the query produces an inference channel before execution, then the results from the queries will as well.

The inference engine presented by Thuraisingham [19] is used to augment the relational database by acting as an intermediary between the queries and the database. The inference engine uses first order logic to represent queries, security constraints, environment information, and real world information. That is, the inference engine converts the current query to first order logic. The first order logic query is then compared against the database constraints to determine if a security constraint will be violated. If a security violation exists, the query is rejected; otherwise, the query is converted into relational algebra and forwarded to the database for execution. The results that are returned from the database are assigned classification labels that ensure that no security violation exists.

Stachour and Thuraisingham propose a system called Lock Data Views (LDV) [16]. This approach to the inference problem is similar to Thuraisingham [19]. That is, the solution proposed by Stachour and Thuraisingham performs query processing that involves converting a query to an internal format, determining if a violation exists by submitting the query to the DBMS and classifying the query results accordingly. Unlike the approach presented by Thuraisingham [19], the approach presented in Stachour and Thuraisingham [16] runs on top of a trusted computing base called LOgical Coprocessing Kernel (LOCK) and is dependent on LOCK functioning correctly (i.e., securely).

Yip and Levitt [21] discuss an inference detection system that utilizes five inference rules to uncover any possible inference channels that may be present. These rules are applied to the initial query and the query results to determine if an inference channel exists. These rules are sound, but not necessarily complete.

A major disadvantage of [11,16,19,21] is that the additional processing time that is introduced during query processing time may have a significant adverse effect on the overall query response time. Our solution does address this disadvantage. In particular, the additional processing time that is introduced by our solution is polynomial in terms of the prerequisites.

7 Conclusion and Future Work

In this paper, we have presented an approach that can be used to increase the performance of a query processing solution to the inference problem. We have presented a solution that forms an index on the history database that contains only hose tuples that can be used in satisfy the database dependencies. We have shown how our approach can be used in a query processing security mechanism called D^2Mon to produce inferences that are sound and complete.

In this paper we have proposed that an index table entry be constructed for each database dependency prerequisite. Then each of these indices would be stored in the prerequisite index table to assist in the inference processing. It may be possible to combine these separate indices into one index structure. We have discussed the construction of one-dimensional indices. Although it is beyond the scope of this paper, we acknowledge that it may be possible to apply multi-dimensional indices to reduce the complexity of our solution even further. Also, we do not consider how our approach can be used in applying tuple generating dependencies. These research questions can be investigated in future work.

References

1. A. Brodsky, C. Farkas, and S. Jajodia. Secure databases: Constraints, inference channels, and monitoring disclosure. *IEEE Trans. Knowledge and Data Eng.*, November, 2000.
2. L.J. Buczkowski. Database inference controller. In D.L. Spooner and C. Landwehr, editors, *Database Security III: Status and Prospects*, pages 311–322. North-Holland, Amsterdam, 1990.
3. S. Dawson, S.De Capitani di Vimercati, and P. Samarati. Specification and enforcement of classification and inference constraints. In *Proc. of the 20th IEEE Symposium on Security and Privacy, Oakland, CA*, May 9–12 1999.
4. D.E. Denning. Commutative filters for reducing inference threats in multilevel database systems. In *Proc. IEEE Symp. on Security and Privacy*, pages 134–146, 1985.
5. C. Farkas and S. Jajodia. The inference problem: a survey. *SIGKDD Explor. Newsl.*, 4(2):6–11, 2002.
6. C. Farkas, T. Toland, and C. Eastman. The inference problem and updates in relational databases. In *Proc. IFIP WG11.3 Working Conference on Database and Application Security*, pages 171–186, July 15-18 2001.
7. J.A. Goguen and J. Meseguer. Unwinding and inference control. In *Proc. IEEE Symp. on Security and Privacy*, pages 75–86, 1984.
8. T.H. Hinke. Inference aggregation detection in database management systems. In *Proc. IEEE Symp. on Security and Privacy*, pages 96–106, 1988.
9. S. Jajodia and C. Meadows. Inference problems in multilevel secure database management systems. In M.D. Abrams, S. Jajodia, and H. Podell, editors, *Information Security: An integrated collection of essays*, pages 570–584. IEEE Computer Society Press, Los Alamitos, Calif., 1995.
10. T. F. Keefe, M. B. Thuraisingham, and W. T. Tsai. Secure query-processing strategies. *IEEE Computer*, pages 63–70, March 1989.

11. D.G. Marks. Inference in MLS database systems. *IEEE Trans. Knowledge and Data Eng.*, 8(1):46–55, February 1996.
12. D.G. Marks, A. Motro, and S. Jajodia. Enhancing the controlled disclosure of sensitive information. In *Proc. European Symp. on Research in Computer Security*, Springer-Verlag Lecture Notes in Computer Science, Vol. 1146, pages 290–303, 1996.
13. S. Mazumdar, D. Stemple, and T. Sheard. Resolving the tension between integrity and security using a theorem prover. In *Proc. ACM Int'l Conf. Management of Data*, pages 233–242, 1988.
14. M. Morgenstern. Controlling logical inference in multilevel database systems. In *Proc. IEEE Symp. on Security and Privacy*, pages 245–255, 1988.
15. G.W. Smith. Modeling security-relevant data semantics. In *Proc. IEEE Symp. Research in Security and Privacy*, pages 384–391, 1990.
16. P.D. Stachour and B. Thuraisingham. Design of LDV: A multilevel secure relational database management system. *IEEE Trans. Knowledge and Data Eng.*, 2(2):190–209, June 1990.
17. T. Su and G. Ozsoyoglu. Inference in MLS database systems. *IEEE Trans. Knowledge and Data Eng.*, 3(4):474–485, December 1991.
18. T.H.Hinke, Harry S. Delugach, and Asha Chandrasekhar. A fast algorithm for detecting second paths in database inference analysis. *Jour. of Computer Security*, 3(2,3):147–168, 1995.
19. B.M. Thuraisingham. Security checking in relational database management systems augmented with inference engines. *Computers and Security*, 6:479–492, 1987.
20. J.D. Ullman. *Principles of Database and Knowledge-base Systems, Volumes 1,2*. Computer Science Press, Rockville, MD, 1988.
21. R. W. Yip and K. N. Levitt. Data level inference detection in database systems. In *Proc. of the 11th IEEE Computer Security Foundation Workshop, Rockport, MA*, pages 179–189, June 1998.

Detecting Privacy Violations in Sensitive XML Databases

Stefan Böttcher and Rita Steinmetz

University of Paderborn (Germany), Computer Science,
Fürstenallee 11, D-33102 Paderborn
stb@uni-paderborn.de, rst@uni-paderborn.de

Abstract. Privacy violations and the exposition of sensitive data to a third party may seriously damage the business of a company. Therefore, it is crucial for the company to identify that set of users that may have exposed the sensitive data. To identify that set of users is a problem, when multiple users must have access rights that allow them to access the exposed sensitive data. Our solution to the problem is based on an analysis of the users' XPath queries. Within a two-step approach, we compare submitted queries with the exposed data to identify suspicious queries.

1 Introduction

1.1 Motivation

Whenever a company has to allow multiple users to access sensitive data, i.e., any information, which through loss, unauthorized access, or modification could adversely affect the privacy of individuals, and some of the sensitive data has been disclosed to a third party, it is important for the company to identify the privacy leak. In such a situation, the company has to determine, who had access to the uncovered sensitive data, i.e., who had the possibility to expose certain data to the third party.

For example, consider a woman – say Jane – who has overdrawn her account at her bank – say MoneyCo – and after a few weeks, she receives advertisements for books on how to reduce debts by a second company. Therefore, Jane might blame MoneyCo for exposing the balance of her bank account to the other company. In such a case, it could be useful if MoneyCo could query its database to identify which database users had access to the concerned data, i.e., which users have posed queries, the results of which contain Jane and the balance of her bank account. In a second step, MoneyCo could interview all suspicious users to detect who might have disclosed the information.

In this scenario, we assume that there exists an access control system within the MoneyCo database, i.e., each database user was only able to access that part of the database he is allowed to. Note however, that not every user really has accessed all the data that he had an access right to. Instead, it depends on the queries that a user submits to a system whether he received sensitive data. In other words, our approach, does not want to prevent anyone who has the access rights from accessing the data, but we want to detect ex post based on the submitted user queries, which user has got

W. Jonker and M. Petković (Eds.): SDM 2005, LNCS 3674, pp. 143–154, 2005.

knowledge of the specified sensitive information, i.e., which user had the opportunity to reveal the specified sensitive information to a third party (which does not have the right to access this information).

1.2 Audit Language

Some requirements to the audit language can be derived from the above given scenario. Jane must be able to express which of her data MoneyCo should audit, i.e., she must be able to submit an audit query to the audit system. Since in this paper we deal with XPath (see [19]) as the system's query language, the language to express audit queries is very similar to XPath. Mainly, an audit query is an XPath expression preceded by a DuringTo-clause and by the keyword 'audit'. It is defined by the following grammar:

```
AuditExp   ::= DuringTo 'audit' XPath
DuringTo   ::= 'during' datetime 'to' datetime
XPath      ::= Path | Path '[' FExp ']'
Path       ::= '/'Path | Path'/'Path | Path'//'Path | Σ | '.'
FExp       ::= XPath | Path Comp constant
Comp       ::= '=' | '<' | '≤' | '>' | '≥' | '≠'
```

datetime is a timestamp, Σ is the set of elements and attributes specified by the DTD of the XML database, and constant is a constant of some standard type, such as String, Long or Integer. Note that our audit language covers a subset of XPath for which an efficient algorithm is presented.

One example of an audit query, which Jane might have posed in the above given scenario is

```
A=during 3pm,01/02/05 to 5pm,08/02/05
  audit /Bank/Department/Customer[./Name="Jane"][.//Balance<0]
```

The DuringTo-clause is used to specify a period in which the suspicious query must have been answered. In the above given scenario, the start time '3pm,01/02/05' would be the time and date when the balance of Jane's bank account got negative and the end time '5pm,08/02/05' would be the time and date when Jane received the advertisement.

The supported set of XPath queries in our system is also defined by the above given grammar when starting with the start symbol XPath. We refer to the supported set of XPath queries as $XP^{\{/, //, [], \geq c\}}$ in the remainder of this paper, where $\geq c$ denotes that comparisons of paths to constants are allowed within predicate filters.

For example, consider the user query

```
            Q1=//Customer[./Account/Balance<0]/Name
```

If within the database there exists an entry of a user with name="Jane" and with balance less than 0 at the time when Q1 has been executed, then Q1 has accessed the data specified by A, i.e., Q1 is returned as a *suspicious query* by our audit system.

1.3 Requirements of Our Audit System

In some situations, additional information can be gained by posing a series of related queries. For example, consider the queries Q2=//Customer/Name and Q3=//Customer[//Balance>=0]/Name. Each of these queries would not be deemed suspicious. However, if outside of the XML database the difference Q1=Q2-Q3 of both queries would be build, the user gains the information specified in the audit query. Nevertheless, in this paper, we limit ourselves to determining whether a single query is suspicious with respect to an audit query, and we do not provide a solution where a combination of queries is suspicious.

Thus, the problem solved in this paper is, given an XML database system, an underlying DTD, and an audit query A, return all user queries, which have accessed data specified in A.

1.4 Paper Organization

The remainder of the paper is organized as follows. Section 2 gives an overview of the system structure designed to fulfill the requirements of our proposed auditing system. Section 3 describes the algorithm to find suspicious queries according to an audit query. Section 4 discusses the related works. Finally, Section 5 concludes the paper.

2 System Structure

The overall system (see Figure 1) is an XML database system which is extended by a query log and a backlog, which are defined as follows.

Query log: The query log stores the queries that have been executed on the XML database together with the IDs of the users who have executed the queries and with timestamps of when the results of the queries were returned to the users.

Backlog: The backlog is used to store all changes to the XML database in order to be able to restore the state of the database at a certain timestamp t.

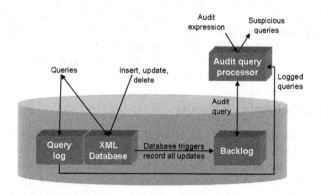

Fig. 1. System architecture (cf. [2])

The backlog is organized as a table where each row contains the following information: an index number identifying the changed XML node, a keyword – either 'delete' or 'insert', depending on the operation performed on the value of the changed node, a value, and the timestamp on when the operation has been performed.

The value is either the new value of the inserted node, if the operation is an insert operation, or the value of the deleted node, otherwise. An update operation on one node is treated as a deletion of the node followed by the insertion of a new node with the same index number and a new value.

An alternative to the use of a backlog to restore the state of a database to the state at a previous timestamp t, is to use a temporal XML database instead, i.e., a database that contains all these states at the same time. For an approach on how to efficiently query temporal XML databases refer to [12]. Note that our algorithms to detect suspicious queries do not depend on the storage approach used for the backlog, i.e., both storage approaches are compatible with our technique to detect suspicious queries.

3 Algorithms

The overall process is as follows: The audit query processor first takes an audit query as input. Then, it searches the query log for possible candidate queries, i.e., it searches for queries that might have accessed information specified by the audit query. Afterwards, the audit query processor restores the database to the time t of each candidate query, i.e., it computes a copy of the database or, in case of a temporal XML database, uses a database view, that represents the state of the database at timestamp t. Finally, the audit query processor returns all suspicious queries, i.e., it returns all the queries that efficiently have accessed the information specified by the audit query. The formal definition of candidate queries will be given in Section 3.1, and the formal definition of suspicious queries will be given in Section 3.3.

In order to test whether a query Q returns the data specified by an audit query A, i.e., whether the query is deemed suspicious, the audit system performs the query A(treeCopyOf(Q(Dt))), and checks whether it returns a non-empty XML node set. Dt is the restored database at timestamp t, where t is the timestamp of the query Q recorded in the query log. The operation treeCopyOf(Q(Dt)) executes the query Q on the database Dt and returns the fragment of Dt that contains all the leaf nodes of Dt that are selected by Q plus all the paths from the root to these selected nodes plus all the nodes that are "selected" by predicate filters plus the paths from the root to these nodes. Our goal is to find all these suspicious nodes.

3.1 Reducing the Number of Queries

One problem of the nested query execution of A(treeCopyOf(Q(Dt))) is that it takes a long time to perform this audit query for all queries Q in the query log, as for each query, the state of the database at the time when the query was answered has to be restored. Therefore, we perform an analysis to filter out some of the non-suspicious queries. The simplest optimization is to perform a static analysis on all queries first, i.e., to filter out all queries, the timestamp of which is not contained within the period specified by the DuringTo-clause of the audit query.

Furthermore, we propose an approach to efficiently identify a set of queries called *candidate queries* that includes all the suspicious queries. These candidate queries can be identified by an analysis of the structure of both queries, the audit query, and the user query. In order to define the set of candidate queries, we need the following definitions:

Definition 1 (Tree Pattern [13]). Let Σ be the set of element names and attributes defined by the underlying DTD. A *tree pattern* is a tree p or a forest F of trees, the nodes of which are labeled with symbols fromΣ, with two distinguished subset of edges, and two distinguished subsets of nodes.

The first distinguished subset of edges is called child edges and it represents the parent-child relationship. It is denoted by a single line. The second distinguished subset of edges is called descendant edges and it represents the ancestor-descendant relationship. It is denoted by a double line.

The first distinguished subset of nodes is called element nodes. It is denoted by a circle. The second distinguished subset of nodes is called comparison nodes. It is denoted by a rectangle. The label of a comparison node is a comparison operator (i.e., $=$, $<, \leq, >, \geq, \neq$) followed by a constant.

Informally, a tree pattern TQ is a tree representation of an $XP^{\{/, //, [], \geq c\}}$ XPath query Q.

A candidate query is a query Q that might have accessed information specified by the audit query, i.e., a query for which a homomorphism from the audit tree pattern to the tree pattern of Q exists.

Definition 2 (Candidate queries). Let TQ be the tree pattern of the query Q, and let TA be the tree pattern of the audit query A. The query Q is a *candidate query* with respect to the audit query A if and only if there exists a homomorphism h:ElementNodes(TA)$\rightarrow$ ElementNodes(TQ) so that

1. h(root(TA)) = root(TQ)
2. $\forall$ x $\in$ ElementNodes(TA) : Label (x) = Label(h(x))
3. $\forall$ x,y $\in$ ElementNodes(TA): if (x,y) is a child edge in TA then (h(x),h(y)) is a child edge in TQ and if (x,y) is a descendant edge in TA then h(y) is a descendant of h(x) in TQ.

In the example of Figure 2, condition 3. is satisfied by the nodes x and y with Label(x)=Customer and Label(y)=Balance in Figure 2(a) and a homomorphism h that maps these nodes to the corresponding nodes h(x) with Label(h(x))=Customer and h(y) with Label(h(y))=Balance in Figure 2(b), because the node h(y) is a descendant of h(x).

3.2 Transformed Tree Patterns

Sometimes a homomorphism h cannot be found just because of some nodes (e.g., the nodes with the labels Bank and Department of the audit pattern of Figure 2(a) cannot be mapped to corresponding nodes in the query pattern of Figure 2(b)). However, there might be a possibility to "map" these nodes to a descendant edge. Therefore, we transform the tree pattern of the user query into an equivalent transformed tree pattern. Equivalent means that the query Q and the transformed query pattern Q' select the same element nodes for each document that is valid according to the given DTD. For example, consider the user query:

```
Q1: //Customer[./Account/Balance<0]/Name
```

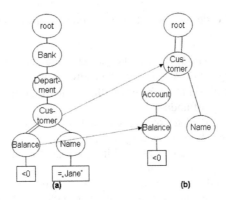

Fig. 2. (a) audit pattern TA, (b) query pattern TQ1

and the following DTD:

```
<!ELEMENT Bank (Department*)>
<!ELEMENT Department (Customer*)>
<!ELEMENT Customer (Name, Account*)>
<!ELEMENT Account (Balance)>
```

As the DTD states that a node Customer can only be reached by the path /Bank/Department/Customer, Q1 is equivalent to the user query

```
Q1'= /Bank/Department/Customer[./Account/Balance<0]/Name.
```

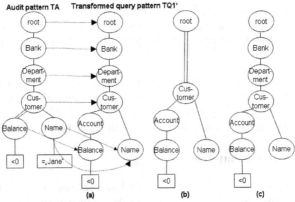

Fig. 3. (a) Homomorphism from audit pattern to transformed query pattern, (b) query pattern, (c) transformed query pattern

In this case, we replace the descendant edge (root, Customer) with a path of nodes root→Bank→Department→Customer. In general, we replace each descendant edge with a set of paths, which is the reduced DTD graph, as introduced in [6].

Figure 3(b) shows the tree pattern TQ1 of the original user query Q1 and Figure 3(c) shows the transformed query tree pattern TQ1' of the transformed user query Q1'.

Figure 3(a) shows a homomorphism between the audit pattern TA of the audit query A and the transformed query pattern TQ1' of the user query Q1. Whether there exists a homomorphism between one audit pattern TA and a transformed tree pattern TQ' of a user query can be tested in $O(|TA||TQ'|)$ time (see [13]), where $|TA|$ is the number of nodes of pattern TA and $|TQ'|$ is the number of nodes of pattern TQ'.

3.3 Suspicious Queries

Definition 3 (treeCopyOf): Let Q be a given query and D be a given document D. Furthermore, let TQ be the tree pattern of the query Q, and let TD be the tree representation of the document D. An embedding from TQ to TD is defined to be a function $e:Nodes(TQ) \rightarrow Nodes(TD)$ with

1. $e(root(TQ)) = root(TD)$
2. $\forall\ x \in ElementNodes\ (TQ) : Label\ (x) = Label(e(x))$
3. $\forall\ x,y \in ElementNodes\ (TQ)$: if(x,y) is a child edge in TQ then (e(x),e(y)) is a child edge in TD and if (x,y) is a descendant edge in TQ then e(y) is a descendant of e(x) in TD.
4. $\forall\ x \in ElementNodes\ (TQ), \forall\ y \in ComparisonNodes\ (TQ)$: if(x,y) is a child edge in TQ, then e(x) has to fulfill the condition stated in label(y).

Let e be such an embedding. Then VED_e is defined as $\{v \in Nodes(TD) \mid v=e(q)$ and $q \in Nodes(TQ)\}$.

Let E be set of all possible embeddings $e:Nodes(TQ) \rightarrow Nodes(TD)$. Let VED be defined as $VED := \cup_{e \in E} VED_e$. Then treeCopyOf(Q(D)) is that subtree of TD that contains all nodes of VED plus all paths from the root node to these nodes.

Definition 4 (Suspicious Query): We call a query Q, the results of which were returned at timestamp t from a database, *suspicious* with respect to an audit query A and a database D, if $A(treeCopyOf(Q(Dt))) \neq \varnothing$, for state Dt of the database D at timestamp t.

Note that the test whether a query is suspicious is completely different from testing query containment which could be used for access control.

3.4 Restoring the Database at Timestamp t

In order to restore the state of the database at timestamp t, we use the backlog. We assume that the backlog is sorted by the timestamps, and we additionally use the eXtended Preorder Numbering Scheme (XPNS) as presented in [11] to implement the index number of each row. The XPNS assigns a tuple (P, R) to each node of the XML database, where P is the preorder number of the node and R is a range. For each node x and each of its descendants y, it holds that $P(x)<P(y)$ and $P(y)+R(y) \leq P(x)+R(x)$, and for each node x and each of its following siblings z, it holds that $P(x)+R(x)<P(z)$. Therefore, given the preorder number P(w) of a node w, w can be found within the XML database by the use of those inequations in $O(log(width(db))*depth(db))$ time, where width(db) is the maximum number of children that one node of the XML database has, and depth(db) is the depth of the XML database.

In order to restore the state of the database for a given query, we first have to check the query log for the timestamp t when the query was answered. Then we check the backlog for all changes from time t to the current time. These changes can be detected quickly as the backlog is sorted by the timestamps. Then we make a copy of the actual XML database and perform all the changes, which are recorded in the backlog, on the copy of the database in reverse order and reverse mode, i.e., if the backlog entry says that a node with preorder number 9 has been inserted, we delete the node, or vice versa.

3.5 Summarized Algorithm

As shown in Figure 4, our algorithm works as follows. First, by a static analysis, we filter out all queries that do not meet the time constraints specified by the audit query (lines (2)-(4)). Then, we generate the transformed query pattern q' for all remaining queries and check if there exists a homomorphism between the audit query pattern and the transformed query pattern (lines (5)-(8)). Finally, we restore the state Dt of the database at timestamp t for each candidate query, and we return all queries for which A(treeCopyOf(Q(Dt)))≠∅ holds.

```
audit(AuditQuery A, querylog QL, DTD D){
(1)  Q,C,S := ∅;
(2)  for each (q ∈ QL) {
(3)      if(A.during ≤ q.timestamp ≤ A.to)
(4)          Q:=Q ∪ {q}; }
(5)  for each (q ∈ Q) {
(6)      q' := transform(q,D);
(7)      if(existsHomomorphism(A,q'))
(8)          C:=C ∪ q; }
(9)  for(q=C.newest;C.moreQueries;C.next)
(10) { Dt:=restoreDB(lastTime,q.timestamp);
(11)     lastTime:=q.timestamp
(12)     if A(treeCopyOf(Q(Dt)))≠∅)
(13)         S:=S ∪ {q}; }
(14) return S; }
```

Fig. 4. Audit algorithm

In this algorithm, q.timestamp is the timestamp stored in the query log for query q. The function transform(q,D) transforms the query q into the transformed query pattern q'.

The overall time complexity of our audit-algorithm is polynomial for the following reasons. Line (3) can be performed in linear time, line (7) can be performed in $O(|A||Q|^2)$ time, as for each query q ∈ C according to [13] the existence of a homomorphism from TA to TQ can be checked in $O(|A||Q|)$ time. Finally, we assume that the query log and therefore as well the sets Q and C are sorted by the timestamps of the query. Therefore, line (10) can be performed in $O(|bl|*log(width(db))*depth(db))$ time, where |bl| is the number of entries in the backlog, width(db) is the maximum number of children that one node of the XML database has, and depth(db) is the depth of the XML database.

3.6 Correctness of Testing Candidate Queries

Within our algorithm, we first filter out all candidate queries and search the suspicious queries only amongst them. Therefore, we have to ensure, that we do not overlook any query.

Theorem 1: Let A be the given audit expression and TD be the tree representation of the XML database D at the time t when the query Q was executed. Let Q be a suspicious query with respect to A and D. Then Q is a candidate query with respect to A.

Proof sketch: Let $Q \in S$ be a suspicious query with respect to A and D. Then there exists at least one embedding e from TQ to TD. Let treeStructureOf(Q(Dt)) be that subtree of treeCopyOf(Q(Dt)) that is generated from treeCopyOf(Q(Dt)) by

1. Deleting all attribute-values
2. Deleting all text-nodes
3. Combining all siblings with the same label into one sibling.

Step 3 is stored within a mapping compress:node→node, i.e. if the nodes x and y are combined within a new node z, we insert x→z and y→z within the mapping compress.

As q is a suspicious query with respect to A, A(treeCopyOf(Q(Dt))) ≠ ∅. Therefore, there exists an embedding e_A from A to treeCopyOf(Q(Dt)). That means, there exists as well a homomorphism h_A from A to treeStructureOf(Q(Dt)) with $h_A(a):=compress(e_A(a))$ for each element node a of the audit pattern TA.

As treeStructureOf(Q(Dt)) contains only paths from the root to nodes compress(e(q)) for each node q of the tree pattern TQ, and TQ' contains all paths that are valid according to the given DTD and that are selected by Q, there exists a homomorphism h_T from treeStructureOf(Q(Dt)) to TQ'.

Then finally, we know that there exists a homomorphism h from the audit pattern TA to the transformed query pattern TQ' with $h(a):=h_T(h_A(a))$ for each element node a of the audit pattern TA. According to Definition 2, q is therefore a candidate query.   □

4 Relation to Other Works

Typical cases of privacy sensitive databases are hippocratic databases. [1] presents an overview of the 10 key privacy principles of such databases. Our work contributes to the principle "compliance", which means, a database shall provide mechanisms so that it can be checked whether the principles – in our case the principle that no sensitive information shall be exposed to a non-authorized third party – are met.

In order to fulfill audit compliance, an "audit log" as the backlog introduced in this paper is needed. One aspect, that has to be considered, but that is not treated in this paper is to detect anyone corrupting the backlog. Snodgrass et al ([15]) contribute to this problem as they propose a mechanism that detects intruders or bugs corrupting the audit log.

Our work has been inspired by the approach to audit compliance for relational databases and SQL presented in [2]. However, we focus on XML databases and XPath expressions. Some issues, such as identifying candidate queries, identifying suspicious queries and the organization of the backlog, are easy to solve for RDBMS, but are more sophisticated for XML databases, as the structure of relational databases are two-dimensional tables, where the structure of XML databases are trees.

Although our approach contributes to the topic privacy, it does not form an approach to access control as e.g. ([4], [5], [7] , and [10]), which contribute to the field of access control for XML data sources and which range from policies, to user groups, to document location, to access control on fragments of XML documents.

Another contribution to these topics [9] concentrates on query rewriting to hide information to the user. However, the problem treated by [9] is fundamentally different from our problem in the following aspect. The problem of [9] is to hide a part of the information from the users submitting queries to the system. In the example taken by [9] a nurse seeing a patient and asking queries about the patient should not get knowledge of whether or not this patient is a trial patient, i.e. this part of the information is hidden by rewriting the queries of the nurse. In comparison, we do not discuss the problem of hiding a part the information from the users that submit queries to the system. In contrast, our problem is that users who are authorized to get knowledge (i.e. "full" access must be granted to them) uncover that knowledge to a third party, i.e. authorized users are a leak. And depending on the queries submitted and answers retrieved by each authorized user, we want to identify the leak. Note that our approach is also significantly different from traditional access control techniques, which provide a technique to prevent some non-authorized users from accessing all the information that is retrievable for authorized users from a database, e.g. from query rewriting techniques like [16].

Containment tests for XPath queries are presented e.g. in ([6], [8], [13], [14], [17], and [18]). Some of them (e.g., the algorithms presented in [8], [17], [18]) restrict the subset of allowed XPath expressions too much, e.g. they do not allow for descendant-axes within the XPath expressions. Others (e.g., the algorithms presented in [6], [13]) present efficient and sound, but incomplete algorithms, i.e., we cannot be sure that each candidate query will be found. Furthermore, other contributions (e.g., [14], [18]) show that for certain classes of XPath expressions, the containment problem gets a too high complexity, i.e., these classes cannot be considered for our algorithm.

In fact, the above-mentioned algorithms deal with containment tests for the results of XPath queries. In our algorithm, a containment test on the structure of the XPath queries is used to detect candidate queries. As our test for candidate queries uses a containment test on the structure of XPath expressions, in this paper, we propose an approach that combines the ideas presented in [3] and [13].

5   Conclusions

Detecting privacy violations is crucial when a company has to allow multiple users to access its sensitive data, and some of the data has been disclosed to a third party. The approach presented in this paper is completely independent from any existing access control system, i.e., we assume, that each database user can only access that part of the database, he is allowed to according to its access rights. In contrast to access control systems, our approach allows the company to check ex post, which user had had access to the specified sensitive part of the database, i.e., which user was able to disclose the specified part of the database to a third party.

In this paper, we have presented an efficient algorithm that identifies a set of suspicious XPath queries with respect to an audit XPath query for an XML database. Our algorithm first restricts the set of relevant queries of the query log by using the timestamp interval given in the audit query. Then it identifies candidate queries by searching a homomorphism between the tree pattern TA of the audit query A and the transformed pattern TQ of each relevant user query Q of the query log. For each query Q where a homomorphism for TA to TQ exists, in a final step, our algorithm checks, whether both queries Q and A access the same data.

In order to keep our presentation as simple as possible, we have restricted it to XPath. However, as XPath forms the major part of other query languages like XQuery and XSLT, we believe that our approach will be easily adaptable to these query languages.

References

[1] Rakesh Agrawal, Jerry Kiernan, Ramakrishnan Srikant, Yirong Xu: Hippocratic Databases. In: Philip A. Bernstein, Yannis E. Loannidis, Raghu Ramakrishnan (Eds.): Proceedings of 28th International Conference on Very Large Data Bases. VLDB 2002, Hong Kong, 2002

[2] Rakesh Agrawal, Roberto J. Bayardo Jr., Christos Faloutsos, Jerry Kiernan, Ralf Rantzau, Ramakrishnan Srikant: Auditing Compliance with a Hippocratic Database In: Mario A. Nascimento, M. Tamer Özsu, Donald Kossmann, Renée J. Miller, José A. Blakeley, K. Bernhard Schiefer (Eds.): (e)Proceedings of the Thirtieth International Conference on Very Large Data Bases. VLDB 2004, Toronto, Canada, 2004

[3] Sihem Amer-Yahia, SungRan Cho, Laks V. S. Lakshmanan, Divesh Srivastava: Minimization of Tree Pattern Queries In: Timos Sellis (Ed.): Proceedings of the 2001 ACM SIGMOD international conference on Management of data. SIGMOD Conference 2001, Santa Barbara, California, United States, 2001

[4] Elisa Bertino, Silvana Castano , Elena Ferrari: On specifying security policies for web documents with an XML-based language In: In Proceedings of the 6th ACM Symposium on Access Control Models and Technologies. SACMAT 2001, Chantilly, Virginia, USA, 2001.

[5] Elisa Bertino, Elena Ferrari: Secure and selective dissemination of XML documents. In: ACM Transactions on Information and System Security. TISSEC, Volume 5, Number 3, pp 290–331, 2002

[6] Stefan Böttcher, Rita Steinmetz: A DTD Graph Based XPath Query Subsumption Test In: Zohra Bellahsene, Akmal B. Chaudhri, Erhard Rahm, Michael Rys, Rainer Unland (Eds.): Database and XML Technologies, First International XML Database Symposium, XSym 2003, Berlin, Germany, 2003

[7] Ernesto Damiani, Sabrina di Virmercati, Stefano Paraboschi, Pierangela Samarati: Securing XML Documents In: Carlo Zaniolo, Peter C. Lockemann, Marc H. Scholl, Torsten Grust (Eds.): Advances in Database Technology - EDBT 2000, 7th International Conference on Extending Database Technology, Konstanz, Germany, 2000

[8] Alin Deutsch, Val Tannen: Reformulation of XML Queries and Constraints In: Diego Calvanese, Maurizio Lenzerini, Rajeev Motwani (Eds.): Database Theory - ICDT 2003, 9th International Conference, Siena, Italy, 2003

[9] Wenfei Fan, Chee Yong Chan, and Minos Garofalakis: Secure XML Querying with Security Views In: Gerhard Weikum, Arnd Christian König, Stefan Deßloch (Eds.): Proceedings of the ACM SIGMOD International Conference on Management of Data. SIGMOD Conference 2004, Paris, France, 2004

[10] Michiharu Kudo, Satoshi Hada: XML document security based on provisional authorization In: In Sushil Jajodia, Pierangela Samarati (Eds.): Proceedings of the 7th ACM Conference on Computer and Communications Security. CCS 2000, Athens, Greece, 2000

[11] Quanzhong Li, Bongki Moon: Partition Based Path Join Algorithms for XML Data In:: Vladimír Marík, Werner Retschitzegger, Olga Stepánková (Eds.): Database and Expert Systems Applications, 14th International Conference, DEXA 2003, Prague, Czech Republic, , 2003

[12] Alberto O. Mendelzon, Flavio Rizzolo, Alejandro A. Vaisman: Indexing Temporal XML Documents In: Mario A. Nascimento, M. Tamer Özsu, Donald Kossmann, Renée J. Miller, José A. Blakeley, K. Bernhard Schiefer (Eds.): (e)Proceedings of the Thirtieth International Conference on Very Large Data Bases. VLDB 2004, Toronto, Canada, 2004

[13] Gerome Miklau, Dan Suciu: Containment and Equivalence for an XPath Fragment. Journal of the ACM, Volume 51, 2004

[14] Frank Neven, Thomas Schwentick: XPath Containment in the Presence of Disjunction, DTDs, and Variables In: Diego Calvanese, Maurizio Lenzerini, Rajeev Motwani (Eds.): Database Theory - ICDT 2003, 9th International Conference, Siena, Italy, 2003

[15] Richard T. Snodgrass, Shilong (Stanley) Yao, Christian S. Collberg: Tamper Detection in Audit Logs In: Mario A. Nascimento, M. Tamer Özsu, Donald Kossmann, Renée J. Miller, José A. Blakeley, K. Bernhard Schiefer (Eds.): (e)Proceedings of the Thirtieth International Conference on Very Large Data Bases. VLDB 2004, Toronto, Canada, 2004

[16] Stonebraker, M.: Implementation of Integrity Constraints and Views by Query Modification In: W. Frank King (Ed.): Proceedings of the 1975 ACM SIGMOD International Conference on Management of Data. SIGMOD Conference 1975, San Jose, California, 1975

[17] Peter T. Wood: Containment for XPath Fragments under DTD Constraints In: Diego Calvanese, Maurizio Lenzerini, Rajeev Motwani (Eds.): Database Theory - ICDT 2003, 9th International Conference, Siena, Italy, 2003

[18] Peter T. Wood: Minimising Simple XPath Expressions In: Giansalvatore Mecca, Jérôme Siméon (Eds.): Proceedings of the Fourth International Workshop on the Web and Databases, WebDB 2001, Santa Barbara, California, USA, 2001

Suppressing Microdata to Prevent Probabilistic Classification Based Inference*

Ayça Azgın Hintoğlu and Yücel Saygın

Sabancı University, Faculty of Engineering and Natural Sciences, Tuzla,
34956 Istanbul, Turkey
{aycah, ysaygin}@sabanciuniv.edu

Abstract. Enterprises have been collecting data for many reasons including better customer relationship management, and high-level decision making. Public safety was another motivation for large-scale data collection efforts initiated by government agencies. However, such widespread data collection efforts coupled with powerful data analysis tools raised concerns about privacy. This is due to the fact that collected data may contain confidential information, or it can be used to infer confidential information. One method to ensure privacy is to selectively hide confidential data values from the data set to be disclosed. However, with data mining technology it is now possible for an adversary to predict the hidden data values, which is another threat to privacy. In this paper we concentrate on probabilistic classification, which is a specific data mining technique widely used for prediction purposes, and propose methods for downgrading probabilistic classification models in order to block the inference of hidden microdata values.

1 Introduction

Data collection is one of the major tasks of enterprises especially after the Internet revolution, which made the data collection task even easier. Collected data is usually stored in data warehouses and, powerful data mining tools are used to turn it into competitive advantage via better business intelligence and customer relationship management. Government agencies are among the most aggressive data collectors especially after the increased threats to safety coming from global terrorist organizations.

The pervasive data collection rally by government agencies and enterprises raised a lot of concerns among people about their privacy. For example, airline companies are obliged by international laws to disclose their passenger information to the officials in the United States and other countries. It is true that privacy of individuals is protected by regulations in Europe and other countries, however such regulations may not be enough to ensure privacy.

Widespread usage of data mining tools as well has contributed to the fears about privacy. This is due to the fact that confidential data mining results can now be ex-

---

* This work is funded by the PIA-BOSPHORUS programme of EGIDE (France) and TÜBİTAK (Turkey).

W. Jonker and M. Petković (Eds.): SDM 2005, LNCS 3674, pp. 155–169, 2005.

tracted with data mining tools, and data mining models themselves can be used to predict confidential data values. Concerns about privacy even caused some data mining projects to be canceled in US. Therefore, privacy issues have become one of the important aspects of data mining research, which has been emphasized in recent panel sessions, and workshops on databases and data mining.

In this paper, we propose new methods for suppressing confidential data values in a data set by modifying it in a way to avoid prediction of confidential data values using probabilistic classification models. As an initial attempt for solving this problem we choose Naïve Bayesian as the representative of probabilistic classification models and propose algorithms based on Naïve Bayesian classification.

The rest of the paper is organized as follows: In section 2, we present an overview of the current approaches on privacy preserving data mining and give some background information on the Naïve Bayesian classification. In section 3, we formally define the problem, and present the algorithms for suppressing probabilistic classification models. In section 4, we present and discuss the experimental results of the algorithms. Section 5 concludes the paper.

2   Background and Related Work

Privacy issues were previously investigated in the context of statistical databases as the inference problem with the aim of blocking attempts to predict confidential information using the results of successive related queries. An extensive survey of statistical database security is provided in [13] and more recent work on statistical disclosure control in databases can be found in [14] and [25]. The issue of preserving the anonymity during the data dissemination process using generalizations and suppressions on the potentially identifying portions of the data was addressed in [10], [17] and [26]. However, in all these works the privacy threats due to inference based on data mining models were not addressed. Therefore, they do not directly apply to our problem.

From the data mining perspective, researchers developed methods to enable data mining techniques to be applied while preserving the privacy. Methods for building classification models on perturbed data were proposed by Agrawal and Srikant in [8]. Association rule extraction methods over encrypted data, which is distributed over multiple autonomous sites, were proposed by Clifton et al. in [2]. Privacy preserving data mining techniques were investigated further in [7], [12], [19], [20], [21], [22] and [23]. These techniques are concentrated on obtaining valid and useful results when the input is private. However, the results might also violate privacy resulting in a potential privacy breach. Kantarcıoğlu et al. explores this issue in [3]. An extensive survey of privacy preserving data mining approaches can be found in [4].

Another issue from the data mining perspective is to protect privacy against data mining techniques. In [5], [6] and [11] methods for protecting confidential data mining results were proposed.

The basic problem of using nonsensitive data to infer sensitive data with the help of data mining has been defined in [1]. In this work, it has been shown how lower bounds from pattern recognition theory can be used to determine sample sizes where data mining tools cannot obtain reliable results. A new paradigm for dealing with the inference problem, which combines the application of decision tree analysis with the concept of parsimonious downgrading, was proposed in [9]. In this work, Chang and Moskowitz showed how classification models can be used to predict suppressed confidential data values and concluded that some feedback mechanism is needed to protect suppressed data values against classification models.

2.1 Naïve Bayesian Classification

Naïve Bayesian Classifier is a statistical classifier that can predict the probability that a given tuple belongs to a particular class. It works with the *class conditional independence* assumption such that the effect of an attribute value on a given class is independent of the values of the other attributes. Moreover, it is based on Bayes theorem. According to this theorem, given a new tuple d whose class label is unknown, the probability that d belongs to some class $c_k \in C$ is equal to the posterior probability of c_k conditioned on d and is given by

$$p(c_k \mid d) = \frac{p(c_k)p(d \mid c_k)}{p(d)} \tag{1}$$

where $p(c_k)$ and $p(d)$ are the prior probabilities of c_k and d respectively, and $p(d \mid c_k)$ is the posterior probability of d conditioned on c_k. Since we made the assumption of class conditional independence, we can write the posterior probability $p(d \mid c_k)$ as

$$p(d \mid c_k) = \prod_{j=1}^{n} p(d_j \mid c_k) \tag{2}$$

where d_j represents the jth attribute value of tuple d.

The Naïve Bayesian classifier will predict that d belongs to the class having the highest posterior probability $p(c_k \mid d)$ as shown below:

$$\text{Most Probable Value} = \arg\max_{c_k}\left(p(c_k \mid d) = \frac{p(c_k)\prod_{j=1}^{n} p(d_j \mid c_k)}{p(d)} \right). \tag{3}$$

A detailed description of Naïve Bayesian classification can be found in [18].

3 Preventing Probabilistic Classification Based Inference

In this section we present the problem of suppressing a confidential data value to prevent probabilistic classification based inference together with the information theoretic evaluation measures used in our experiments. We also introduce the strategies for preventing classification based inference with the algorithms implementing these strategies with a discussion on the effectiveness of the suppression algorithms.

3.1 Problem Formulation

Classification is the process of finding a set of classification models using a training data set in order to predict the class label of a given tuple based on its attribute values. In this study, we aim at preventing probabilistic classification models to predict a *confidential data value*. Formally, the problem of suppressing a confidential data value to prevent probabilistic classification based inference can be stated as follows:

> Let $A = \{a_1, ..., a_n\}$ be the set of attributes and, let C be the set of class labels that a confidential data value might take. Let $D = \{d_1, ..., d_m\}$ be the data set where each tuple $d_i \in D$ is an n dimensional row vector (d_{i1} d_{i2} ... d_{in}). Given such a data set D where the jth attribute of the ith tuple, denoted by $d_{ij}^{\,1}$, contains a confidential data value, how can we modify the data set D to form a new data set D' with as little information loss as possible, such that the confidential data value d_{ij} used to contain cannot be predicted by a probabilistic classification model formed using D'.

As an initial attempt for solving this problem we choose Naïve Bayesian classification model as the representative of probabilistic classification models and develop the suppression algorithms based on this model.

3.2 Evaluation Measures

One of the issues in suppressing a confidential data value is to minimize the information loss by minimizing the number of data values modified. Therefore, the proposed algorithms are assessed by measuring information loss apart from the CPU time requirements and success rate. In order to measure the information loss, two metrics is used.

The first and the simplest metric is the direct distance. Direct distance finds the number of data values hidden after suppressing the confidential data value.

Definition 1 (Direct Distance). Given two data sets D and D' representing the original and new data sets with m tuples and n attributes respectively, the direct distance between them can be defined as

$$DD(D, D') = \sum_{i=1}^{m} \sum_{j=1}^{n} dist_{ij} \tag{4}$$

where

$$dist_{ij} = \begin{cases} 0 & if \ d_{ij} = d'_{ij} \\ 1 & otherwise \end{cases} \tag{5}$$

The second metric is the sum of Kullback Leibler distances. This metric is based on the Kullback Leibler distance which is defined within the scope of information theory and heavily used to assess information loss in several contexts. It measures the information loss by finding the distance between the first order probability distributions of the original and the new data sets. A detailed description of Kullback Leibler distance can be found in [24].

---

[1] Note that, d_{ij} is used to denote the location of the confidential data value in the rest of the paper.

Definition 2 (Kullback Leibler Distance). Let $X \in A$ be an attribute from the original data set D with probability distribution $p_x(x)$ and X' be the corresponding attribute from the new data set D' with probability distribution $p_{x'}(x)$. Moreover, let the domain of X and X' be $\aleph$. Then, the Kullback Leibler distance between the original and the new data sets in terms of attributes X and X' can be defined as

$$D(p_X \parallel p_{X'}) = \sum_{x \in \aleph} p_X(x) \log \frac{p_X(x)}{p_{X'}(x)}. \tag{6}$$

Definition 3 (Sum of Kullback Leibler Distances). Given the original data set D with n attributes $A = \{a_1, \ldots, a_n\}$ and the new data set D' with the corresponding n attributes $A' = \{a'_1, \ldots, a'_n\}$, the sum of Kullback Leibler distances can be defined as

$$SKLD(D, D') = \sum_{i=1}^{n} D(p_{a_i} \parallel p_{a'_i}). \tag{7}$$

3.3 Algorithms for Preventing Probabilistic Classification Based Inference

One method of suppressing confidential data values in a data set is to replace them with a special symbol NULL or "unknown" denoted by a question mark. As a more general scheme the confidential data values could be generalized to non-confidential data values from a concept hierarchy. Within the scope of this study, we use the simpler method of replacing confidential data values with a question mark which is also referred to as *hiding*.

Suppressing a confidential data value alone by replacing it with a question mark may not be enough to protect it if the whole data set is going to be disclosed. This is due to the fact that an adversary can build a classification model using the rest of the data as the training data set and can use the resulting classification model to predict the actual confidential data value. In order to avoid such attacks, we propose three algorithms for preventing probabilistic classification based inference using the Naïve Bayesian classification.

DECP Algorithm
The DECP algorithm tries to decrease the probability of the tuple containing the confidential data value being a member of class t, $p(t \mid d_i)$, below the probability of it being a member of class random next best guess t_{rnbg}, $p(t_{rnbg} \mid d_i)$.

Definition 4 (Random Next Best Guess). Let C be the set of possible class labels, and $d_i \in D$ be the tuple containing a confidential data value $t \in C$, such that the most probable value for the class label of d_i is equal to t. Then, the random next best guess t_{rnbg} for the tuple d_i is a randomly selected class label such that the probability of d_i being a member of class t_{rnbg} is smaller than that of class t and greater than zero as shown below:

$$t_{rnbg} = rand(c_k \mid c_k \in C - \{t\}, p(t \mid d_i) > p(c_k \mid d_i) > 0). \tag{8}$$

In order to decrease $p(t|d_i)$ below $p(t_{mbg}|d_i)$, the attribute values with largest impact on probability coefficient $p(d_i|t)$ can be replaced with a question mark in the tuples with class label t.

Definition 5 (Largest Impact Attribute). The attribute with largest impact on probability coefficient $p(d_i|t)$ is the one that satisfies

$$\left\{ a_l \in A \middle| \arg\min_{a_l} \left(\left\| D_{C=t \& a_l=d_{il}} - \{d_i\} \middle| \middle| \middle\| D_{C=t \& a_l=d_{il}} - \{d_i\} \middle| > 1 \right) \right\} \tag{9}$$

where $D_{C=t}$ denotes the set of tuples with class label t, d_{il} denotes the lth attribute value of tuple d_i, $D_{a_l=d_{il}}$ denotes the set of tuples having the same l^{th} attribute value as d_i, and $D_{C=t \& a_l=d_{il}}$ denotes the set of tuples having the same l^{th} attribute value as d_i among the ones with class label t.

Definition 6 (Largest Impact Data Values). Let a_l be the largest impact attribute. Then, the largest impact data values are the set of occurrences of the lth attribute values in tuples $D_{C=t \& a_l=d_{il}}$ excluding d_i.

$$\text{Largest Impact Data Values} = \left\{ d_{kl} \middle| d_k \in D_{C=t \& a_l=d_{il}} - \{d_i\} \right\} \tag{10}$$

As we replace the occurrences of data values which impact the probability coefficient most with a question mark, we achieve the maximum reduction in probability.

Theorem 1. Let a_l be the largest impact attribute satisfying

$$\left\{ a_l \in A \middle| \arg\min_{a_l} \left(\left\| D_{C=t \& a_l=d_{il}} - \{d_i\} \middle| \middle| \middle\| D_{C=t \& a_l=d_{il}} - \{d_i\} \middle| > 1 \right) \right\} \tag{11}$$

where $D_{C=t}$ denotes the set of tuples with class label t, d_{il} denotes the lth attribute value of tuple d_i which contains a confidential value, $D_{a_l=d_{il}}$ denotes the set of tuples having the same l^{th} attribute value as d_i, and $D_{C=t \& a_l=d_{il}}$ denotes the set of tuples having the same l^{th} attribute value as d_i among the ones with class label t. And, let the lth attribute values of tuples in $D_{C=t \& a_l=d_{il}} - \{d_i\}$ be the largest impact data values. Then, every replacement of a largest impact data value with a question mark causes the maximum reduction in probability $p(t|d_i)$, resulting in fewer data values to be modified.

Proof. Let us first find the effect of hiding a largest impact data value on $p(t) p(d_i|t)$. Remember that since $p(d_i)$ does not change with class label it can be ignored when calculating $p(c_k|d_i)$ for all $c_k \in C$. Let the size of $D_{C=t \& a_l=d_{il}} - \{d_i\}$ be $Freq_{a_l}$ and p_{org} denote the initial probabilities before suppression. Then,

$$p(t) p(d_i|t) = p(t) \prod_{k=1}^{n} p(d_{ik}|t) \tag{12}$$

$$= p_{org}(t) \left(\prod_{k=1}^{l-1} p_{org}(d_{ik}|t) \right) p(d_{il}|t) \left(\prod_{k=l+1}^{n} p_{org}(d_{ik}|t) \right). \tag{13}$$

Single replacement of a largest impact data value causes $p(d_{il}|t)$ to decrease from $\dfrac{Freq_{a_l}}{|D_{C=t}|}$ to $\dfrac{Freq_{a_l}-1}{|D_{C=t}|}$. And, this decreases $p(t|d_i)$ by $\dfrac{Freq_{a_l}-1}{Freq_{a_l}}$.

$$p(t)p(d_i \mid t) = p_{org}(t) \prod_{k=1}^{l-1} p_{org}(d_{ik} \mid t) \left(p_{org}(d_{il} \mid t) \frac{Freq_{a_l} - 1}{Freq_{a_l}} \right) \prod_{k=l+1}^{n} p_{org}(d_{ik} \mid t) \qquad (14)$$

$$= p_{org}(t) \prod_{k=1}^{n} p_{org}(d_{ik} \mid t) \left(\frac{Freq_{a_l} - 1}{Freq_{a_l}} \right) \qquad (15)$$

Now, let there be another attribute a_k which causes a higher reduction in $p(t \mid d_i)$ than that of a_l. This implies the following:

$$\frac{(Freq_{a_k} - 1)}{Freq_{a_k}} > \frac{(Freq_{a_l} - 1)}{Freq_{a_l}} \qquad (16)$$

$$(Freq_{a_k} - 1)Freq_{a_l} > (Freq_{a_l} - 1)Freq_{a_k} \qquad (17)$$

$$Freq_{a_l} > Freq_{a_k} \qquad (18)$$

which contradicts the definition of the largest impact attribute. So, we can conclude that every replacement of a largest impact data value with a question mark causes the maximum reduction in $p(t \mid d_i)$ implying fewer number of data values should be modified.   □

The algorithm works as follows: Let d_{ij} contain the confidential data value t which is assumed to be the class label of d_i. In order to suppress d_{ij} by decreasing the probability coefficient $p(d_i \mid t)$, the algorithm first finds the probabilities $p(c_k \mid d_i)$ for each $c_k \in C$. If it decides that it is necessary to suppress the confidential data value by hiding other data values, it picks a random next best guess t_{rnbg} from C, and decreases the probability $p(t \mid d_i)$ until it is less than $p(t_{rnbg} \mid d_i)$ by finding the largest impact data values and replacing them with a question mark. An overview of this algorithm is depicted in Fig. 1. As can be seen from the pseudocode, the hiding decision is randomized if the number of different class labels a confidential data value might take is equal to 2. In such a case, suppressing the actual confidential value might result in an adversary guessing it correctly with a confidence equal to the success rate of the algorithm. In order to avoid this situation, the decision to suppress a confidential data value is randomized in all algorithms for the case $|C| = 2$. This results in an adversary guessing the actual confidential data value with 50% confidence which is the maximum uncertainty we could achieve.

Lemma 1. Let d_{ij} contain the confidential data value t with probability $p(t \mid d_i)$ and, let t_{rnbg} be the random next best guess with probability $p(t_{rnbg} \mid d_i)$. Moreover, let the number of tuples in D with class label equal to t be N_t excluding d_i. Then, the upper bound for the number of target data values that will be replaced with a question mark will be equal to $(n - 1)(N_t - 1)$ where n is equal to the number of attributes.

Proof. The proof of this statement is straightforward. DECP algorithm hides the largest impact data values from tuples with class label equal to t. If the number of such tuples is N_t, then the maximum number of possible largest impact data values is also equal to N_t. The algorithm hides $N_t - 1$ of these largest impact data values for a single largest impact attribute. After, hiding $N_t - 1$ data values it picks another attribute as the largest impact attribute and starts hiding data values of this attribute. Since, we assumed from the beginning that the number of attributes is $n-1$ excluding the class attribute, then the DECP algorithm hides at most $(n-1)(N_t-1)$ data values for suppressing a single confidential data value.   □

```
INPUT: the data set D, the confidential data d_ij with actual value t
OUTPUT: the new data set D'
Begin
Place a question mark for the confidential value d_ij
Find the probabilities p(c_k | d_i) for each c_k ∈ C
If most probable value of d_ij == actual value t {
   If | C | = 2
      Randomly decide to continue suppression
   Pick a random next best guess t_rnbg
   Do {
      Find the largest_impact_attribute
      Find the largest_impact_data_values
      Count = number of data values in largest_impact_data_values
      While p(t | d_i) • p(t_rnbg | d_i) and Count > 1 {
         Place a question mark for the next data value in
                      largest_impact_data_values
         p(t | d_i) = p(t | d_i) * (Count - 1) / Count
         Count = Count - 1
      }
   }
   While p(t | d_i) • p(t_rnbg | d_i) & candidates for
              largest_impact_attribute exist
}
End
```

Fig. 1. Pseudocode of Algorithm DECP

INCP Algorithm

An alternative to decreasing the probability of the actual confidential value is the INCP algorithm which increases the probability of the next best guess set, S_{nbg}, over $p(t \mid d)$.

Definition 7 (Next Best Guess Set). Let C be the set of class labels, and $d_i \in D$ be the tuple containing a confidential data value $t \in C$, such that the most probable value for the class label of tuple d_i is equal to t. And, let t_{rnbg} be a random next best guess. Then, the next best guess set, S_{nbg}, for the tuple d_i is the set of all class labels $c_k \in C$ such that the probability of d_i being a member of c_k is smaller than that of class t and greater than or equal to than that of class t_{rnbg}.

$$S_{nbg} = \left\{ c_k \mid c_k \in C - \{t\}, p(c_k, d_i) \ge p(t_{rnbg}, d_i) \right\} \qquad (19)$$

In order to achieve this, for each class label $c_k \in S_{nbg}$, the class labels of tuples in $D_{C=c_k}$ which have no common data values with d_i are hidden. The algorithm works as follows: Let d_{ij} contain the confidential data value t that will be suppressed. The algorithm suppresses d_{ij} by increasing the probability coefficient $p(d_i \mid c_k)$ for all $c_k \in S_{nbg}$. As the first step, it finds the probabilities $p(c_k \mid d_i)$ for each $c_k \in C$. If it decides that it is necessary to suppress the confidential data value by hiding other data values, it picks a random next best guess t_{rnbg} from $C - \{t\}$, and finds all class labels $c_k \in C$ satisfying $p(t \mid d_i) > p(c_k \mid d_i) \ge p(t_{rnbg} \mid d_i)$. These class labels form the next best guess set. Next, for each $c_k \in S_{nbg}$ the algorithm finds the tuples in $D_{C=c_k}$ which have no common data values with d_i and replaces the class labels of these tuples with a question mark until $p(t \mid d_i)$ is less than or equal to $p(c_k \mid d_i)$. Finally, it checks whether the most probable value of d_{ij} is equal to t. If this is the case, DECP algorithm is called to complete this algorithm. An overview of the INCP algorithm is shown in Fig. 2.

```
INPUT: the data set D, the confidential data d_{ij} with actual value t
OUTPUT: the new data set D'
Begin
Place a question mark for the confidential value d_{ij}
Find the probabilities p(c_k | d_i) for each c_k ∈ C
If most probable value of d_{ij} == actual value t {
  If | C | = 2
    Randomly decide to continue suppression
  Pick a random next best guess t_{rnbg}
  S_{nbg} = All class labels c_k ∈ C satisfying p(t | d_i) > p(c_k | d_i) •
                                                        p(t_{rnbg} | d_i)

  For Each c_k in S_{nbg} {
    Find the tuples in D_{C=ck}
    While  p(t | d_i) • p(c_k | d_i) And D_{C=ck} != ∅ {
      T = next tuple in D_{C=ck}
      If  T ∩ d_i = ∅ {
        Place a question mark for the class label of T
        Recalculate probabilities p(c_k | d_i) for each c_k ∈ C
      }
    }
  }
  If  most probable value of d_{ij} == actual value t
    Run Algorithm DECP
}
End
```

Fig. 2. Pseudocode of Algorithm INCP

Lemma 2. Let d_{ij} contain the confidential data value t with probability $p(t \mid d_i)$, and let S_{nbg} be the next best guess set. Moreover, let the number of tuples in data set D be m, and the number of tuples in D with class label equal to t be N_t (excluding d_i). Assuming that there are enough number of tuples that can be used for the suppression process (no need for DECP execution) the upper bound for the number of target data values that will be replaced with a question mark is equal to $m - N_t - 1 - \mid S_{nbg} \mid$.

Proof. The proof of this statement is straightforward. DECP algorithm removes only the data values from the tuple set $D_{C=c_k}$ which have no common data values with d_i where $c_k \in S_{nbg}$. In the worst case, S_{nbg} contains all class labels except t. This implies that the sum of all tuples with class label equal to one of the class labels in S_{nbg} is equal to $m - N_t - 1$. Moreover, for all $c_k \in S_{nbg}$, the probabilities $p(c_k \mid d_i)$ must be greater than zero due to the definitions of next best guess set and random next best guess. This means that, in the worst case there exists at least one tuple having the same data values with d_i (except the class label) for each $c_k \in S_{nbg}$. So, the number of target data values that will be hidden is bounded by $m - N_t - 1 - \mid S_{nbg} \mid$.   □

DROPP Algorithm

This algorithm suppresses a confidential data value contained in d_{ij} by decreasing the probability of tuple d_i being a member of class t below the probability of it being a member of class random next best guess t_{rnbg}. In order to achieve this, the algorithm hides the data values d_{ik} for $1 \le k \le n$ & $k \ne j$ satisfying the inequality $p(d_{jk} | t) > p(d_{jk} | t_{rnbg})$. The data values satisfying this inequality are the ones that increase the probability of the actual confidential data value t above the probability of the random next best guess t_{rnbg}. The algorithm works as follows: Let d_{ij} contain the confidential data value t that will be suppressed. The algorithm first finds the probabilities $p(c_k | d_i)$ for each c_k $\in$ C. If it decides that it is necessary to suppress the confidential data value by hiding other data values, it picks a random next best guess t_{rnbg} from C. Then, it finds repeatedly the data values d_{ik} for $1 \le k \le n$ & $k \ne j$ that have a higher probability of occurrence in tuples with class label t than in tuples with class label t_{rnbg} and hides these data values. An overview of this algorithm is shown in Fig. 3.

```
INPUT: the data set D, the confidential data d_ij with actual value t
OUTPUT: the new data set D'
Begin
Place a question mark for the confidential value d_ij
Find the probabilities p(c_k | d_i) for each c_k ∈ C
If most probable value of d_ij == actual value t {
   If | C | = 2
   Randomly decide to continue suppression
   Pick a random next best guess t_rnbg
   While   p(t | d_i) • p(t_rnbg | d_i) {
      k = next attribute index for which corresponding data value in
                  d_ik is not hidden yet
      If   p(d_ik | t) > p(d_ik | t_rnbg) {
         Place a question mark for the data value d_ik
         Recalculate probabilities p(c_k | d_i) for each c_k ∈ C
      }
   }
}
End
```

Fig. 3. Pseudocode of Algorithm DROPP

Lemma 3. Let d_{ij} contain the confidential data value t with conditional probability $p(t | d_i)$ and, let t_{rnbg} be the random next best guess with conditional probability $p(t_{rnbg} | d_i)$. If the number of attributes is n, then the upper bound for the number of target data values that will be replaced with a question mark is equal to $n - 1$ excluding the confidential data value.

Proof. The proof of this statement is straightforward. DROPP algorithm replaces only the data values that are contained in d_i with a question mark. We assumed that the number of attributes is n which means that d_i contains $n - 1$ data values excluding the confidential data value. So, the DROPP algorithm hides at most $n - 1$ data values for suppressing a single confidential data value.   □

3.4   Discussion on the Effectiveness of Suppression Algorithms

The motivation of the suppression algorithms presented in this paper is to make a given set of confidential data values non-discoverable, while minimizing the side effects. But how can we be sure that an adversary would not be able to predict the suppressed confidential data values? Certainly this might be a problem if randomization is not employed in various stages in the algorithms. Now, let us assume that the transformed database D' and the set of class labels C, a confidential data value might take, are known by an adversary and, analyze how the randomization techniques used avoid the adversary from guessing the actual confidential data value.

First, let us assume that instead of the random next best guess the class label having the second highest probability among C, denoted by t_{nbg}, is used in suppressing the confidential data value t. This results in an exchange between the actual confidential data value t and t_{nbg}. Knowing this fact, the adversary can predict the actual confidential data value with a confidence equal to the success rate of the algorithm. Since this problem is inherent in all suppression algorithms, we employed a random next best guess in order to reduce the confidence of an adversary predicting the actual confidential value.

The second issue that needs to be discussed occurs when the number of class labels is equal to 2. Assume that the algorithms are not randomized in deciding to suppress a confidential data value. In this case, the algorithms will try to suppress the confidential data value. Knowing this fact, the adversary will be able predict the actual confidential data value with a confidence equal to the success rate of the algorithm. In order to avoid this type of attacks, we randomly decide to suppress a confidential data value or not for data sets with 2 class labels.

The final issue that needs to be discussed is the side effects of the algorithms which are related to the number of data values hidden including the confidential data value. According to the upper bounds we derived for the number of data values that will be hidden; we can say that, for the INCP algorithm the number of data values that will be hidden depends on the number of transactions m. On the contrary, for the DROPP algorithm, the number of data values that will be hidden depends on the number of attributes n. And, finally for the DECP algorithm the number of data values that will be hidden depends on both the number of transactions m and the number of attributes n. Now, let us assume that $m \gg n$. In this case, the worst case performance of the DROPP algorithm will be much better than the worst case performance of the DECP and INCP algorithms with respect to the side effects. However, for data sets satisfying $n \gg m$, like the ones containing gene expression data, the worst case performance of the INCP algorithm will outperform the DECP and DROPP algorithms with respect to the side effects. It must be noted that, the DECP algorithm will perform very similar to the other algorithms it is grouped with, because in both cases either m or n will lose its significance with respect to the other term.

4 Experimental Results

In order to conduct the experiments we select the Wisconsin Breast Cancer data set [15] with 699 instances, 10 attributes and 16 unknowns from the University of California at Irvine repository [16]. We implemented the proposed algorithms using the C++ programming language. To evaluate the performance of the algorithms, we performed experiments on a 2.20 GHz Celeron PC with 256 MB of memory running the Windows operating system.

The first performance criterion we measured is the average CPU time required to suppress a single confidential data value. The CPU time results for each suppression strategy are depicted in Table 1. In order to find the average CPU times we suppressed a data value from each tuple of the data sets and averaged the CPU time results. Since the suppression algorithms contain random components, all the experimental results we present are averages of five realizations unless stated otherwise. As can be seen from the table, all the algorithms suppress a single confidential data value in less than a second, with INCP and DECP algorithms performing slightly better than the DROPP algorithm.

Table 1. Average CPU times(in msecs)

DECP	INCP	DROPP
156.2	154.5	159

Another performance criterion is the rate of successful suppressions with respect to the Naïve Bayesian classification model. Rate of successful suppressions is the percentage of suppressed data values that cannot be predicted using Naïve Bayesian classification after suppression. The performance of the algorithms in terms of success rate is shown in Table 2. As can be seen from the table, the DECP and INCP algorithms suppress the confidential data values with 100% success rate, followed by the DROPP algorithm with 51% success rate. Since the number of attributes is very small compared to the number of transactions, the DROPP algorithm performs relatively worse compared to the INCP and DECP algorithms. In order to guarantee 100% success rate, the tuples containing confidential data values that cannot be hidden by the corresponding suppression algorithm can be completely removed from the data set. However, in order to justify our discussions on success rate and side effects we leave these tuples as they are. Finally, it must be noted that the decision to suppress the confidential data values is not randomized, because the number of possible class labels confidential data values can take is greater than two.

Table 2. Rate of Successful Suppressions

DECP	INCP	DROPP
100%	100%	51%

The next performance criterion is the information loss caused by the suppression algorithms. In order to measure information loss, we use direct distance and sum of Kullback Leibler distances. As a benchmark, we use the naive Row Deletion (RD) algorithm which suppresses a confidential data value by hiding the whole instance containing the confidential data value.

The first metric used to measure the information loss is the average direct distance which finds the average number of unknowns introduced due to suppression of a single confidential data value. The average direct distance of the suppression algorithms is shown in Table 3. As can be seen from the table, the DROPP algorithm causes the least amount of information loss in terms of direct distance followed by the RD algorithm. Actually, the DROPP algorithm is bounded by the RD algorithm, because both algorithms suppress a confidential data value by hiding the data values from the instance containing the confidential data value. On the other hand the DECP and INCP algorithms perform relatively worse, because they aim at distorting the classification model in a randomized manner. Total direct distance versus number of confidential data values to suppress for a group of randomly selected 30 confidential data values is shown in Fig. 4.

Table 3. Average Direct Distance

DECP	INCP	DROPP	RD
78.8	63.5	1.7	10

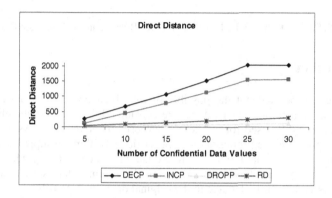

Fig. 4. Direct Distance for Breast Cancer Wisconsin Data Set

The second information loss metric used is the sum of Kullback Leibler distances which measures the total distance between the first order probability distributions of the original and the new data sets. The performance of the suppression algorithms in terms of average sum of Kullback Leibler distances is shown in Fig. 5. Similar to direct distance results, the DROPP algorithm causes the least amount of information loss in terms of sum of Kullback Leibler distances followed by the RD, INCP and DECP algorithms.

To sum up, the experimental results for the suppression algorithms show that there is a tradeoff between the rate of successful suppressions and the information loss caused by the suppression process. Moreover, it can be clearly seen that the algorithms distorting the classification model, the DECP and INCP algorithms, achieve a higher success rate leading to a high amount of information loss. On the other hand, the DROPP algorithm achieves a lower success rate leading to a low amount of information loss. However, it must be noted that the reason why the information loss caused and success rate achieved by the DECP and INCP algorithms is higher than that of the DROPP algorithm is that the data set used in experiment satisfy the inequality $m \gg n$ (number of transactions in the data set is much more than the number of attributes). And finally, the information loss results of the RD algorithm show that it provides an upper bound for the DROPP algorithm.

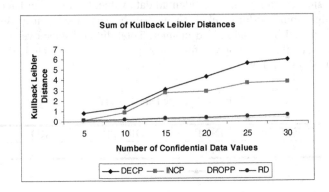

Fig. 5. Sum of Kullback Leibler Distances for Breast Cancer Wisconsin Data Set

5   Conclusion

In this paper we pointed out the possible privacy breaches induced by data mining algorithms on hidden microdata values. We considered the probabilistic classification model which could be used for prediction purposes by adversaries. As an initial step to attack the problem, we proposed some heuristic algorithms to suppress the selected classification model so that the hidden microdata values cannot be predicted with this model. Our methods are based on modifying the original data set by inserting unknown values with as little damage to the original data set as possible.

Our experiments with a real data set showed that the proposed algorithms are effective in blocking the inference channels based on the probabilistic classification model. From the success rate and side effects results we observed that there is a tradeoff between the rate of successful suppressions and the information loss caused by the suppression process. Moreover, these results verify our statement that; the side effects of the DECP algorithm depend both on the number of transactions and number of attributes while the side effects of the INCP and DROPP algorithms depend on the number of transactions and the number of attributes respectively.

In order to ensure that a confidential data value cannot be recovered later on by any alternative prediction method, we need to develop a more general technique based directly on information theory concepts, which we consider as a future work.

References

1. Clifton, C. Using Sample Size to Limit Exposure to Data Mining. Journal of Computer Security, v.8, n.4, p. 281-307, Dec. 2000.
2. Kantarcioglu, M., Clifton, C. Privacy-Preserving Distributed Mining of Association Rules on Horizontally Partitioned Data. IEEE TKDE, Vol. 16, No. 9, September 2004.
3. Kantarcioglu, M., Jin, J., Clifton, C. When do data mining results violate privacy? KDD 2004.
4. Verykios, V. S., Bertino, E., Parasiliti, L., Favino, I. N., Saygin, Y., Theodoridis, Y. State-of-the-Art in Privacy Preserving Data Mining. SIGMOD Record, Vol. 33, No. 1, 2004.

5. Verykios, V. S., Elmagarmid, A., Bertino, E., Saygin, Y., Dasseni, E. Association Rule Hiding. IEEE TKDE, Vol. 16, No. 4, 2004.
6. Saygin, Y., Verykios, V. S., Elmagarmid, A. Privacy Preserving Association Rule Mining. Proceedings of the 12th International Workshop on Research Issues in Data Engineering (RIDE'02), IEEE Computer Society Press, 2002.
7. Vaidya, J., Clifton, C. Privacy-Preserving K-Means Clustering over Vertically Partitioned Data. SIGKDD 2003
8. Agrawal, R., Srikant, R. Privacy Preserving Data Mining. SIGMOD 2000, p. 45-52.
9. Chang, L., Moskowitz, I. S. Parsimonious Downgrading and Decision Trees Applied to the Inference Problem. Proceedings of the Workshop of New Security Paradigms, 1999.
10. Iyengar, V. S. Transforming data to satisfy privacy constraints. SIGKDD 2002.
11. Oliveira, S. R. M., Zaiane, O. R. Protecting Sensitive Knowledge by Data Sanitization. Proceedings of the 3rd IEEE International Conference on Data Mining (ICDM'03), 2003.
12. Rizvi, S. J., Haritsa, J. R. Privacy-Preserving Association Rule Mining. Proceedings of the 28th International Conference on Very Large Data Bases, Hong Kong, China, August 2002.
13. Adam, N. R., Wortmann, J. C. Security-Control Methods for Statistical Databases: A Comparative Study. ACM Computing Survey. 21(4): 515-556 (1989).
14. Domingo-Ferrer, J. (editor). Inference Control in Statistical Databases, Lecture Notes in Computer Science, vol. 2316, Berlin: Springer-Verlag, 2002.
15. Mangasarian, O. L., Wolberg, W. H. Cancer diagnosis via linear programming, SIAM News, Volume 23, Number 5, September 1990, pp 1 & 18.
16. UCI Machine Learning Repository. http://www.ics.uci.edu/~mlearn/MLSummary.html.
17. Samarati, P. Protecting respondents' identities in microdata release. IEEE TKDE, 2001.
18. Han, J., Kamber, M. Data Mining Concepts and Techniques. Morgan Kaufmann Publishers. 2001.
19. Du, W., Zhan, Z. Using Randomized Response Techniques for Privacy-Preserving Data Mining. SIGKDD 2003.
20. Kargupta, H., Liu, K., Ryan, J. Privacy Sensitive Distributed Data Mining from Multi-party Data, ISI 2003, p. 336-342.
21. Kargupta, H., Datta, S., Wang, O., Sivakumar, K. On the privacy preserving properties of random data perturbation techniques, Data Mining, 2003, ICDM 2003.
22. Polat, H., Wenliang, D. Privacy-preserving collaborative filtering using randomized perturbation techniques, Data Mining, 2003, ICDM 2003.
23. Evfimievski, A. V., Gehrke, J., Srikant, R. Limiting privacy breaches in privacy preserving data mining, PODS 2003, p. 211-222.
24. Cover, T. M., Thomas, J. A.Elements of Information Theory. John Wiley & Son, 1991.
25. Farkas, C., Jajodia, S. The inference problem: A survey. SIGKDD Explorations, Jan 2003.
26. Sweeney, L. k-Anonymity: A model for protecting privacy. International Journal on Uncertainty, Fuzziness and Knowledge-based Systems, 10(5), 2002; 557-570.

On Deducibility and Anonymisation
in Medical Databases

David Power, Mark Slaymaker, and Andrew Simpson

Oxford University Computing Laboratory,
Wolfson Building, Parks Road, Oxford OX1 3QD, United Kingdom

Abstract. The utilisation of real medical data in research projects is becoming evermore widespread, and a clear duty of care towards such data is mandatory. To this end, anonymisation is essential. It is well understood that a conflict between functionality and confidentiality exists within this context: while patients' confidentiality must be preserved, restricting access can reduce the value of the data that is available to researchers. As such, limiting access so that confidentiality is preserved while still ensuring a high degree of functionality should be a key aim of every designer of medical research databases. In this paper, we outline an approach developed within the e-DiaMoND project that combines anonymisation and query modification to manage this conflict.

1   Introduction

The utilisation of real data in medical research projects is becoming increasingly widespread as is the use of IT within healthcare delivery, and the two areas appear to be on a convergence path. The linking of personal data from various sources gives rise to many promising research opportunities. Such integration requires the striking of a balance between functionality—in maximising the use of such data to support research that may lead to improved healthcare—and ethical and legal concerns—ensuring that the rights of the participants are respected. Within the UK, legal protections can be derived from (at least) the Human Rights Act of 1998 [21] and the Data Protection Act of 1998 [13].

Within the UK, the National Health Service (NHS) comprises a number of hospital trusts, each of which is an independent legal entity. Each hospital trust is legally responsible for the data held at its sites: this data is released only with respect to the principles of the Caldicott Guardian [5], which include "don't use patient-identifiable information unless it is absolutely necessary" and "use the minimum necessary patient-identifiable data".

When real patient data is used in research projects, *anonymisation* is essential. It is acknowledged that the simple removal of a patient's name and address from a record is not sufficient to guarantee anonymisation: there may be further information that enables one to deduce the patient's identity, such as, for example, date and place of birth. Those fields that are anonymised or removed have no research value, while those fields that remain constitute a useful resource; eliminating more information than the bare minimum is essential to prevent information flow—the deducing of answers to illegal queries from the results of

W. Jonker and M. Petković (Eds.): SDM 2005, LNCS 3674, pp. 170–184, 2005.
© Springer-Verlag Berlin Heidelberg 2005

legal ones (see [11] for an overview of such issues) while eliminating too much will reduce the value of the data that has been captured. The consideration of *tracker attacks* [12], which may be characterised by the submission of successive queries over different subsets of data to determine specific values of sensitive data, is also of concern.

In this paper, we reprise the approach to query modification of [24], describe a formal framework for reasoning about inferences, and then consider how they can be used together. Our inference framework draws upon concepts and theory from the areas of information security (specifically, the notion of information flow [10]) and relational database design (specifically, the notion of functional dependencies—a concept first described in [1]), and is presented in terms of the formal description technique Z [29].

The motivation for this work comes from the authors' involvement in the e-DiaMoND project [4], the primary aim of which is the development a prototype for a national database of mammograms to support applications for training, breast screening, epidemiological studies, and data mining. The e-DiaMoND grid consists of a number of nodes each of which contains data belonging to a single hospital. If a user wishes to access this data they cannot connect to the database directly, but must instead access the data via a *grid service*. If the user sends an SQL query to the database it is modified by the grid service in accordance with the access control policy of that hospital. If a user wishes to access data stored at multiple hospitals, then the query must be sent to each hospital where it is subject to the local access control policy. As the user is not aware of their exact access permissions at each hospital it would not be possible to construct a query based on the views they have access to; instead they just write the query they wish to run and the grid service will either modify it so that it can be run, or reject it. This allows the hospitals to dynamically change their access control policies without having to inform the users. (The reader is referred to [28] for a detailed overview of this architecture.) If the e-DiaMoND database [23] is to support epidemiological studies, then it is essential that access to data is provided in accordance with appropriate ethical and legal guidelines. That is, it is essential that the identities of patients cannot be deduced from the information provided to researchers undertaking such studies unless explicit consent has been given.

2 Terminology

Disclosure control (see, for example, [2] or [32]) is the term given to the activity that is concerned with the alteration of data containing information pertaining to individuals that may be considered confidential with a view to ensuring that third parties working with this altered information cannot recognize the individuals—thereby arriving at confidential information.

Microdata is the term given to a series of records, where each record in the series contains information pertaining to an indvidual entity; *masked* (or *released*) *microdata* (see, for example, [8]) refers to microdata that has been masked to reduce the possibility of disclosure; [35] contains a survey of statistical disclosure control techniques for the masking of microdata.

Disclosure risk is the risk that a particular type of disclosure will occur if masked microdata is released [7]. Disclosure risk can be measured in numerous ways: as a matter of perception [22], in terms of the probability of population uniqueness [2,19], in terms of the proportion of sample records that are population unique [16,26], or as the proportion of correct matches among the records in the population that match a sample unique masked microdata record [15].

Overviews of related security research may be found in [3] and [34].

We concern ourselves with the automated discovery of the potential for information leakage. A key difference between the work described in this paper and that of those mentioned above is that the literature is typically concerned with determining risk on the basis of the *actual* data contained in a database, whereas our focus is the *semantics* of the information model under investigation.

3   Query Modification

3.1   Motivation

The use of query modification was first proposed by Stonebraker and Wong [31,30] for use with the query language QUEL, and was implemented as part of the original INGRES database management system. Other work in which the concept of query modification has played a significant role includes [20], [6], [33], [18], [14], and [17]. While essentially similar to views, the application of query modification differs in several ways.

First, the user makes a query against the underlying tables as if there was no access restriction taking place. This query is intercepted by the access control mechanism and the query is then modified so that the user can only access the data that they have permission to access. As an example, it could be that the DBA wishes to restrict access to a table containing information pertaining to patients from two departments. Typically, a DBA might create two views of the table, with each view presenting information associated with one of the two departments. The users would only be given permission to use one of the views and they would then make their query against that view. When using query modification the user would make their query against the underlying tables and would not be aware of the modification made to their query. For example, a nurse from one department might only see information pertaining to that department. In this example, the results of the two queries would be identical: the effect of query modification was just to hide the views from the user.

Second, while the added flexibility of query modification may make it slightly more difficult to administer, it does have another advantage over views. For example, there is no need for the query modification to take place inside the DBMS: the query can be intercepted at any point between the user and the DBMS. In a system such as e-DiaMoND this can take place in a trusted internal grid service. (See [27] and [28] for more details.)

3.2 Stonebraker's Approach to Query Modification

What restrictions are placed on a query depends on which columns of which tables are accessed. This includes not just the columns that are returned, but also columns that are used as part of a WHERE clause. This is an important restriction as the values in other columns could be deduced by using them as part of a WHERE clause. Each combination of columns has an associated WHERE clause which is added to the WHERE clause of the original request using a logical *and*. If a user tries to access a combination of columns that are not listed for that user then access will be denied. If more than one combination of columns is applicable, then the WHERE clauses are combined using a logical *or*.

As an example consider the following table, *Patient*,

ID	DOB	Occupation	Postcode	Gender	MaritalStatus
P_1	03/04/1950	Plumber	OX1 3QD	F	Married
P_2	12/11/1934	Dentist	SE1 9RT	F	Single
P_3	27/07/1956	Butcher	SW17 0QT	M	Divorced
P_4	07/06/1942	Builder	OX3 7LJ	F	Widowed

Consider also the following rules:

$$\{DOB, Occupation\} \mapsto DOB < 01/01/1950$$
$$\{DOB, MaritalStatus\} \mapsto DOB > 01/01/1940$$
$$\{Postcode, Gender, MaritalStatus\} \mapsto 1 = 1$$

Given the above rules, the following original queries

- SELECT Postcode, Gender FROM Patient;
- SELECT DOB FROM Patient;
- SELECT DOB FROM Patient WHERE Occupation = 'Plumber';

become

- SELECT Postcode, Gender FROM Patient WHERE 1 = 1;
- SELECT DOB FROM Patient
  WHERE (DOB < 01/01/1950) OR (DOB > 01/01/1940);
- SELECT DOB FROM Patient
  WHERE (Occupation = 'Plumber') AND (DOB > 01/01/1940);

3.3 Query Modification for Medical Research Databases

If multiple views are allowed of the same table, then it is essential that they do not feature the primary key of the table—this is because they could then be used to uniquely identify the same row in two or more views. This can cause a problem if one wishes to perform a join as the primary key is needed.

In Stonebraker's query modification scheme [31], tables can only be joined if a user is given simultaneous access to a query involving both tables. The consequence of this is that all joins are explicitly defined; it also gives access to the primary key/foreign key pair as this will form part of the WHERE clause. If one wished to use views to restrict access to the data then there would not be the same problem: this is because the joining columns do not need to be included in the view. It should be noted that there is little point in restricting joins if users have access to the primary key/foreign key pair. In this case, the user could manually perform the join themselves, by asking for the entire contents of both tables and then performing the join outside of the database. Similarly with sub-queries, one could always perform the sub-query separately though this may involve many queries, hence each sub-query can be treated as a separate request.

We consider two methods that a user can use to perform a join. In the first method, a user has already been given access to the primary key/foreign key columns. In this case, the access restriction for the two tables are joined using a logical *and*. This differs from the case when there are multiple access restrictions on one table where a logical *or* is used to join them.

In the second method, explicit access is given for the join, with possibly stricter restrictions than the user has for the underlying tables. If the user is not to be able to see the primary key of a table used in a join the standard rules for allowing access to data cannot be applied, instead the primary key and foreign key columns are not counted when the join is performed, as long as they are only used as part of the joining condition. This only applies for rules involving explicit joins and not in general.

To see the need for control over joins, consider the following table, *Symptom*.

ID	Date	Symptom
P_1	04/08/1998	Back Pain
P_1	10/11/1998	Fainted
P_1	23/11/1998	Heart Attack
P_3	07/01/1997	Nausea
P_3	28/02/1999	Nausea
P_4	14/06/2003	Fractured Leg

This table relates the identifier of a patient with a symptom and a date. Consider now that we have the same restriction on access that we discussed previously, and that total access to this new treatment table has been granted. This alone would not allow a join to take place as the user does not have access to the *ID* column of the *Patient* table.

It would, of course, be possible to create a new view of the *Patient* table that included the *ID* column: this would have the benefit of allowing the user to join the two tables together, but would have the drawback of also allowing the user to join to any other table which they have access to the *ID* column of, which may or may not be desirable.

It is also possible to create an explicit join view that would allow one to choose the exact combination of permissable columns. This is much safer but it still could lead to problems: if two different explicit join views were allowed that mirrored the two original allowable views, then the user could use the unique nature of the list of conditions to identify an individual row in the patient table.

By doing this using both the permitted accesses of the patient table a unique patient could be identified, and—even worse—the user would know sensitive information about their symptoms. What may be safe, however, is to permit just access to say the *occupation* column of the *Patient* table and the *symptom* column of the *Symptom* table: this would permit queries without the negative effect of giving away too much information about the patient.

4 A Formal Approach to Anonymisation and Information Flow

In this section, we introduce a framework for anonymisation and information flow. We do not consider, for example, how dependencies are determined—that is, after all, a property of the specific domain; nor do we consider how anonymisation is carried out. Although the framework is presented formally, the intention is that the surrounding narrative should be sufficient to aid those readers who are unfamiliar with the Z notation.

4.1 Capturing Inferences

Our language of anonymisation is concerned primarily with pieces of information. We express the collection of all possible pieces of information within a particular context in abstract fashion in terms of the set *Tag*. For this discussion, we shall assume that each tag is associated with an attribute of a relational model. It should be noted that the relationships between tags depends entirely upon the semantics of the model under consideration.

If it is possible for the value of one tag, B, to be inferred from another tag, A, then we shall write this potential inference as $A \rightarrow B$. We choose this notation to be evocative of the notion of a functional dependency from the relational database design literature. For example, it is possible that someone's sex may be determined by their title; as such, we have $title \rightarrow sex$. Even though there are cases where this is not the case (such as, for example, if an individual's title is 'Dr') there are, of course, cases where it most certainly is possible: we identify the *potential* inference.

It is sometimes the case that the value of a tag, C, cannot be inferred directly from the value of A but can be inferred from the combination of A and another tag, B. We express this via *conjunction*: $A \wedge B \rightarrow C$. For example, assume that each hospital assigns unique patient numbers—that is, patient numbers are unique within individual hospitals. Furthermore, each hospital has a unique number to distinguish it from other hospitals. As such, assuming that *HNum* denotes the hospital number attribute, *PNum* denotes the patient number attribute and *PNam* denotes the patient name attribute, neither $HNum \rightarrow PNam$ nor $PNum \rightarrow PNam$ holds, but $HNum \wedge PNum \rightarrow PNam$ does hold.

It is sometimes the case that the value of a tag, C, can be derived from either A or B. We express this via *disjunction*: $A \vee B \rightarrow C$. For example, it may be possible to derive a patient's condition from either their symptoms or their treatment; as such, $symptoms \vee treatment \rightarrow condition$ holds.

We can capture the set of such inferences formally in Z in terms of a *relation*, i.e., a set of pairs:

$$| \quad inferences : (\mathbb{P}\ Tag) \leftrightarrow Tag$$

We move from the domain to which the dependencies pertain to the set *inferences* in the following fashion:

- If $A \rightarrow B$, then $\{A\} \mapsto B \in inferences$.
- If $A \rightarrow B \wedge C$, then $\{\{A\} \mapsto B, \{A\} \mapsto C\} \subseteq inferences$.
- If $A \wedge B \rightarrow C$, then $\{\{A, B\} \mapsto C\} \in inferences$.
- If $A \vee B \rightarrow C$, then $\{\{A\} \mapsto C, \{B\} \mapsto C\} \subseteq inferences$.

Furthermore, $X \mapsto T \in inferences$ only if it can be derived from the set of dependencies in the manner described above. As an example, if our dependencies are $A \rightarrow B$, $B \wedge C \rightarrow D$, $D \vee E \rightarrow F$ and $F \rightarrow G \wedge H$, then we arrive at the following set of pairs:

$$inferences = \{\{A\} \mapsto B, \{B, C\} \mapsto D, \{D\} \mapsto F,$$
$$\{E\} \mapsto F, \{F\} \mapsto G, \{F\} \mapsto H\}$$

Having introduced the notion of tags, together with the potential relationships between them, we now consider two subsets of *Tag*. The first, *critical*, is the set of tags that we wish to remain undiscovered; the second, *anonymised*, is the set of anonymised tags.

$$| \quad critical, anonymised : \mathbb{P}\ Tag$$

Within a particular context, then, we can represent the set of known, i.e., immediately visible, facts as *known*:

$$known : \mathbb{P}\ Tag$$
$$known = Tag \setminus anonymised$$

That is, *known* contains all elements of *Tag* that are not anonymised.

4.2   An Axiomatic Approach to Information Flow

We have seen that we can express the set of all direct inferences within a particular context via the set *inferences*. So, for example, if the dependency *title* $\rightarrow$ *sex* holds within the domain, then $\{title\} \mapsto sex \in inferences$. What is more interesting, though, is the set of *derived* inferences.

As we have seen, it is possible to capture domain-specific information in the guise of sets and relations. This approach has much in common with the established theory of functional dependencies; as such, it is natural to consider some of the results of that area here.

Consider the following simple example.

$$Tag = \{A, B, C, D, E, F, G, H\}$$
$$critical = \{D\}$$
$$anonymised = \{C, D\}$$
$$inferences = \{\{A\} \mapsto B, \{B\} \mapsto C, \{C\} \mapsto D\}$$

Here, D is critical, and—as such—been anonymised. It is fairly straightforward to see that—even though D has been removed from the interface—it can be derived easily enough: from A, via B and C. (One can imagine, though, that in more complex domains such information flow could not be detected so trivially.) Thus, it is not sufficient to consider the obvious dependencies captured from the domain, but also the non-obvious dependencies that can be derived from the original ones. As such, we need to consider more than simply the set of *inferences*: we need to consider a collection of rules—or axioms—underpinning this set to determine which tags can be *derived*.

Armstrong's axioms for functional dependencies [1] are appropriate within this context and allow one to determine the closure of a set of dependencies.

We shall let *closure* determine the closure of a set of inferences:

$$| \quad closure : ((\mathbb{P}\ Tag) \leftrightarrow Tag) \twoheadrightarrow ((\mathbb{P}\ Tag) \leftrightarrow Tag)$$

Here, *closure* (*inferences*) represents the closure of the set *inferences*, i.e., the collection of all inferences that can be derived from the original ones.

We consider each of Armstrong's axioms in turn.

The first axiom, *reflexivity*, can be captured as a predicate on *closure*:

$$\forall r : (\mathbb{P}\ Tag) \leftrightarrow Tag \bullet (\forall s : \mathbb{P}\ Tag;\ t : Tag \mid t \in s \bullet s \mapsto t \in closure\ (r))$$

As an example, this axiom may be characterized by "if one knows a patient's name and their address, then one knows their name."

The second axiom, *augmentation*, can be captured as a predicate on *closure*:

$$\forall r : (\mathbb{P}\ Tag) \leftrightarrow Tag \bullet$$
$$(\forall s_1, s_2 : \mathbb{P}\ Tag;\ t : Tag \mid s_1 \mapsto t \in r \bullet (s_1 \cup s_2) \mapsto t \in closure(r))$$

As an example, this axiom may be characterized by "if it is true that one can deduce a patient's name from their photograph, then it is also true that one can deduce a patient's name and address from their photograph and address."

The third axiom, *transitivity*, can be captured as a predicate on *closure*:

$$\forall r : (\mathbb{P}\ Tag) \leftrightarrow Tag \bullet \forall s_1, s_2 : \mathbb{P}\ Tag;\ t_1 : Tag \bullet$$
$$(s_1 \mapsto t_1 \in closure\ (r) \wedge s_1 \subseteq (closure\ (r))(\!(\{s_2\}\!)) \Rightarrow$$
$$s_2 \mapsto t_1 \in closure\ (r)$$

As an example, this may be characterized by "if it is possible to deduce a patient's name from their photograph and it is also possible to deduce a patient's address from their name, then it is possible to deduce a patient's address from their photograph."

Together these axioms ensure that *closure* gives us the closure of *inferences*. Armstrong's axioms provide us with a closure that is both sound, i.e., all captured inferences genuinely are inferences, and complete, i.e., all genuine inferences are captured [9].

We can, then, extend our definition of *closure* as follows:

$$
\forall r : (\mathbb{P} \; Tag) \leftrightarrow Tag \bullet \forall n : \mathbb{N} \mid n > 1 \bullet
$$
$$
closure^0 \, (r) = \{t : Tag; \; s : \mathbb{P} \; Tag \mid t \in s \bullet s \mapsto t\}
$$
$$
closure^1 \, (r) = closure^0 \, (r)
$$
$$
\cup
$$
$$
\{s_1, s_2 : \mathbb{P} \; Tag; \; t : Tag \mid s_1 \mapsto t \in r \bullet (s_1 \cup s_2) \mapsto t\}
$$
$$
closure^n \, (r) = closure^{n-1} \, (r)
$$
$$
\cup
$$
$$
\{s_1, s_2 : \mathbb{P} \; Tag; \; t : Tag \mid
$$
$$
s_1 \mapsto t \in closure^{n-1} \, (r) \wedge
$$
$$
s_1 \subseteq (closure^{n-1} \, (r)) (\!| \{s_2\} |\!) \bullet
$$
$$
s_2 \mapsto t\}
$$

We can, then, define *closure* as

$$
closure : ((\mathbb{P} \; Tag) \leftrightarrow Tag) \twoheadrightarrow ((\mathbb{P} \; Tag) \leftrightarrow Tag)
$$
$$
\forall r : (\mathbb{P} \; Tag) \leftrightarrow Tag \bullet closure \, (r) = \bigcup\{n : \mathbb{N} \bullet closure^n \, (r)\}
$$

Recalling that *known* is the set of Tags that we know and *critical* is the set of things that we do not wish to give away, it follows that confidentiality is satisfied exactly when

$$
critical \cap ((closure \, (inferences)) (\!| \{known\} |\!)) = \emptyset
$$

That is, confidentiality is guaranteed exactly when no critical facts can be derived from known ones. We note that in extreme cases, the satisfaction of this equality will result in a collection of information that is useless: this is, of course, an extreme manifestation of the conflict between functionality and privacy.

4.3   Minimal Additions

While the consideration of closures is effective from a theoretical point of view, there must, of course, be a tractable representation to ensure a practical manifestation of the concept: in reality, any closure will grow exponentially as via the reflexivity axiom, it will contain entries for all possible subsets of tags mapping to each of their members.

As such, we would like to define a set of inferences that is equivalent to the closure set—the set that is typically referred to as the *minimal set of functional dependencies* in the functional dependency context.

We term this set *onepass*, and its relationship with *closure* is as follows:

$$\forall\, r : (\mathbb{P}\ Tag) \leftrightarrow Tag;\ s_1 : \mathbb{P}\ Tag;\ t : Tag\ \bullet$$
$$s_1 \mapsto t \in onepass\,(r) \Leftrightarrow$$
$$(s_1 \mapsto t \in closure\,(r) \wedge$$
$$t \notin s_1 \wedge$$
$$\neg\,(\exists\, s_2 : \mathbb{P}\ Tag\ \bullet\ s_2 \mapsto t \in closure\,(r) \wedge s_2 \subset s_1))$$

The following property should be evident from the above:

$$\forall\, r : (\mathbb{P}\ Tag) \leftrightarrow Tag;\ s : \mathbb{P}\ Tag\ \bullet$$
$$(closure\,(r))(\!(\,\{s\}\,)\!) = (onepass\,(r))(\!(\,\mathbb{P}\,s\,)\!) \cup s$$

We would, for obvious reasons, like our definition of *onepass* to be independent of the set *closure*. As such, we define two new functions—*removes* and *combine*.

The function reduce *removes* all the redundant maplets that are not needed:

$$reduce : ((\mathbb{P}\ Tag) \leftrightarrow Tag) \twoheadrightarrow ((\mathbb{P}\ Tag) \leftrightarrow Tag)$$

$$\forall\, r : (\mathbb{P}\ Tag) \leftrightarrow Tag\ \bullet$$
$$reduce\,(r) = \{s_1 : \mathbb{P}\ Tag;\ t : Tag\ |\ s_1 \mapsto t \in r \wedge t \notin s_1 \wedge$$
$$\neg\,(\exists\, s_2 : \mathbb{P}\ Tag\ \bullet\ s_2 \mapsto t \in r \wedge s_2 \subset s_1)\ \bullet\ s_1 \mapsto t\}$$

The function *combine* adds the maplets which can be deduced by combining any two existing maplets:

$$combine : ((\mathbb{P}\ Tag) \leftrightarrow Tag) \twoheadrightarrow ((\mathbb{P}\ Tag) \leftrightarrow Tag)$$

$$\forall\, r : (\mathbb{P}\ Tag) \leftrightarrow Tag\ \bullet$$
$$combine\,(r) = r$$
$$\cup$$
$$\{\, s_1, s_2 : \mathbb{P}\ Tag;\ t_1, t_2 : Tag\ |$$
$$s_1 \mapsto t_1 \in r \wedge s_2 \mapsto t_2 \in r \wedge$$
$$t_1 \in s_2 \wedge t_1 \notin s_1 \wedge t_2 \notin s_2\ \bullet$$
$$(s_1 \cup (s_2 \setminus \{t_1\})) \mapsto t_2\}$$

We can, then, define *onepass* in the following fashion.

$$onepass : ((\mathbb{P}\ Tag) \leftrightarrow Tag) \twoheadrightarrow ((\mathbb{P}\ Tag) \leftrightarrow Tag)$$

$$\forall\, r : (\mathbb{P}\ Tag) \leftrightarrow Tag\ \bullet$$
$$onepass\,(r) = onepass^{\,min\,\{n:\mathbb{N}\,|\,onepass^n\,(r)=onepass^{n+1}\,(r)\}}\,(r)$$

where

$$\forall\, r : (\mathbb{P}\ Tag) \leftrightarrow Tag\ \bullet\ \forall\, n : \mathbb{N}\ |\ n > 1\ \bullet$$
$$onepass^0\,(r) = \emptyset \wedge$$
$$onepass^1\,(r) = reduce\,(r) \wedge$$
$$onepass^n\,(r) = reduce\,(combine\,(onepass^{n-1}\,(r)))$$

5   Combining Inferences and Query Modification

In this section we outline an approach to query modification that takes into account known and calculated inferences. Together, these go some way to realising the notion of an *ethical firewall*, as described in [25]. Aspects that are not directly relevant to our discourse, such as, for example, the auditing and analysis of past queries with a view to preventing the aforementioned tracker attacks, are not discussed here.

We assume that the data owner has described what access is permitted. This is achieved by specifying combinations of columns which may be queried as well as any restrictions that should be placed on those queries. Conceptually, these restrictions depend on the individual concerned. These query modification rules do not need to take into account any inferences between columns and as such can be written in a reasonably simplistic fashion. In addition, the data owner has to produce a set of inferences between columns to be used by the system. Recall that we concern ourselves with the *possibility* of information flow, i.e., we concern ourselves with the semantics of relations and not with the contents of tables.

It would be possible to use the inference rules to re-write the query modification rules, but this would be rather time consuming and could lead to a large set of query modification rules. It would be preferable for the set of inferences to have the function *onepass* applied to them, and for these calculated inferences to be captured.

When a query is received by a user, the normal procedure of creating a set of columns that are used by the query is performed. Rather than applying the query modification rules to this set of columns straight away, each inference from the output of *onepass* is compared with the set to see if it is applicable. By definition, each inference need only be considered once, so a single pass through the set will give a definitive set of columns that can be inferred from the original set. It is the union of the original set and the infered set that is then used as input to the next step of the query modification system. This separation of concerns is preferable to calculating a resultant set of query modification rules as it allows new unknown inferences to be added without affecting the query modification rules; it also allows new query modification rules to be added without concern for inferences.

If the set of inferences includes $\{DOB\} \mapsto MaritalStatus$ and we again consider the following two queries

- SELECT DOB FROM Patient;
- SELECT DOB FROM Patient WHERE Occupation = 'Plumber';

then the effective sets of columns would become

- $\{DOB, MaritalStatus\}$
- $\{DOB, MaritalStatus, Occupation\}$

due to the fact that

$$onepass\,(\{\{DOB\} \mapsto MaritalStatus\})\, (\!|\; \mathbb{P}\,\{DOB\}\;|\!)$$
$$= onepass\,(\{\{DOB\} \mapsto MaritalStatus\})\, (\!|\; \mathbb{P}\,\{DOB, Occupation\}\;|\!)$$
$$= \{MaritalStatus\}$$

The first query will not be affected by the addition of the inferences, but the second query would be blocked as there is no rule containing all three columns.

Of course, difficulties arise when one has to consider more complicated queries that involve more than one table. As an example, consider the following tables, *Patient* and *Child*,

ID	DOB	Surname
P_1	12/04/1972	Power
P_2	23/10/1965	Slaymaker
P_3	06/08/1971	Simpson

ID	DOB	Surname	ParentID
C_1	03/04/1990	Power	P_1
C_2	12/11/1984	Slaymaker	P_2
C_3	27/07/1982	Jones	P_2

together with the associated inference, $\{Patient.Surname\} \mapsto Child.Surname$.

Using the first style of join described in Section 3 the following two rules may have been defined:

$$\{Patient.ID, Patient.Surname\} \mapsto 1 = 1$$
$$\{Child.ParentID, Child.DOB\} \mapsto 1 = 1$$

These allow the surname of a patient to be related to the dates of birth of the children. As such, without the inference, the following query is allowed:

- `SELECT Patient.Surname, Child.DOB FROM Patient, Child`
  `WHERE Patient.ID = Child.ParentID`

However, the inference will lead to the set of used columns growing from

$$\{Patient.Surname, Patient.ID\} \cup \{Child.ParentID, Child.DOB\}$$

to

$$\{Patient.Surname, Patient.ID\} \cup$$
$$\{Child.Parent.ID, Child.DOB, Child.Surname\}$$

This set of columns would not be permitted as there is no applicable rule for the *Child* table.

The same result is achieved when an explicit join is permitted. Considering the explicit join version of the rules defined above we have:

$$JOIN(\{Patient.ID, Child.PatientID\} \mapsto Patient.ID = Child.PatientID)$$
$$\{Patient.Surname, Child.DOB\} \mapsto 1 = 1$$

where the first line represents the allowed joining condition and the second line represents the columns that can be referenced and any resulting restriction.

Again, without the inference rule the query would be allowed due to the fact that after the join is taken into account the set of referenced columns is *{Patient.Surname, Child.DOB}*. However, if the inference rule is taken into account, the set of referenced columns after the join is performed would become *{Patient.Surname, Child.DOB, Child.Surname}*, and, as such, the query will not be allowed.

6   Discussion

The work described in this paper was motivated by the authors' involvement with the e-DiaMoND project. Within systems such as e-DiaMoND, each database is owned by a hospital that is legally and ethically responsible for the data. A user would typically want to run the same query on many databases. As all access to the database in the e-DiaMoND grid is via grid services it is possible to modify all queries before they are submitted to the database. This is a more ideal solution than using views due to the fact that the access control policy will differ between hospitals, and hence the user will not be aware of which view they should be using. It should be noted that there is only one grid service per database and hence there is no possibility of the access permissions differing between applications, it should also be noted that each hospital will have full control of the policy used by this grid service. A benefit of the e-DiaMoND grid approach is that the user can be authenticated using a certificate based system. This is more flexible than using passwords as a trusted certificate authority can give access to the database without the need to create multiple accounts on the database, or the need for many users to use the same account.

Our approach to query modification offers flexibility in comparison to access control based on views, while retaining the same level of functionality. It is significantly easier for the users as they only have to know one version of the database schema as opposed to a possibly disjoint set of views, based on a range of roles that they may have access to. Furthermore, the impact of updates to policies are easier to manifest using this approach. The contribution of this paper is to build upon our previous work on query modification to consider potential inferences.

We have adopted a characterisation of information flow in terms of Armstrong's axioms of functional dependencies. Although the system is adapted from another domain it works well for our needs. The approach described is distinct from previous work in the domain, in that it utilises formal description techniques. In addition, it is concerned with the automated discovery of the potential for information leakage, rather than identifying risk.

With respect to the validation of our approach, establishing appropriate mappings between the real world domain and the formal representation of those concepts will be key, as will the provision of appropriate tool support for the end users.

References

1. W. W. Armstrong. Dependency structures of data base relationships. In *Proc. IFIP Congress, Stockholm, Sweden,* 1974.
2. J. G. Bethelehem, W. J. Keller, and J. Pannekoek. Disclosure control of microdata. *Journal of the American Statistical Association,* 85:38–45, 1990.
3. J. Biskip and P. A. Bonatti. Controlled query evaluation for enforcing confidentiality in complete information systems. *International Journal of Information Security (Special issue on ESORICS 2002,* 2(1):14–27, October 2004.
4. J. M. Brady, D. J. Gavaghan, A. C. Simpson, M. M. Parada, and R. P. Highnam. e-DiaMoND: A Grid-enabled federated database of annotated mammograms. In F. Berman, G. C. Fox, and A. J. G. Hey, editors, *Grid Computing: Making the Global Infrastructure a Reality,* pages 923–943. Wiley Series, 2003.
5. The Caldicott Report. www.publications.doh.gov.uk/ipu/confiden, December 1997.
6. S. Chauduri. Generalization and a framework for query modification. In *Proceedings of the IEEE International Conference on Data Engineering,* 1990.
7. G. Chen and S. Keller-McNulty. Estimation of deidentification disclosure risk in microdata. *Journal of Official Statistics,* 14(1):79–95, 1998.
8. T. Dalenius and S. P. Reiss. Data-swapping: a technique for disclosure contol. *Journal of Statistical Planning and Inference,* 6:73–85, 1982.
9. C. J. Date. *An Introduction to Database Systems.* Addison Wesley, seventh edition, 2000.
10. D. E. Denning. A lattice model of secure information flow. *Communications of the ACM,* 19(5):236–243, May 1976.
11. D. E. Denning and P. J. Denning. Data security. *ACM Computing Surveys,* 11(3), September 1979.
12. D. E. Denning, P. J. Denning, and M. D. Schwartz. The tracker: a threat to statistical database security. *ACM Transactions on Database Systems,* 4(1):7–18, 1978.
13. Data Protection Act 1998. The Stationery Office Limited, London, 1998.
14. K. Du. *On automated query modification techniques for databases.* PhD thesis, Case Western Reserve University, May 1993.
15. M. J. Elliot. Dis: a new approach to the measurement of statistical disclosure risk. *International Journal of Risk Management,* pages 39–48, 2000.
16. S. E. Feinberg and U. E. Markov. Confidentiality, uniqueness, and disclosure information for categorical data. *Journal of Official Statistics,* pages 385–397, 1998.
17. D. Florescu, L. Raschid, and P. Valduriez. Query modification in multidatabase systems. *International Journal of Intelligent and Cooperative Information Systems (Special Issue on Formal Methods in Cooperative Information Systems: Heterogeneous Databases),* 5(4), December 1996.
18. M. M. Fonkam and W. A. Gray. Employing integrity constraints for query modification and intensional answer generation in multi-database systems. In *Advanced Database Systems: Proceedings of the 10th British National Conference on Databases,* pages 244–260. Springer-Verlag Lecture Notes in Computer Science, volume 618, 1992.
19. B. Greenberg and L. Zayatz. Strategies for measuring risk in public use microdata files. *Statistica Neerlandica,* pages 33–48, 1992.
20. D. Harman. Relevance feedback and other query modification techniques. In W. B. Frakes and R. Baeza-Yates, editors, *Information retrieval: data structures and algorithms.* Prentice Hall, 1992.

21. Human Rights Act 1998. The Stationery Office Limited, London, 1998.
22. D. Lambert. Measures of disclosure risk and harm. *Journal of Official Statistics*, 9:313–331, 1993.
23. D. J. Power, E. Politou, M. A. Slaymaker, S. Harris, and A. C. Simpson. An approach to the storage of dicom files for grid-enabled medical imaging databases. In *Proceedings of the ACM Symposium on Applied Computing*, pages 272–279, 2004.
24. D. J. Power, M. A. Slaymaker, E. A. Politou, and A. C. Simpson. Protecting sensitive patient data via query modification. In *ACM Symposium on Applied Computing*, pages 224–230, 2005.
25. A. C. Simpson, D. J. Power, M. A. Slaymaker, S. L. Lloyd, and E. A. Politou. GIMI: Generic infrastructure for medical informatics. In *IEEE Computer-Based Medical Systems (to appear)*, 2005.
26. C. J. Skinner, C. Marsh, S. Openshaw, and C. Wymer. Disclosure control for census microdata. *Journal of Official Statistics*, pages 31–51, 1994.
27. M. A. Slaymaker, E. Politou, D. J. Power, S. L. Lloyd, and A. C. Simpson. Security aspects of grid-enabled digital mammography. *Methods of Information in Medicine (to appear)*, 2004.
28. M. A. Slaymaker, D. J Power, E. A. Politou, and A. C. Simpson. A vision for secure grid-enabled healthcare. In *Workshop on Grid Security Practice and Experience*. Technical Report YCS-2004-380, University of York, June 2004.
29. J. M. Spivey. *The Z Notation: A Reference Manual*. Prentice-Hall International, second edition, 1992.
30. M. Stonebraker. Implementation of integrity constraints and views by query modification. In *Proceedings of ACM SIGMOD International Conference on the Management of Data*, pages 65–78, 1975.
31. M. Stonebraker and E. Wong. Access control in a relational data base management system by query modification. In *ACM/CSC-ER Proceedings of the 1974 annual conference*, 1974.
32. P. Tendick and N. Matloff. A modified random pertubation method for database security. *ACM Transactions on Database Systems*, 19(1), 1994.
33. A. Walker and S. C. Salveter. Automatic modification of transactions to preserve data base integrity without undoing updates. Technical Report 81/026, State University of New York, Stony Brook, New York, June 1981.
34. L. Wang, S. Jajodia, and D. Wijesekera. Securing OLAP data cubes against privacy breaches. In *Proceedings of the 2004 IEEE Symposium on Security and Privacy*, pages 161–175, 2004.
35. L. Willemborg and T. Waal. *Elements of statistical disclosure control*. Springer-Verlag, 2001.

Protecting Privacy Against Location-Based Personal Identification*

Claudio Bettini[1], X. Sean Wang[2], and Sushil Jajodia[3]

[1] DICo, University of Milan, Italy
bettini@dico.unimi.it
[2] Dept of CS, University of Vermont, Vermont
xywang@cs.uvm.edu
[3] CSIS, George Mason University, Virginia
jajodia@gmu.edu

Abstract. This paper presents a preliminary investigation on the privacy issues involved in the use of location-based services. It is argued that even if the user identity is not explicitly released to the service provider, the geo-localized history of user-requests can act as a quasi-identifier and may be used to access sensitive information about specific individuals. The paper formally defines a framework to evaluate the risk in revealing a user identity via location information and presents preliminary ideas about algorithms to prevent this to happen.

1 Introduction

There are currently over 1.5 billion mobile phone users worldwide and the numbers are still growing very fast. Location technologies can be currently used by wireless carrier operators to provide a good estimate of the user location. These techniques are being refined in order to meet the requirements imposed by federal institutions both in US and Europe for location-enhanced emergency services. Significantly more precise positioning is obtained by GPS technology which is already integrated in some mobile phones and it is likely to become a common feature of mass product phones. Indoor positioning is also available based on a wide range of enabling technologies including ultrasounds, Wi-Fi, and Bluetooth. Considering that mobile phones are rapidly evolving into multipurpose devices that can access a wide range of services, there is a general concern about how positioning information is stored, managed and released to possibly untrusted service providers.

This paper considers the privacy issues involved in accessing location-based services, i.e., services that, based on the user current position, can provide location-aware information. Typical examples are map and navigation services, services that provide information on close-by public resources (e.g., gas stations, pharmacies, ATM machines, ...), services that provide localized news (e.g.,

---

* This work is partially supported by NSF under grants IIS-0430402 and IIS-0242237. The work of Bettini is also partially supported by the Italian MIUR (FIRB "Web-Minds" project N. RBNE01WEJT_005).

W. Jonker and M. Petković (Eds.): SDM 2005, LNCS 3674, pp. 185–199, 2005.

weather forecasts, road constructions, etc.), as well as more personalized services like proximity marketing or friend-finder.

In principle, most location-based services do not require the personal identification of the user. However, better service may be provided if personalization is allowed. In order to obtain personalized service without revealing personal information, we may use a trusted middleware infrastructure to make sure that only pseudonyms are sent to the service providers, hence making the service requests anonymous for them. Such pseudonyms can also be helpful when the accounting of service usage is performed.

The problem, however, is that positioning information, in the form of a specific location or of a movement trace, can actually lead to personal identification, hence revealing the association between a pseudonym and a real person. For example, a service request containing as location information the exact coordinates of a private house provides sufficient information to personally identify the house's owner since the mapping of such coordinates to home addresses is generally available and a simple look up in a phone book (or similar sources) can reveal the people who live there. If several requests are made from the same location with the same pseudonym, it is very likely that the user associated with that pseudonym is a member of the household.

An obvious solution might be to make all requests very coarse in terms of spatial and temporal resolution. However, for some services to be useful, sufficiently fine resolution must be used. With fine resolution, however, location data may become a quasi-identifier. A quasi-identifier (see Section 4 for more details) is similar to a social security number in that with some external information source, a specific person can be identified. Any service request containing data that becomes sensitive once associated with a user's identity is a potential threat to the user's privacy. Hence, the challenge is to obtain useful service without revealing personal privacy.

By sensitive data we mean information of general concern, like medical information or financial data that could be transmitted as part of a service request; but it may also be the spatio-temporal information regarding the user, as possibly collected by a location-based service provider. Examples include a) information on the specific location of individuals at specific times, b) movement patterns of individuals (specific routes at specific times and their frequency), c) personal points of interest (frequent visits to specific shops, clubs, or institutions).

The problem we are addressing can be stated as follows:

> *We must ensure that no sensitive data is released to a service provider when the data can be personally identified through a location-based quasi-identifier.*[1]

The main contributions of this paper are the following:

- By defining location-based quasi-identifiers and by introducing the notion of Historical k-anonymity, we provide a formal framework to evaluate the risk of revealing personal sensitive information based on location data.

---

[1] See Section 4 for a formal definition of location-based quasi-identifiers.

- We propose a technique to preserve a specified level of anonymity, and identify several promising research directions on this topic.

The rest of the paper is organized as follows. In Section 2 we discuss related work. In Section 3 we present the service delivery model we are taking as a reference in our work. In Section 4 we define location quasi-identifiers, while in Section 5 the central notion of historical k-anonymity is presented. In Section 6 we present preliminary ideas about algorithms for preserving historical k-anonymity, and we mention several issues that deserve further investigation. Section 7 concludes the paper.

2   Related Work

The problem we are addressing has many analogies with the problem of guaranteeing anonymity of personal data extracted from a relational database (see e.g., [14]). Typical solutions involve either the de-identification of data, essentially avoiding the presence of quasi-identifiers, the obfuscation of sensitive data, or the separation of quasi-identifiers from sensitive data. The first two solutions are usually based on the generalization or suppression of attribute values. Despite we will show that there are specific issues that distinguish the location-based problem from the analogous one in the relational database scenario, similar techniques can be applied. Indeed, the dynamic change of spatio-temporal resolution that we illustrate in Section 6 is an obfuscation technique based on generalization.

Considering the delivery of positioning data, the IETF Geopriv working group [7] has focused on the design of protocols and APIs that enable devices to communicate their location in a confidential and integrity-preserving manner to a location server. Then, the location server is assumed to deliver data to other services accordingly to the user's privacy policies, possibly including the use of pseudonyms instead of the real user identity. This work can be considered complementary to ours.

The idea of adapting spatio-temporal resolution to provide a form of location k-anonymity can be found in [11]. This work is extended in [9] to support the use of a different value of k for different requests. However, the notion of k-anonymity used in [9] is slightly different: the authors consider a message sent to a service provider to be k-anonymous, only if there are other k-1 users in the same spatio-temporal context that actually send a message. This is a debatable interpretation of the k-anonymity concept, and differs from the one used in our paper as well as in [11]. We only require the presence in the same spatio-temporal context of k-1 *potential* senders, which is a much weaker requirement.

Independently from the above issue, [11] and [9] address a special case of the problem considered in this paper, characterized by assuming that each location is a quasi-identifier, and that the simple fact of issuing a request is sensitive information. We believe that this assumption on the quasi-identifier is actually a very strong one, similar to assuming that an external source (e.g. a camera) would be available at each location allowing the identification of all users that were at that location in any given time interval. The solution proposed in [11] ensures that the request may have been issued by anyone of k users present at a certain location in the time interval specified in the request. With respect to this work, our framework addresses the issue of defining what a location-based quasi-identifier is, enabling a wide range of assumptions about how easy it would be to re-identify a subject in a specific context. Moreover, we extend to traces the notion of k-anonymity.

Location privacy issues have also been addressed in [2,1]. In particular, the authors propose and deeply investigate the notion of a *mix-zone*. A mix-zone is analogous to a mix node in communication systems [6], and can be intuitively described as a spatial area such that, if an individual crosses it, then it won't be possible to link his future positions (outside the area) with known positions (before entering the area). Here, "link" means the association of different requests to the same user. While it is not the focus of this paper to analyze mix-zones, we consider it a very useful notion, and we use it in Section 6 as part of algorithmic solutions for the preservation of historical k-anonymity.

3   The Anonymous Location-Based Service Model

Our investigation assumes a specific service provisioning model described by the following scenario (see Figure 1). This model is assumed as well in [11,9], and it closely reflects the reality of current systems. Although a trusted server presents risks in terms of a single-point trust, since mobil devices are usually limited in their capabilities, the assumed model as we adopt here is a reasonable assumption.

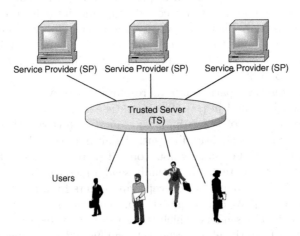

Fig. 1. Service provisioning model

– Users invoke or subscribe to location-based remote services that are going to be provided to their mobile devices. Users can turn on and off a privacy protecting system which has a simplified user interface with qualitative degrees of concern: low, medium, high. The user choice may be applied uniformly to all services or selectively. More expert users can have access to more involved rule-based policy specifications.

- User sensitive information, including user location at specific times and possibly other data needed for the service request, is collected and handled by a Trusted Server (TS). TS has the usual functionalities of a location server (i.e., a moving object database storing precise data for all of its users and the capability to efficiently perform spatio-temporal queries). Qualitative privacy preferences provided by each user are translated by the TS into specific parameters. The TS has also access to the location-based quasi-identifier specifications (see Subsection 6.1).
- Service Providers (SP) receive from TS service requests of the form

$$\text{(msgID, UserPseudonym, } \langle \text{Area, TimeInterval} \rangle, \text{Data)}.$$

The **msgID** is used to hide the user network address and will be used by the TS to forward the answer to the user's device; **UserPseudonym** is used to hide the user identity while allowing the SP to authenticate the user, to connect multiple requests from the same user, and possibly to charge the user for the service (through a third party which has the mapping to identity and payment instruments). The field $\langle$**Area, TimeInterval**$\rangle$ defines a spatio-temporal context in which the request was issued. While the TS knows the exact point and exact time when the user issued a request, both **Area** and **TimeInterval** provide possibly generalized information in the form of an area containing the exact location point, and of a time interval containing the exact instant. Finally, **Data** is a set of attribute-value pairs depending on the specific service and request.

- Service providers fulfill the requests sending the service output to the user's device through the trusted server.

4 Location-Based Quasi-Identifiers

In a database table storing personal information about individuals, a set of attributes is called a *quasi-identifier* [8] if their values, in combination, can be linked with external information to reidentify the respondents to whom the information refers. A typical example of a single-attribute quasi-identifier is the Social Security Number, since knowing its value and having access to external sources it is possible to identify a specific individual. In this work we consider in particular the possibility of reidentifying the respondents based on attributes revealing spatio-temporal data, possibly considering histories of attribute values. A relevant issue, not actually addressed in previous work, is how to define and how to represent such location-based quasi identifiers (LBQIDs in the sequel). Since the choice of an LBQID implies certain assumptions on the accessibility of external sources to identify the user, we believe that this is a crucial point in defining what is really a privacy concern for location-based services.

We propose to represent LBQIDs as spatio-temporal patterns, as intuitively illustrated in Example1.

Example 1. A user may consider the trip from the condominium where he lives to the building where he works every morning and the trip back in the afternoon as an LBQID if observed by the same service provider for at least 3 weekdays in the same week, and for at least 2 weeks.

The derivation of a specific pattern or a set of patterns acting as LBQIDs for a specific individual is an independent problem, and is not addressed in this paper. However, it should be clear that the derivation process will have to be based on statistical analysis of the data about users movement history: If a certain pattern turns out to be very common for many users, it is unlikely to be useful for identifying any one of them. The selection of candidate patterns may also possibly be guided by the user. Since in our model it is the TS which stores, or at least has access to, historical trajectory data, it is probably a good candidate to offer tools for LBQID definition.

Definition 1. *A* Location-Based Quasi-Identifier *(LBQID) is a spatio-temporal pattern specified by a sequence of spatio-temporal constraints each one defining an area and a time span, and by a recurrence formula.*

Each location in the sequence is represented analogously to the spatio-temporal context used in each request, i.e., ⟨**Area, U-TimeInterval**⟩ where **Area** identifies a set of points in bidimensional space (possibly by a pair of intervals $[x_1, x_2][y_1, y_2]$), and **U-TimeInterval** is a *unanchored* time interval $[t_1, t_2]$. Differently from the specification of the time interval at request time, here the values t_1 and t_2 represent unanchored instants of time. For example, the **U-TimeInterval** = [7am,9am] defines the time span of two hours starting at 7am and ending at 9am in a *generic* day. This interval is called unanchored since it does not identifies a specific time interval on the timeline, but an infinite set of intervals, one for each day.

A recurrence formula is associated with each location sequence and it follows the following syntax:

$$r_1.G_1 * r_2.G_2 * \ldots * r_n.G_n$$

where for each $i = 1 \ldots n$, r_i is a positive integer, and G_i is a time granularity, as formally defined in [3].

The intuitive semantics is the following: each sequence must be observed within a single granule of G_1. The value r_1 denotes the *minimum* number of such observations. All the r_1 observations should be within one granule of G_2, and there should be at least r_2 occurrences of these observations. The same semantics clearly extends to n granularities.

Example 2. The LBQID intuitively described in Example 1 can be formally defined as follows:

⟨**AreaCondominium [7am,8am], AreaOfficeBldg [8am,9am],
AreaOfficeBldg [4pm,6pm], AreaCondominium [5pm,7pm]**⟩
Recurrence: 3.Weekdays * 2.Weeks

Accordingly to the semantics of this expression, each round-trip from home to office and vice versa should be observed in the same weekday, there should be 3 observations in the same week, and for at least 2 weeks.

Considering the given language syntax and semantics, we can observe that any subexpression $1.G_n$ at the end of a recurrence formula can be dropped, since it is implicit. For the formula to be satisfied, it is also implicitly necessary that there are at least r_i granules of G_i, each containing at least r_{i-1} granules of G_{i-1}. If the recurrence formula is empty, it is assumed equivalent to $1.\top$, hence the sequence can actually appear just once at any time.

Note that if user-defined time granularities are allowed, recurrence formulas can also express patterns like "same weekday for at least 3 weeks", or "at least two consecutive days for at least 2 weeks". In the first case we may use the granularities Mondays, Tuesdays, etc., and use a different LBQID for each one of them. The second pattern may require a special granularity having each granule composed of 2 contiguous days.

However, the formalism we propose is only one among many that could be used to represent recurring spatio-temporal sequences. Some of the work on recurring temporal patterns may also be considered [13,10]. The choice of a particular formalism is not crucial for our approach, as long as there are algorithms to continuously verify if the patterns are matched by the positioning data associated with the users' requests.

Considering the language proposed above, a timed state automata [4] may be used for each LBQID and each user, advancing the state of the automata when the actual location of the user at the request time is within the area specified by one of the current states, and the temporal constraints are satisfied. Details about monitoring LBQIDs are outside the scope of this paper.

For specifying our framework we only need to define the notion of a set of requests *matching* an LBQID.

Definition 2. *If $\langle x_i, y_i, t_i \rangle$ is the exact location and time of a request r_i, as seen by the TS, r_i is said to* match *an element E_j of an LBQID if $\textbf{Area}_j$ contains $\langle x_i, y_i \rangle$ and t_i is contained in one of the intervals denoted by $\textbf{U-TimeInterval}_j$.*

Definition 3. *A set of requests R' is said to* match *an LBQID Q if the following conditions hold: (1) each request r_i in R' matches an element E_j of Q, and vice versa each element E_j is matched by a request r_i in R'; (2) if t_i is the time instant of a request r_i matching E_j, the set of t_i's for all $r_i \in R'$ must satisfy the temporal constraints imposed by the recurrence formula of Q.*

5   A Privacy Preservation Framework Based on k-Anonymity

In this section we present the principles defining our framework for privacy preservation. The framework has the main goal of enabling a quantitative evaluation of the effectiveness of privacy preservation solutions.

5.1   The Notion of k-Anonymity for Location-Based Services

As mentioned earlier, when a user does not want to be recognized when performing an action, like issuing a service a request, making a call, or informing a service provider of the present location, one general solution is to make requests anonymous with pseudonyms. The reason that pseudonyms lead to anonymity is because there exists a set of many individuals, each of whom could have used any given pseudonym. Hence, anonymity can be intuitively described as the property of being indistinguishable among a set of individuals. The *anonymity set* concept was probably first defined in [5] in an analogous context as *the set of participants who could have sent a certain request, as seen by a global observer.* According to this definition the cardinality of the anonymity set gives a measure of anonymity level. The greater the k value, the higher the level of anonymity. In our context, the anonymity of the service requests may be obtained as follows:

Given a measure k of desired anonymity level, algorithms should be applied at the TS to guarantee that the SP will not be able, using location data, to bind a request to an anonymity set with fewer than k users.

A location-based anonymization algorithm based on this notion was first proposed in [11]. The main idea is to forward a request to the SP only when at least k different subjects have been in the space defined by **Area** in anyone of the subintervals of **TimeInterval**. Since any of the subjects may have issued the request, even if the SP had access to a direct observation of the area, the SP may not determine which of the subjects actually issued the request.

Note that this approach has an implicit assumption (not mentioned in [11]): There is a very low probability that all the individuals in the anonymity set will actually make exactly the same request in the same time interval. Indeed, if this is not the case, the cardinality of the set is irrelevant, since it would be sufficient to know that an individual belongs to the set in order to know that he/she actually issued the request. A similar assumption is made when dealing with k-anonymity in relational databases. In the following we also make this assumption and we assume that it has been validated by a data statistical analysis. Note that [9] requires that.

In this paper we also take into account sequences of requests issued by the same individual. These sequences are usually identified by service providers when the service requires authentication, since each request is explicitly associated with a userid. We remind that in our model, a **UserPseudonym** is included in each request and it is also used to authenticate the user. Central to our framework are the notions of *Service Request Linkability* and *Historical k-anonymity*.

5.2   Service Request Linkability

Intuitively, service request linkability (*linkability* for shortness) is a measure of the possibility, by looking at the set of service requests issued to a service provider, to guess that two requests have been issued by the same user. Any two requests with the same UserPseudonym are clearly linkable, since we assume that pseudonyms are not shared by different individuals. Using different pseudonyms for the same individual may not be sufficient to make his/her requests unlinkable. In general computing linkability is not a trivial task, since various techniques can be used to link two requests. The issue has been investigated in [12] considering multi target tracking techinques to associate the location of a new request with an existing trace; if this association succeeds, the new request is considered linkable (with a certain probability) to all the requests used in the trajectory. However, many other techniques could also be applied, including pattern matching of traces (to guess, for example, recurring traces), or probability-based techniques considering most common trajectories based on physical constraints like roads, crossings, etc.. While it is out of scope in this paper to consider specific linking techniques, we assume the TS can replicate the techniques used by a possible attacker, hence computing a likelihood value for the linkability of any pair of issued requests.

Definition 4. *Given the set $R = \{r_1, \ldots, r_n\}$ of all requests issued to a certain SP, linkability is represented by a partial function $Link()$ from $R \times R$ to $[0, 1]$, intuitively defining for a pair of requests r_i and r_j in R the likelihood value of the two requests being issued by the same individual.*

The $Link()$ function is assumed to have some simple properties: $Link(r_i, r_j) = Link(r_j, r_i)$ (symmetricity), and $Link(r_i, r_i) = 1$ (reflexivity).

For each request we can define the set of all requests linkable to it as follows.

Definition 5. *Let R be the set of all the requests issued to a certain SP and $R' \subseteq R$. Then we say R' is link-connected with likelihood Θ if for each pair r_i and r_j of requests in R', there exist $r_{i_1}, \ldots, r_{i_k}$ in R', where $r_{i_1} = r_i$ and $r_{i_k} = r_j$, such that $Link(r_{i_l}, r_{i_{l+1}}) \geq \Theta$ for all $l = 1, \ldots, k-1$.*

Note that we may say that the $Link()$ function is *correct* if, for each set R' of requests, the following holds: all the requests of R' belong to the same user if and only if R' is link-connected with $\Theta = 1$.

5.3   Historical k-Anonymity

In order to define historical k-Anonymity we need some preliminary definitions.

The trusted server not only stores in its database the set of requests that are issued by each user, but also stores for each user the sequence of his/her location updates. We call this sequence *Personal History of Locations*.

Definition 6. *The sequence of spatio-temporal data associated with a certain user in the TS database is called his/her Personal History of Locations (PHL), and it is represented as a sequence of 3D points $(\langle x_1, y_1, t_1 \rangle, \ldots, \langle x_m, y_m, t_m \rangle)$, where $\langle x_i, y_i \rangle$, for $i = 1, \ldots, m$, represents the position of the user (in two-dimensional space) at the time instant t_i.*

Note that a location update may be received by the TS even if the user did not make a request when being at that location. Hence, for each request r_i there must be an element in the PHL of $User(r_i)$, but the vice versa does not hold. This has an intuitive motivation in the fact that the anonymity set for a certain area and a certain time interval is the set of users who were in that area in that time interval, and who could *potentially* make a request.

We also need to define the following relationship between PHLs and sets of requests issued to the SP.

Definition 7. *A PHL* $(\langle x_1, y_1, t_1 \rangle, \ldots, \langle x_m, y_m, t_m \rangle)$ *is said to be* location-time-consistent, *or* LT-consistent *for short, with a set of requests* $r_1, \ldots, r_n$ *issued to an SP if for each request* r_i *there exists an element* $\langle x_j, y_j, t_j \rangle$ *in the PHL such that the area of* r_i *contains the location identified by the point* x_j, y_j *and the time interval of* r_i *contains the instant* t_j.

We can now define Historical k-Anonymity.

Definition 8. *Given the set R of all requests issued to a certain SP, a subset of requests* $R' = \{r_1, \ldots, r_m\}$ *issued by the same user U is said to satisfy* Historical k-Anonymity *if there exist* $k - 1$ *PHLs* $P_1, \ldots, P_{k-1}$ *for* $k - 1$ *users different from* U, *such that each* P_j, $j = 1, \ldots, k - 1$, *is LT-consistent with* R'.

What we want to do below is to make sure that if a set of requests R' matches an LBQID and is link connected with a certain likelihood, then R' satisfies historical k-anonymity. This means that if an SP can successfully track the requests of a user through all the elements of an LBQID, then there would be at least $k - 1$ other users whose personal history of locations is consistent with these requests; in other words, from the SP perspective, there would be at least k users who may have issued those requests.

From the above definitions it should be clear that the two main parameters defining a "level of privacy concern" in our framework are k, the anonymity value, and Θ, the linkability likelihood.

6   Preserving Historical k-Anonymity

While several strategies may be devised for privacy preserving in our framework, here we illustrate a simple approach that may be used as a starting point to develop more sophisticated techniques.

6.1   A Simple Strategy

We assume that each location-based service has some *tolerance constraints* that define the coarsest spatial and temporal granularity for the service to still be useful. For example, consider a service that returns information on the closest hospital. For the service to be useful, it should receive as input a user location that is at most in the range of a few square miles, and a time-window for the actual request time of at most a few minutes. On the contrary, a service providing localized news may even work reasonably with much coarser spatial and temporal granularities.

Our strategy can be summarized as follows:

1. The TS monitors all incoming user requests for the possible release of LBQIDs. While the TS knows the exact position and time ($\langle x, y, t \rangle$) associated with a request r, they are generalized when r is forwarded to the SP in the following case: r matches an element E_j of an LBQID for $User(r)$ such that (1) either E_j is the first element or (2) a previous request r' by the same user has matched E_{j-1} and the time instants associated with r' and r satisfy the temporal constraints specified in Q between E_{j-1} and E_j. The generalization essentially consists in enlarging the Area and TimeInterval, hence increasing the uncertainty about the real user location and time of request. Generalization is performed by an algorithm that tries to preserve Historical k-Anonymity of the set of requests that have matched the current partial LBQID.

2. If, for a particular request, generalization fails, (i.e., historical k-anonymity is violated), the system will try to unlink future requests from the previous ones by changing the pseudonym of the user. If unlinking succeeds before a complete LBQID is matched, all partially matched patterns based on old pseudonym for that user are reset. Otherwise, the user is considered at risk of identification, and notified about it so that he may refrain from sending sensitive information, disrupt the service, or take other actions.

Clearly, if the generalization algorithm succeeds for each LBQID sub-pattern, k-historical anonymity is satisfied. If the algorithm fails, it does not mean that an LBQID would be revealed. Indeed, if Step 2 succeeds in changing the pseudonym of the user before a complete LBQID is matched, no further requests with the old pseudonym will occur and the partially matched patterns would have no chance to be completed.

We now show the generalization algorithm explaining how it can guarantee Historical k-Anonymity. For simplicity, we make the assumption that each request can match an element in only one of the LBQIDs defined for a certain user. The algorithm can be easily extended to consider multiple LBQIDs.

6.2   A Spatio-Temporal Generalization Algorithm

Algorithm 1 is composed of two main steps (lines 1 and 8 in the listing). If the current request matches the first element in an LBQID, then steps at lines 5 and 6 are executed selecting from all the user PHLs the k points (each one from a different user) that are closest to the point corresponding to the request. For requests matching intermediate elements in an LBQID, Steps at lines 2 and 3 are performed using the PHLs of the k users selected when the request matching the first element of the LBQID has been processed. The second main step (line 8) simply checks if the generalization satisfies the tolerance constraints. If it doesn't, in order not to disrupt the service, the computed area and time interval are

---

algorithm 1. The generalization algorithm

Input: $\langle x, y, t \rangle$ as position and time of request r, k user-ids (if r matches the initial element of an LBQID) or a parameter k, tolerance constraints;

Output: $\langle$ **Area, TimeInterval** $\rangle$, boolean value for HK-anonymity, k user-ids (if r matches the initial element of an LBQID);

Method:

1: **if** k user-ids are given as part of the Input **then**
2:     For each of the k user-ids, find the 3D point in its PHL closest to $\langle x, y, t \rangle$.
3:     Compute $\langle$ **Area, TimeInterval** $\rangle$ as the smallest 3D space containing these points
4: **else**
5:     Compute $\langle$ **Area, TimeInterval** $\rangle$ as the smallest 3D space (2D area + time) containing $\langle x, y, t \rangle$ and crossed by k trajectories (each one for a different user)
6:     Store the ids of the k users.
7: **end if**
8: **if** $\langle$ **Area, TimeInterval** $\rangle$ satisfies the tolerance constraints **then**
9:     HK-anonymity := True
10: **else**
11:     HK-anonymity := False
12:     **Area** and **TimeInterval** are uniformly reduced to satisfy the tolerance constraints
13: **end if**

---

shrunk as much as required to satisfy the constraints. A *False* value is returned for the variable HK-anonymity to notify the failure in proper generalization.

The most time consuming step is the one at line 5. This can be performed using a brute-force algorithm by simply considering the nearest neighbor in the PHL of each user and then taking the closest k points. In this case, the worst case complexity of this step is $O(k * n)$ where n is the number of location points in the TS. Optimizations may be inspired by the work on indexing moving objects. The computation necessary for steps at lines 2 and 3 is quite simple, considering that it is restricted to the traces of k users, and that this number is usually much smaller than the total number of users.

In order to make the algorithm practical several issues still have to be addressed. The most relevant one is the trade-off between quality of service (i.e., how strict tolerance constraints should be), degree of anonymity (i.e., choice of k), and frequency of unlinking (i.e., number of possible interruptions of the service). These parameters must be considered carefully, possibly based on the user policies. Based on specific objective functions, several techniques can then be applied to improve the algorithm. For example, if we want to ensure historical k-anonymity, we should probably use an initial parameter k' larger than k. Indeed, the longer the trace, the less are the probabilities that the same k individuals will move along the same trace (even considering generalizations along the space and time dimensions). Starting with a larger k and decreasing its value at each point in the trace, until k is reached, should increase the probability to maintain historical k-anonymity for longer traces. Guidance on the choice of k' and on the value by which it should be decremented at each step should come from the analysis of historical data.

6.3   Unlinking Techniques

Unlinking is performed by changing the pseudonym of the user, possibly doing it when he crosses a mix-zone [2] (see Section 2), in order for the SP not to be able of binding the different pseudonyms to the same user. Mix-zones have been defined as "natural" locations where no service is available to anybody and specific conditions are satisfied such that it becomes very difficult for an SP to link two requests from the same user if the user has crossed the mix-zone. The definition is partly due to the fact that the class of services considered in [2] are specific to certain areas (e.g., all branches of a department store), leaving most of the remaining space unserviced.

We are interested in defining mix-zones on-demand, for example temporarily disabling the use of the service for a number of users in the same area for the time sufficient to confuse the SP. Technically, we may define the problem as that of finding, given a specific point in space, k diverging trajectories (each one for a different user) that are sufficiently close to the point. The "diverging" feature should capture the intuitive idea that these users, once out of the mix-zone, will take very different trajectories.

We abstract the above into an action called "Unlinking with a likelihood parameter Θ". This action will make sure that two requests, when unlinked, will (1) have two pseudonyms pID_1 and pID_2, and (2) $Link(r_1, r_2) < \Theta$ for all requests r_1 and r_2 having pID_1 and pID_2, respectively.

We can now state our correctness result for our algorithm:

Theorem 1. *If we apply our strategy with Algorithm 1, and we assume we can always perform Unlinking for a certain likelihood parameter Θ, then, given an anonymity value k, any set of requests issued to an SP by a certain user that matches one of his/her LBQIDs and is link connected with likelihood Θ, will satisfy Historical k-anonymity.*

By choosing an appropriate k, Theorem 1 ensures that no SP may use an LBQID to personally identify a user.

7   Conclusions and Open Issues

In this paper we have formally defined the problem of the personal identification of sensitive data in location-based services. We believe that the formal framework we have defined can be used for two very different purposes:

(a) to enforce a certain level of privacy – possibly disabling the service when the level cannot be guaranteed –, and

(b) to evaluate if the privacy policies that a location-based service guarantees are sufficient to deploy the service in a certain area. This may be achieved by considering, for example, the typical density of users, their movement patterns, their concerns about privacy, as well as the spatio-temporal tolerance constraints of the service and the presence of natural mix-zones [1] in the area.

While in this paper we presented preliminary results about (a), we consider (b) as another promising research direction.

Regarding a) we already pointed out several issues that deserve further investigation, including monitoring multiple LBQIDs, efficient generalization algorithms and unlinking techniques. In addition, randomization should be used as part of the TS strategy to prevent inference attacks.

Another interesting open issue regards user interfaces. On one side, very simple tools should be provided to define LBQIDs and verify them based on statistical data. On the other side, simple and effective interfaces are needed to specify the level of anonymity required by the user, as well as to notify when identification is at risk. Graphical solutions, like the open and closed lock in an internet browser should be considered.

References

1. A. Beresford, F. Stajano, Mix Zones: User Privacy in Location-aware Services. In Proc. IEEE Workshop on Pervasive Computing and Communication Security (PerSec), pp. 127-131, IEEE, 2004.
2. A. Beresford, F. Stajano. Location Privacy in Pervasive Computing. IEEE Pervasive Computing, 2(1):46-55, 2003.
3. C. Bettini, S. Jajodia, X.S. Wang, Time Granularities in Databases, Data Mining, and Temporal Reasoning, Springer, 2000.
4. C. Bettini, X. Wang, and S. Jajodia. Testing complex temporal relationships involving multiple granularities and its application to data mining, in Proc. of ACM Symposium in Principles of Database Systems (PODS), ACM press, 1996.
5. D. Chaum, The Dining Cryptographers Problem: Unconditional Sender and Recipient Untraceability. Journal of Cryptology 1(1): 65-75, 1988.
6. D. Chaum, Untraceable Electronic Mail, Return Addresses, and Digital Pseudonyms. Communications of the ACM, 24(2): 84-88, 1981.
7. J. Cuellar, J. Morris, and D. Mulligan. Internet Engineering task force geopriv requirements. http://www.ietf.org/html.charters/geopriv-charter.html, 2002.
8. T. Dalenius. Finding a needle in a haystack – or identifying anonymous census record. Journal of Official Statistics, 2(3):329–336, 1986.
9. B. Gedik, L. Liu. A Customizable k-Anonymity Model for Protecting Location Privacy. The 25th International Conference on Distributed Computing Systems (IEEE ICDCS 2005).
10. I. Goralwalla, Y. Leontiev, M. Özsu, D. Szafron, Carlo Combi, Temporal Granularity: Completing the Puzzle, J. Intell. Inf. Syst. 16(1): 41-63, 2001.
11. M. Gruteser, D. Grunwald, Anonymous Usage of Location-Based Services Through Spatial and Temporal Cloaking. In Proc. of MobiSys 2003.

12. M. Gruteser, B. Hoh, On the Anonymity of Periodic Location Samples In Proc. of 2nd International Conference on Security in Pervasive Computing, LNCS series, Springer, 2005.
13. L. Khatib, R. Morris Generating Scenarios for Periodic Events with Binary Constraints, In Proc. of TIME, pp. 67–72, IEEE, 1999.
14. P. Samarati, Protecting Respondents' Identities in Microdata Release, IEEE Trans. Knowl. Data Eng. 13(6): 1010–1027, 2001.

Information SeeSaw: Availability vs. Security Management in the UbiComp World

Boris Dragovic and Calicrates Policroniades

Systems Research Group, The Computer Laboratory,
University of Cambridge, United Kingdom
{Firstname.Lastname}@cl.cam.ac.uk

Abstract. The ubiquitous computing vision brings about a number of
information security and privacy challenges, some of which we already
face in the mobile computing arena. This work focuses on a context-
specific class of information leakage threats not involving a malicious
custodian. *Information exposure threats* arise as a side effect of a particular choice of data management procedures employed during legitimate
information use or possession in a specific context. They affect, in different forms, information throughout its lifetime in a ubiquitous computing environment. To maximize information availability, and thus its
value to user, under unpredictably varying threat models, we depart form
static and inflexible approaches to secure data management to provide
for continuous and adaptive information exposure protection. We outline
a means of structured reasoning about information exposure and introduce a metric for its quantification. An approach to threat mitigating
information management operations discrimination based on *information utility change* is also presented. To unify the introduced concepts
into a coherent big picture we form a *Levels of Exposure* model. On the
implementation side, we overview a type aware, sub-file granularity data
repository system that meets the requirements implied in the paper.

1 Introduction

Ubiquitous computing vision [1] has brought about a number of challenges for
information security and privacy stemming from a number of technological and
socio-technological reasons [2] [3] [4] [5]. Some of the problems can be solved by
adapting existing solutions from traditional distributed systems while the others
need novel solutions.

Context represents a significant factor in establishing a threat model for an
asset. Every contextual state can be attributed with a set of threats and their
respective likelihoods, as seen from the point of view of an sensitive asset. Vari-
ability in context thus implies threat model changes. Information omnipresence,
its anywhere and anytime availability to end users, in the ubiquitous computing
world leads to dissolution of the notion of secure perimeter. Consequently, information is subjected to unpredictable context changes, and thus threat models,
throughout its lifetime.

Our work focuses on, what we call, *Information Exposure Threats*. Information exposure threats are a subset of information leakage threats and impact on

W. Jonker and M. Petković (Eds.): SDM 2005, LNCS 3674, pp. 200–216, 2005.

information confidentiality. Their distinguishing characteristic is that they do not involve a malicious custodian[1]. Information exposure threats represent information leakage into the environment as a side-effect of the information management and handling procedures deployed in a particular context. They stem from a mismatch between: information sensitivity; context surrounding the information - determining the threat model; and a particular information management procedure employed - granting a level of protection in the context. Simple instances of the threat class involve sensitive information being: displayed in a form and on a screen visually accessible by a third party [6] [7]; taken out of a secure perimeter on a mobile computing or storage device unaccounting for the shift in threat model; transmitted in plain-text over a corporate wireless link whose signal penetrates into a publicly accessible area, etc.

Addressing information exposure threats requires continuous threat monitoring and application of adequate protective measures in the face of threat changes. In contrast to access control mechanisms, triggered at the point of access, continuous information exposure protection has to be provided in pre- during- and post-access phases. Threat mitigating operations, thus, have to be available whether information is on a storage device, in virtual memory, or being displayed or transmitted.

Information security and privacy protection mechanisms are frequently at odds with both information availability and system usability. This undermines the very vision of ubiquitous computing. Reasoning about threat mitigating operations in terms of the degree and the nature of protection they provide in contrast to their impact on information availability allows for maximising information availability while ensuring adequate levels of information security and privacy - balancing the seesaw.

In this paper we extend our previous work [8] [9] to meet the challenges of the continuous information exposure threats mitigation while maximising information availability. Section 2 contrasts our work with related research. Section 3 provides a brief overview of an approach to modeling the world based on the notions of *container* and *containment* that allows for structured and continuous fine-grained reasoning about threats information is exposed to. In Section 4 we outline a method for quantifying information exposure, an approach to threat mitigation actions discrimination based on their *impact*, most notably on *information utility* and unification of the concepts through the *Levels of Exposure* modeling. Section 5 outlines a type-aware storage subsystem that allows for fine-grained, per sensitivity level, data manipulation matching the information centric nature of our approach to information security and privacy protection.

2   Related Work

The most prominent instance of information exposure threats is information leakage due to unprotected storage on lost and stolen mobile devices. Thus, a

---

[1] A person in a legitimate possession or access to information as determined by external authentication and authorisation mechanisms.

wide body of research has been focused on data storage protection. This has resulted in a wide variety of cryptographic and information hiding file systems. Furthermore, a number of commercial vendors offer solutions based on mandatory data storage encryption.

Data storage protection affects threats relevant to only a segment of information lifetime. Once data is read from a protected storage it becomes possibly affected by a plethora of other information exposure threats. Furthermore, indiscriminate data storage security management procedures may prove too restrictive and resource costly for application on constrained ubiquitous devices.

Provos [10] realises the vulnerability of information beyond storage and extends cryptographic protection to swap-space. As such, the protection provided covers another aspect of information lifetime only. The mandatory, cryptographic-only approach, retains the previously outlined issues.

A step forward in "on-demand" encryption is made by Corner and Noble in their work on Zero Interaction Authentication [11]. They use transient association between a storage hosting device and a token, signifying user presence, to encrypt stored data on user absence. In [12] Corner and Noble build on their previous work to provide for on-demand process state and virtual memory encryption as well. They also allow for selective data encryption by designing an API that allows aware applications to be notified on user-absence and take relevant application-specific actions. The threat model space, as seen by Corner and Noble, is binary - determined by the state of user presence. We see user presence as only one of the possible contextual factors which may impact on the likelihood of a set of information exposure threats. Thus, our approach enables reasoning about threats on a much finer granularity. Furthermore, Corner and Noble do not provide for alternatives in security-relevant data management procedures.

In [13] Patwardhan et al. develop a deontic policy language *Rei* and show how it can be employed for securing information in pervasive environments. Among their objectives are: accountability, by which an administrator may specify a policy for safe use of the device to limit the damage in case it is lost or stolen; automatic guards, providing for automatic security-relevant event-triggered device reconfiguration; and capability restriction, limiting a device's software or hardware capabilities according to the automatic guards. Unlike the previously mentioned work, this approach allows for flexible context-based threat reasoning. However, rather than offering a method for context-aware information security reasoning or analysis the work offers solely a framework for policy enforcement. As such, it resembles work done on Ponder [14].

In summary, current approaches, to the best of our knowledge, lack holistic, continuous and data item centric, fine-grained, information protection throughout information lifetime. In general, they aim at providing information protection through a combination of platform functionality restriction and deployment of inflexible, generalised, data management and handling mechanisms. Not only does this inhibit information availability and system usability but without means of estimating the level of risk in a methodic way, by only assessing the possibility of a threat, the protection provided may well be without a cause.

3   The Role of Containment

To provide for continuous structured reasoning about information exposure threats on per data item granularity we developed a way of modeling the world based on the notions of a *container* and *containment*. The model facilitates localized threat mitigation.

3.1   Characterizing Threats

For the sake of clarity we firstly define threats as used in the rest of the paper. We characterize threats with two values: *type* and *effect*. With respect to the class of unintentional information leakage, or information exposure, threats the type is intended to denote the nature of the channel, or means, by which information leaks form a data item to an unauthorized entity. For the purpose of clarity of this paper, as an example illustration, we can typify information exposure as: *physical, visual, audio* and *network*. The threat effect describes the *impact* of a threat. Threat effect is expressed using an appropriate metric, Section 4, and has unified semantics across all threats recognized by the system.

3.2   Container - The Basic Building Block

We define a *container* to be a virtual or physical enclosure, a bounded region, in which a piece of information, or another container, may exist. The semantics of an enclosure imply that migrations as well as destruction of a container assume its contents. Containers can be classified into a hierarchy based on their nature. The three top level classes we define are: *physical container, virtual container* and *intermediate container*. Physical containers refer to enclosed physical spaces such as e.g. an office, space within a secure perimeter, etc. Virtual containers, on the other hand, do not have dimensions in the physical world e.g. a file, a file system, an TCP packet, an IPSEC tunnel, a GUI window, etc. Intermediate containers act as a bind between the physical and virtual worlds by being physical phenomena but able to contain only virtual containers e.g. a storage device, a display, a keyboard, a wireless communications link etc. Container class *data item* is special in a sense that it serves as a direct representation of information. We introduce *containable* relationship to denote container classes that a container of a particular class may contain.

The fundamental characteristic of a container is its *transparency*. Container transparency represents filtering characteristics that its boundary poses for different types of contextual factors, and thus for implied information exposure threats. For example: an sound-proof enclosure filters out threats of audio access to information originating from outside; a size of a GUI window and information rendering characteristics determine relative distance and angle required for the information to be accessed visually; tamper resistance of a storage device, file or communications channel encryption increase the level of effort, knowledge and determination needed for physical access to information, etc. Container transparency may change depending on container's state, e.g. size of a GUI window, open vs. closed door of a room etc. Based on this observation we define for each of the container classes a *transparency function* that, given a set of container characteristics and a threat specification, determines the impact of the container's boundary on the threat's effects.

3.3   Containment - The Model of the World

The state of the world at any point in time can be represented, in a graph-theoretic way, as a forest of finite-path-length finite-degree rooted trees with directed edges. Nodes of the tree represent containers while the edges denote *contains* relationship. For a containment tree to be well structured it has to obey the containable relationship. Containers of class data item are always leaf nodes. *Containment* of an entity (a container of a data item) represents a sequence of nested containers leading from the tree root to the entity in question. Detailed formal specification of the model can be found in [8].

To evaluate effects of a threat occurring somewhere in a containment tree on a data item we successively apply the transparency function for each of the containers on a path from the threat source container to the data item.

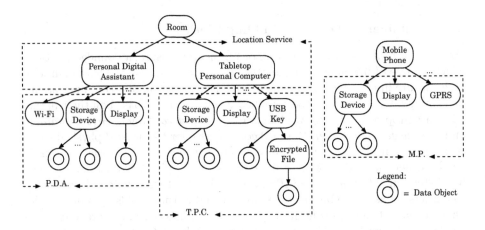

Fig. 1. Containment model of the world snapshot

The model is intended to be established and maintained independently on individual ubiquitous computing devices - called *model authorities*. Figure 1 shows a partial containment-based model of the world denoting, as labeled on the dashed boxes, model authorities and their respective model portions.

4   From Exposure Quantification to Threat Mitigation

4.1   Quantifying Information Exposure

The first and essential step towards our aim of matching threats and protective actions on fine grained basis is derivation of a threat exposure metric. In

Section 3 we have outlined how a container may impact on a threat effect which allows us to reason about information exposure threats on per data item basis. The approach, as presented, assumes that the threat has materialized and does not account for two specific factors: context sensing uncertainty and the likelihood of a particular threat materializing in the given context. Context sensing uncertainty stems from characteristics of sensors and deployed context inference methods; it has been a topic of interest of a wide body of research in the area of context-aware computing. The likelihood of a threat materializing in a context depends on a particular set of contextual fragments forming the context. In other words, it represents probabilistic correlation between contextual fragments and threat occurrence. As the setting makes experimentation close to impossible other methods based on, for example, prior experiences and historical information, expert opinions, cost/benefit analysis or attacker profiling have to be used to arrive at threat likelihood values.

We propose the following general form of the metric for quantifying information exposure:

$$exposure(u, l, e)$$

where u represents context sensing uncertainty, l is the perceived likelihood of threat occurrence while e is the threat effect as experienced by a data item in a particular containment upon threat materialization. Exact functional dependence between the parameters, their domains as well as the metric semantics and cardinality are application specific.

In general, context-threat mapping is many-to-many. It is realistic to expect a number of threats of the same and different types to co-occur in a context. As the exposure metric is threat specific the following table defines a simple algebra for combining exposure values of different types:

$\oplus$	$e_1^{t_1}$	$e_1^{t_2}$
$e_2^{t_1}$	$max(e_1^{t_1}, e_2^{t_1})$	$[e_2^{t_1}, e_1^{t_2}]$
$e_2^{t_2}$	$[e_2^{t_2}, e_1^{t_1}]$	$max(e_2^{t_2}, e_1^{t_2})$

where $e_n^{t_x}$ denotes an exposure value enumerated as n and resulting from a threat type x. The algebra shows that exposure values due to different threat types can not be added but are preserved separately. The table also shows that given several exposures of the same time the joint exposure is just as significant as the highest value individual exposure on its own. The motivation and the consequence of the algebra specification are shown in section 4.4.

4.2 Controlling Information Exposure - The Protective Actions

The role of protective actions is to lower exposure experienced by a piece of information to what is considered to be an "acceptable" level with respect to a security policy. Protective actions can be grouped as:

  – Container manipulation:
    • Container modification.
    • Container creation.
    • Containment migration.
  – Information manipulation:
    • Information reduction.
    • Information subsetting.

Container manipulation actions rely on container transparency to mitigate threats. *Container modification* exploits dependencies between a container's characteristics and its boundary's transparency to impact on a threat effect propagation, e.g. resizing a GUI window decreases its visibility radius. Insertion of a container, i.e. its *creation*, in a threat propagation path down a containment tree is equivalent to adding a filter for the threat effects, e.g. file encryption - regarded as "enclosing" a file within a cryptographic container. Lastly, threat effects may be mitigated by *migration* of a portion of a data item's containment to a different point in the containment tree, e.g. migration of a GUI window from an wall-mounted display to a PDA's built-in display.

Unlike container modification actions, information manipulation operations do not act to lower exposure but to make information more "tolerable"[2] to the experienced exposure. To increase the exposure "tolerance" information manipulation actions impact on data sensitivity by decreasing the quality and quantity of data items' information content. *Information reduction* techniques [15] assume direct transformations of data items' content such as e.g. JPEG image degradation. *Information subsetting* consists of fully omitting sensitive pieces of information, e.g. map feature selection as in [16]. Information subsetting may be seen as a coarse-grained form of information reduction providing only a binary, full content or none, alternative.

4.3   The Choice of Action

Given the variety of possible protective actions there is likely to be multiple alternatives to mitigating any single threat. For example, in case of a threat of visual information exposure the actions of resizing the GUI window, hiding the GUI window, blanking the whole screen or migrating the window to a more restricted display are viable. The ability to reason about "appropriate" action given a threat is one of the fundamental contributions of our work. To meet the stated goal of maximizing information availability while adequately protecting its security and privacy with respect to information exposure threats we introduce the measure of information *utility*.

Information Utility Measure. Information utility measure is envisaged to capture the following properties of a piece of information affected by a protective action execution:

---
[2] As defined by a wider security policy.

- Information content.
- Locality of information.
- Information Accessibility.
- User Perceived Quality of Service.

We reason about impact of protective actions on information utility given, what we call, assumption of general "rational" behavior of a system and a user with respect to information utility. We say that a system or a user behaves in a "rational" manner if any information management decision taken and operation performed strives to maximize information utility. For example, if a user opts for a particular display to view a piece of information or a system chooses a specific link to transfer data we assume that both decisions maximize information utility under a relevant set of constraints. An information manipulation action is likely to impact on *information content* of affected data. We introduce *Information Loss Factor* as a measure of relative change of information content pre- and post- protective action execution. *Locality of information* is introduced to characterize change of containment of a piece of information. Given the "rationality" assumption it is intended to favorise actions that cause no containment shift as shown in the table below. *Information accessibility* captures *delay* and *cost* of accessing a piece of information as well as general information *availability* post-execution of a protective action. Finally, it is well known in the human-computer interaction that human perceptions of the quality of service vary subjectively and are difficult to generalize. *User Perceived Quality of Service* expresses user preferences towards the form in which and means by which information is managed and presented. For example, while one user would be happy to trade off some of information content for keeping the information on the same display another may favor the opposite. Even more straightforward, given a laptop, a PDA and a mobile phone different users may voice different preferences towards using their resources.

Information Utility Measure is introduced to combine the above four factors in order to obtain a ranking of protective actions with respect to their impact on information utility. The level of measure (ordinal, interval or ratio) used for expressing each of the above factors is application specific. While, for example, the natural way to express ILF is in percentage (ratio level of measurement) the locality may be expressed ordinally, as in the following table:

	Local	Collaborative	Remote
== cclass	6	5	4
!= cclass	3	2	1

where the local container of the same class is the most preferred (preference value 6). The *collaborative* category represents containers that are part of different, trusted and highly available, ubiquitous computing devices. In general, given the "rationality" assumption, the information utility measure should be designed to favorise actions that: make information at least as available as it was; do not reduce information content; and make information available through means and in a form preferred by user.

Other Properties. Besides the information utility measure which enables balancing the level of protection and the information utility there are several other protective action properties that may influence the discrimination process. *Reversibility* represents the *cost* and *degree* to which a protective action may be undone. Reversibility is important as, due to the "rationality" assumption, we may expect that once an information exposure threat becomes inactive the system will try to return to its "pre-protective-action-execution" state. Other two important aspects are protective action *cost*, resource and/or monetary, and its impact on system usability in general. For example, locking up a mobile phone has a wider system usability impact than erasing a single data item.

Action Impact. We define *impact* of an action to be a function of the information utility measure, its cost, reversibility, system usability impact and the perceived threat duration, if available. Threat duration may play a significant role in weighing individual factors that contribute to an action's impact: for short lived threats actions with greater information utility impact, reversibility factor and lower cost may be sensible to perform; for longer lived threats, on the other hand, information utility may be considered as the single most important factor.

If we consider A to be the set of all actions, $A^\circ \subset A$ to be a set of alternative actions to mitigate a threat and ι the action impact function then we define:

$$A^{\circ\circ} = \{a \mid a \in A^\circ \wedge \iota(a,c) = max_{x \in A^\circ}[\iota_{avg(sum)}(x,c)]\}$$

where c is a containment path expression that the action applies to. $\iota_{avg(utility)}$ is a function that expresses action impact taking into account the average of information utility measure on per affected data item basis. This form of the action impact function is to be used when a protective action impacts multiple data items at once, e.g. blanking of a screen containing multiple GUI windows, encrypting a file system as a whole, etc. The averaging form of the ι function is, thus, likely to be used for any container manipulation action. Averaging in this manner is necessary in cases where the utility measure is to be weighed differently depending on the affected data items' sensitivity classification level.

$A^{\circ\circ}$ therefore represents a set of optimal actions given a threat and a particular containment configuration. If $\mid A^{\circ\circ} \mid > 1$ then $\forall a \in A^{\circ\circ}$, a is an optimal choice according to the above criteria.

4.4 Levels of Exposure Modeling

A *Level of Exposure* (LoE) represents a range in information exposure which requires the same security and privacy *handling procedure*. A handling procedure assumes a set of protective actions matching the exposure level denoted by a LoE and any auxiliary actions. The latter represent non threat relevant actions to be performed on LoE activation such as e.g. logging, user notification, etc. LoE defining exposure regions are non-overlapping.

In general, LoEs are defined on per information sensitivity level. This is because of two reasons. Firstly, a security policy may define different exposure thresholds for information of different sensitivity. And secondly, a specific set of protective actions may be mandated for information of certain sensitivity e.g. encryption algorithm of a specific key length. At any point in time, i.e. in every context, all containments in a containment model are associated with a set of LoEs denoting exposure for data items of each sensitivity level.

LoEs Model. All LoEs that are part of the same security policy form a *LoE Model*. A LoE model is defined as a directed multigraph $G = (V, E)$ where V is a set of vertices, each representing a LoE, and E is a set of labeled edges, each representing an action. In any one context each LoE is associated with none or more containments relevant to the local model authority - denoting exposure of the contained data items. The graph edge configuration is relative to a context and is based on a set of available protective actions. Each edge is directed towards a node (LoE) signifying a lower exposure. Edge labels consist of source and destination containments, which may be the same in case of information reduction actions, and the respective action impact, as defined in Section 4.2.

The simplest conceivable LoE model has two levels: "exposed" and "not-exposed", for each of the information sensitivity levels. The latter signifies exposure values not "endangering" information confidentiality while the former requires a mitigating action to be taken. All approaches of Section 2 implicitly assume a single bi-LoE model for data items of all sensitivity levels without any flexibility in choosing protective actions.

LoEs Modeling Granularity. A number of subtleties exist which require departure from the simple bi-LoE approach.

Situations may arise in which performing actions to fully mitigate information exposure impacts severely on a progress of a task dependent on an affected data item. To address this issue, a security policy may define additional LoEs that denote exposures that are sustainable under a set of constraints e.g. temporal. For example, consider an exposure metric in volume of information leakage per unit time. Then a three level LoE sub-model for one of information sensitivity levels may be defined as: LoE *Low* - 0 to 5 bits/sec; LoE *Medium* - 5 to 10 bits/sec; and LoE *High* - more than 10 bits/sec. The medium LoE can further have a constraint associated that bounds amount of time it can be sustained for e.g. 10 seconds, time required for a proportion of the overall information content to leak etc.

The exposure algebra, defined in Section 4.1, specifies that exposure values due to threats of different types can not be added i.e. it preserves the type. The primary reason for this is that the handling procedures assigned to a exposure value range (a LoE) may be threat type specific. Furthermore, LoE defining information exposure ranges may also vary depending on the threat type and the exposure metric semantics. Thus, in general case, a LoE is defined for any possible combination exposure value ranges due to threats of different types. This approach avoids the possibility of a single data item being under multiple LoEs in a context. It also enables model representation of protective actions that affect "multi-typed" exposures by a single edge. However, the approach increases size of the LoE space. In the worst case scenario a number of LoEs required to represent n threat types and m exposure ranges per type, for a single sensitivity level, is given by n^m. The average case is influenced by a particular container classification granularity and threat typification which may render certain combinations of threat types occurring concurrently for a specific container impossible. For example, it is unlikely that a data item may be both "visually" and "audibly" exposed at the same time and under the same containment.

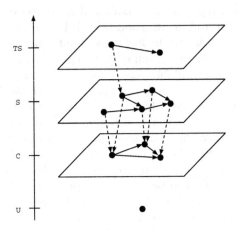

Fig. 2. A LoEs model example

Figure 2 depicts an abstract representation of a partial LoE model (see below). Dots representing LoEs, i.e. graph nodes, are grouped in planes which represent information sensitivity levels (U, C, S and TS). Unclassified (U) information is never considered exposed in a sense that it would need a threat mitigating operation and thus only a single LoE associated with it. The LoE is also used as the destination node of actions that cause complete information loss i.e. information content destruction. Thus, there should be an edge from every LoE to the single LoE at the bottom of the diagram. These edges, as well as the edges connecting LoEs associated with non-adjacent information sensitivity levels are not shown for the diagram clarity. Coplanar graph edges denote container manipulation actions while the edges connecting planes correspond to information manipulation actions. In other words, staying within a plain assumes no information loss. Note that a particular graph configuration always corresponds to a particular context and model authority.

5   Enforcing Data Security

In our previous work [9] we concentrated on the overall system architecture and an appropriate formal policy model to address the specific requirements posed by the target setting, the ubiquitous computing world. The work is particularly focused on enabling the system deployment on widely heterogeneous platforms with substantial and variable resource constraints. The proposed architecture and the policy model fully support the concepts presented in the previous chapters.

As justified in [9], mainly due to resource requirements and complexity issues, we split the system into two: the *management* side and the *client* side. The former handles computationally heavy and centralizable tasks related to policy specification and formulation tailored to the capabilities of a policy enforcement device, conflict resolution etc. The *client* side is deployed on ubiquitous devices where tasks such as context establishment, policy evaluation, user preference analysis and enforcement actually happen.

5.1   Policy Enforcement - An Overview

The formal policy model employed is based on *Deterministic Finite State Transducers* (DFST). For DFST policy representation we use the model presented in [17] that is a modification of predicate augmented FSTs (Finite State Transducers) [18] to provide intrinsic support for conflict resolution via *tautness functions*. The policy model supports consideration of user preferences and device constraints in discriminating between the protective actions (Section 4.2).

Figure 3 depicts client components that take part in the policy enforcement process and their relevant interactions. The policy enforcement process assumes the execution of protective actions as determined by *Policy Evaluation Master* (PEM) - a client side component in charge of policy evaluation.

As for the container manipulation actions, both the application and the system layers may be responsible for their execution. This is as containers of classes intermediate and virtual may originate from both an application or a system

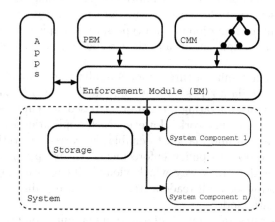

Fig. 3. Policy enforcement component architecture

component. For example, while a SSL tunnel and a GUI window are application level containers, a IPSEC tunnel and swap space encryption are system level containers. Thus, when a container manipulation is required *Enforcement Module* (EM) enquires with *Containment Model Manager* (CMM) to learn the "owner" of a respective container and instructs them accordingly - as shown by the interaction arrows in the figure.

In case of information manipulation actions, the atomic unit of policy enforcement is a data item. It denotes an entity that binds related information of the same security and privacy sensitivity level. As such it is conceptually different from the traditional notion of a monolithic file - which may well represent a collection of data items with different sensitivity levels. Such approach allows for fine-grained policy enforcement that affects only the "threatened" information.

5.2   Data Model: Requirements and Implications

Information manipulation actions are performed on per data item basis. They have a generic description and data item type specific implementation. To avoid imposing otherwise unnecessary overheads and functionality requirements on the application space and burdening application designers with additional complexity we offload the support for information manipulation actions into the data storage system. Such an approach causes a shift in roles and responsibilities of both the applications and the data repository.

Data Repository. For a data repository to support the information manipulation actions it needs to be able to recognize, at a fine-grained level, application specific data types and respective internal data layouts. By internal data layout we assume its data item substructure. Understanding of the data layouts also ensures the compatibility of the transformed data. Means of associating individual data items with sensitivity levels, with respect to a security policy, need to exist. Identification of data items for information manipulation purposes is done on information sensitivity level basis. The data repository, further, has to support a mechanism for provision of data type specific implementations of generic information manipulation actions and their respective mappings.

Applications. Upon a shift in threat model applications should simply be able to retrieve, from the data repository, an "updated" version of any of the threat affected data they are operating on. An event-based system to accomplish this is outside the scope of this work. However, each application-specific data type should include enough information to enable the correct operation of the data repository with respect to policy enforcement. An exception are applications that do not alter data in a way which violates its relevant layout, e.g. data viewers such as browsers, pdf readers etc. These can remain utterly unaware of the underlying data model.

Figure 4 illustrates an example information manipulation process at the data repository level. It represents the data item structure of a document prior to and post a set of information manipulation actions, depicted on the left and on the

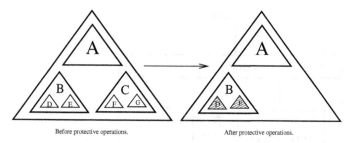

Before protective operations.   After protective operations.

Fig. 4. A data transformation scenario

right of the arrow respectively. To address a particular information exposure, as instructed by the EM, the data repository adapts the document by: fully omitting data entity labeled C, containing data items F and G, and reducing the information content of data items labeled D and E.

5.3   Data Layout Specification

To address the issue of data layout specification we leverage the capabilities of XML [19] data representation. XML allows for applications and standards bodies to produce data layout descriptions which can be interpreted by the data repository in a systematic fashion. XML data representations are seen as matching our requirements for several reasons. Firstly, they facilitate efficient inspection and identification of data content, both automatic and manual, aiding choice and design of applicable information manipulation actions. Secondly, the XML approach enables easy protective actions validation through XML schemas to ensure application specific data compliance of transformed data. Thirdly, XML file formats being built upon a set of standards implies the ability to reuse data type specific information manipulation actions for all applications' data that uses standardized data types. Finally, we have at hand a number of standard XML tools that greatly facilitate generic data access.

5.4   Storage Subsystem Architecture

Figure 5 shows the component structure of the storage subsystem. It is comprised of: a Generic Interface, pluggable Type Wardens and the Data Store. The Data Analyser and the Type Wardens perform the protective operations cooperatively. The Enforcement Module (EM) interacts with the storage subsystem by invoking generic calls. Generic calls are internally mapped to data-type specific implementations that obey certain data structuring rules. These are provided by pluggable modules known as Type Wardens.

Generic Interface. Generic interface provides a set of generic calls as invoked by the EM. An example of the interface is a set of calls of the form `degrade_levelX` (`sensitivity`), where X represents Information Loss Factor (Section 4.3) and `sensitivity` denotes the level of sensitivity of data items that the operation should be applied to.

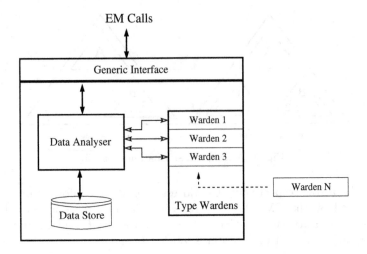

Fig. 5. Storage enforcement system architecture

Data Analyser. The role of the Data Analyser is coordination of an information manipulation procedure. Firstly, it identifies target data items and retrieves them from the store. Secondly, it invokes appropriate operations for each of the data items. Finally, it either: stores the data; passes the data to the EM for application update, in case it is the data an application was using that was under exposure; or does both.

Type Wardens. The role of Type Wardens is to provide data-type specific implementations of the generic information manipulation actions. The data-type specific actions can be either provided along the type definition by standards' bodies or application designers or they me be custom-made by security administrators. The latter is facilitated by the existence of standard XML tools (i.e. DOM, SAX, XPath) that can be used as data manipulation interface to application-specific data types. The ability to provide for type wardens in an "on-demand" fashion significantly facilitates the deployment of the storage system on resource constrained ubiquitous devices.

Data Store. For the purposes of the proposed system the data store is used solely as a persistent data repository.

6   Conclusion

Traditionally, the notion of secure data management was assumed to point towards data storage. The peculiarities of the ubiquitous computing vision, reflected largely on its prime forerunner, mobile computing, have both raised novel information security and privacy issues and have brought into spotlight some that were previously considered attention unworthy. Information exposure threats, as introduced in our work, extend the semantics of secure data management to represent a means of both maximizing information availability at any one time and providing adequate information exposure protection throughout information lifetime.

To facilitate structured and methodic reasoning about information exposure threats and localized threat mitigation we have outlined a model of the world based on a naturally-occurring notion of a container and containment. Essential for flexible and context-adaptive information exposure threat mitigation was conception of the information exposure and mitigating operations' impact metrics. The level of abstraction at which both are introduced paves the way for application-specific specializations. The previously introduced concepts are fused in a Levels of Exposure Model, a structured representation of degrees of information exposure as formed with respect to particular information classification policy and available data management procedures. From the practical perspective, we have presented a data repository system that greatly facilitates the system implementation.

As our prototype is in its early stages, being developed at the time of writing of this document, the paper lacks any usability, computational complexity or related overheads evaluation. The prototype fuses the work presented in this paper as well as our previous publications on the topic. The overall practical evaluation is the first item on our future work agenda. Theoretical evaluation of relevant aspects, however, is available in our previous work.

Acknowledgments

We would like to thank Jon Crowcroft and Ian Pratt for support in the research that led to the publication of this paper. Boris Dragovic is a Benefactors' Scholar of St John's College, Cambridge, UK. Calicrates Policroniades has a scholarship from the Mexican government through the National Council of Science and Technology (CONACyT). Last but not the least, we would like to express our gratitude to the anonymous reviewers who have provided valuable advice on how to improve the paper and the research in general.

References

1. Weiser, M.: The computer for the 21st century. Scientific American **265** (1991) 94–104
2. Thomas, R., Sandhu, R.: Models, protocols, and architectures for secure pervasive computing: Challenges and research directions. In: IEEE PerSec'04. (2004)
3. Stajano, F., Crowcroft, J. In: The Butt of the Iceberg: Hidden Security Problem of Ubiquitous System. Kluwer (2003)
4. Stajano, F.: Security for Ubiquitous Computing. Wiley (2002)
5. Nixon, P., Wagealla, W., English, C., Terzis, S.: Security, privacy and trust issues in smart environments. Technical report, SmartLab, Dept of Computer Science, Uni of Strathclyde, UK (2004)

6. Tan, D.S., Czerwinski, M.: Information voyeurism: Social impact of physically large displays on information privacy. In: Short paper at CHI 2003 Conference on Human Factors in Computing Systems. (2003)
7. Kuhn, M.G., Anderson, R.J.: Soft tempest: Hidden data transmission using electromagnetic emanations. In: Information Hiding, Second International Workshop. (1998)
8. Dragovic, B., Crowcroft, J.: Containment: from context awareness to contextual effects awareness. In: 2nd Intl Workshop on Software Aspects of Context (IWSAC'05). (2005)
9. Dragovic, B., Baliosian, J., Vidales, P., Crowcroft, J.: Autonomic system for context-adaptive security in ubiquitous computing environments. Submitted for publication at ESORICS 2005, notification: May 30. (2005)
10. Provos, N.: Encrypting virtual memory. In: USENIX Security Symposium. (2000)
11. Corner, M., Noble, B.D.: Zero-interaction authentication. In: 8th ACM Conf. on Mobile Computing and Networking (MobiCom '02). (2002)
12. Corner, M., Noble, B.D.: Protecting applications with transient authentication. In: The 1st Intl. Conf. on Mobile Systems, Applications, and Services (MobiSys '03). (2003)
13. Patwardhan, A., Korolev, V., Kagal, L., Joshi, A.: Enforcing policies in pervasive environments. In: International Conference on Mobile and Ubiquitous Systems: Networking and Services. (2004)
14. Damianou, N., Dulay, N., Lupu, E., Sloman, M.: The ponder policy specification language. In: Workshop on Policies for Distributed Systems and Networks. (2001)
15. Heuer, A., Lubinski, A.: Data reduction - an adaptation technique for mobile environments. In: Interactive Apllications of Mobile Computing (IMC'98). (1998)
16. Chalmers, D.: Contextual Mediation to Support Ubiquitous Computing. PhD thesis, Department of Computing, Imperial College London (2002)
17. Baliosian, J., Serrat, J.: Finite state transducers for policy evaluation and conflict resolution. In: Proceedings of the Fifth IEEE International Workshop on Policies for Distributed Systems and Networks (POLICY 2004). (2004)
18. van Noord, G., Gerdemann, D.: Finite state transducers with predicates and identities. Grammars **4** (2001) 263–286
19. XML: eXtensible Markup Language. http://www.w3.org/XML (2004)

XML Security in the Next Generation Optical Disc Context

Gopakumar G. Nair[1], Ajeesh Gopalakrishnan[1], Sjouke Mauw[1], and Erik Moll[2]

[1] Eindhoven University of Technology (TU/e),
Eindhoven, The Netherlands
{G.gopakumar, A.gopalakrishnan, S.mauw}@tue.nl
[2] Philips Applied Technologies,
Eindhoven, The Netherlands
Erik.moll@philips.com

Abstract. The Extensible Markup Language (XML) is considered as the de facto standard for information processing and exchange on the Internet and in the enterprise services domain. It is widely regarded that XML has the potential of being an interoperable standard for interactive applications in the next generation connected Consumer Electronic devices. A key industry concern in using XML in CE devices is that how basic security requirements pertaining to the above said domain can be met. Notably, the standardization bodies of the Internet domain such as W3C and OASIS have defined specifications for cryptography-based security solutions using XML technology that is mainly aimed for web applications. This paper investigates and presents various scenarios where XML Security can be applied to markup based interactive applications in the context of a next generation Consumer Electronic Optical Disc Player. We conclude the paper by presenting a prototype establishing how these scenarios could be realized in practice.

1 Introduction

Until recently, the diverse and well-established domains of Personal Computers (PC), Web (Internet), Consumer Electronics (CE) and Broadcast domains have had their own autonomous realms of existence. Each of these domains spawned their own characteristic and individualistic ways of managing and doing things, with examples as diverse as the application specification to the very notion of interactivity. However, lately there has been considerable interest among these domain communities to share and adopt inter-domain best practices and knowledge. As an illustration, the content creators could create applications for one domain, which could be seamlessly integrated or be transferred to other domains. Such integration could provide new usage models in the CE optical disc domains [2]. As a fleshed out example, the content creators could author multi-domain interoperable applications which could be packaged in a disc and additional application extensions such as bonus materials, clips etc could be downloaded from a content server or a set top box in a home network, thus borrowing the ideas from Web and Broadcast domains. One of the possible candidates

W. Jonker and M. Petković (Eds.): SDM 2005, LNCS 3674, pp. 217–233, 2005.
© Springer-Verlag Berlin Heidelberg 2005

for this cross-domain sharing is the XML and its related technologies, which entails the core theme of discourse in this paper.

XML is emerging as the de-facto standard for storing, managing, and communicating information on the Internet [1]. In addition, XML is the basis for markup applications and a wide range of XML based languages [7] for various web services. Several standardized interfaces, tools, techniques and their programming language bindings are available, both commercial and open source. This makes XML a serious contender for being considered as a standard for creating consumer interactive multimedia systems, the market where disc based systems mainly belong. A well-known example of such a standard is DVB-HTML [8], an XML based interactive application specification for Multimedia Home Platform [8] which has been existing for several years. With such pervasive and proven applications and usage scenarios of XML in a myriad of domains, it is without doubt a pick while considering the specification for Interactive Applications in next generation optical discs. Certainly, in combination with a procedural language, such as Java such a standard would open up new possibilities in bringing interactivity to such devices.

Next generation optical disc formats such as Blu-ray disc (BD) [2], High Definition (HD) DVD, and enhanced DVD (eDVD) [31] are reckoned as the natural successors of DVD as a medium for storage, playback and distribution of digital media [2].

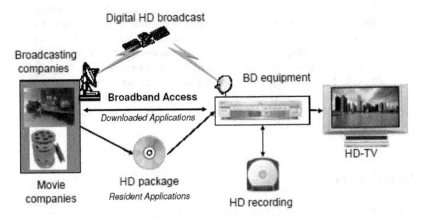

Fig. 1. End-to-End Usage Model (based on [1])

Figure 1 depicts the end-to-end usage model of the next generation optical discs based players in a consumer home. The movie companies distributes the High Definition (HD) content via optical discs as medium or via HD broadcast and the optical disc player equipment at the consumer home can playback the content on HD Televisions. As a consequence, the consumers get High Definition (HD) video experience, the content providers (movie companies) get the opportunity to store and distribute high quality videos and games and the independent content creators and vendors have the opportunity to provide value-added media based services. Additionally, due to the wide availability and growth of broadband connections, new Internet based usage models to download applications from content servers are foreseen for such devices due to the perceived characteristics of these devices to connect to Internet. In order to realize this, the next generation optical discs would need an interoperable interactive application specification with adequate considerations for security.

In the context of next generation optical disc players, careful consideration should go into the interactive application security issues while considering the usual issues of copy protection of audio and video content. In this case, the applications could also be copyrighted and could be subjected to malicious usage. To give an example, consider a malicious application loaded from an external server that could corrupt the local storage of the player. As another example, the user could try to create his/her own application, load to the system and try to access content where he has no access rights. The security mechanisms that could prevent such issues must be non-invasive to the users, should be capable of being applied easily by the content creators and be necessarily future proof. Additionally, the opted security mechanism should be flexible, interoperable, and widely supported with appropriate tools and libraries in order to be accepted by the manufacturers.

W3C [22] and OASIS [18], the major standardization bodies within the Internet domain, have been working on creating XML based security standards for web-based applications. We foresee that these standards can be applied with the XML based interactive applications for the next generation optical disc systems. In this paper we discuss which are these standards, what problems they can solve in a disc player context and how we can establish the end-to-end security. We also see whether these mechanisms are realizable in an embedded system context.

This paper first portrays a typical markup based Content Hierarchy depicting the Interactive Applications in the next generation optical discs. Further to that, we characterize the security profile of a connected player by applying analytical Threat Modeling and ascertaining the detailed security requirements for this paper from the Threat model, which will be used for the rest of the discussions. Various XML Security standards are presented with their proposed solutions for the above said security requirements. Additionally, an end-to-end security scenario is presented and a proposal of how all the security standards could be brought together to guarantee an end-to-end security solution is exposed. Finally, to substantiate the proposal, a prototype implementation is detailed on a next generation optical disc reference platform.

2 A Markup Based Content Hierarchy

Optical discs are intended to store digital content, the term, used to describe any kind of collection of functional work, artwork, or other creative content, copyrighted or otherwise distributed in an optical disc. In this section, we introduce the content hierarchy in the next generation optical discs; in particular, the markup based application hierarchy, which can be used for representing Interactive applications. The Interactive Application refers to a part of the overall content that can be executed by the optical disc player.

At the top of the content hierarchy (see Figure 2) is the *Interactive Cluster*, which is the generic representation of packaged content, including Video, Audio and markup Application. The *Interactive Cluster* contains several *Tracks*, which form chapters for *Video/Audio Playlist* [23] and optionally *manifest* (application). The playlists contain meta-information about the play items and refer to *Clip Information*, which ultimately links to the Mpeg-2 Transport Stream file [24]. It is the *Application Manifest* that represents the Interactive Application in the hierarchy and captures its essence.

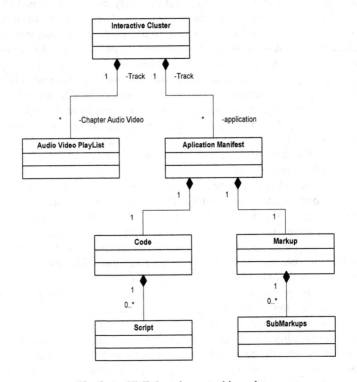

Fig. 2. An XML based content hierarchy

The manifest file consists of two distinct parts, namely the *Markup* and the *Code*. The Markup part captures the static composition of the application, which includes layout, timing model. The Code part provides flexibility by adding programmability and dynamics to the overall interactive experience. In turn the markup part could contain "*SubMarkups*" helping the separation of various characteristics of the application. For e.g. the layout can be captured in one SubMarkup and the timing issues in another. On the same lines, the code part can contain none or more scripts. As long as the overall structure and representation is respected, these subtle choices are entirely up to the discretion of the content author.

The choice of the markup for next generation optical discs may be from the following XML based languages, such as Synchronized Multimedia Integration Language (SMIL) [9], Scalable Vector Graphics (SVG) [26], Extended Hypertext Markup Language (XHTML) [27] and Extended Style Sheet Language (XSL) [28]. Additionally, ECMAScript [10] could be considered for the programmable part of the manifest.

3   Identifying Security in an Optical Disc Player Context

As pointed out in Section 1, next generation optical discs can be used to distribute HD video [3] content, along with interactive applications packaged in the disc and additional resources may be downloadable from an external location. The disc players can represent a myriad of devices ranging from Consumer Electronics devices to PC drives and mobile systems such as portable game stations. To get a complete picture of security requirements in such varied usage contexts, a complete threat characterization, and analysis is necessary. As a result, a Threat Modeling approach based on STRIDE [15] has been applied in order to make a methodical analysis of the security threats for optical disc based systems– especially with regard to the accession of interactive applications.

3.1   Threat Modeling for Next Generation Optical Disc Player

The Threat Model [12] provides us with a comprehensive list of threats to the application security and the various mitigation strategies that can be applied. We intend not to present the full results from the model [12], since the model per se is out of scope of this paper. Nevertheless, using the model we select a subset of the requirements and investigate how XML security mechanisms could be used to mitigate certain risks. In particular, the requirements of Authentication, Application Integrity, Content Secrecy, and Access control management ([4]) were under scrutiny.

Some of interesting inferences resulting from the investigative study of the model [12] about threats and their widely adapted mitigation strategies [4] are presented below in the context of next generation optical disc and players.

- *Authentication & Integrity*:   The markup applications or resources loaded from the disc need to be authenticated by the player in order to guarantee that only trusted applications are executed. Additionally, the applications or their parts or downloaded resources [3] may need to pass integrity checks [4] to detect (malicious) tampering before being used by the disc player.
- *Encryption*: Applying encryption techniques [4] can allow content authors to avoid wiretapping (man-in-the-van attack) and application sources/resources protection. This is important in the context of markup and script applications because they are essentially verbose.
- *Key Management:* Key Management includes all the services pertaining to key handling, registration, revocation and updates of cryptographic public keys, which are used in authentication and encryption mechanisms. In particular, appropriate Key Management procedures [4] must be in place to circumvent the causes of illegal creation, exchange, repudiation, replacement, protection, storage, and usage of keys used in the scenarios of optical disc application authentication and encryption.
- *Access Control:* The access control mechanisms [4] allow the next generation optical disc player to give access rights to the markup based on certain predetermined policies. As a result, it can provide or restrict access to certain resources, as requested by the application author or under certain conditions.

In the subsequent sections, we see various XML security standards and examine their usage in satisfying the requirements (identified in Section 3.1) in an optical disc usage context.

4 Overview of the Applicable XML Based Security Mechanisms

In this section, an overview of the standardized XML security mechanisms, proposed by W3C and OASIS, is presented.

The issues of Authentication and Integrity identified in Section 3.1 can be mitigated by Digital Signatures, which can be used to verify the integrity of the Interactive Application or associated content assets. To this end, XML Digital Signature [5] proposes a specific syntax to represent a Digital Signature [4] over arbitrary digital content. Furthermore, the XML Digital Signature is in itself a well-formed XML document and carries all the information needed to process the signature, including the verification information. The XML Digital Signature specification also recommends a mechanism for signature creation and verification of XML based markup. It is useful for signing and verifying entire or portion of the markup, which may be of binary content and/or include multiple documents.

Another point identified for elaboration in Section 3.1 was the issue of encryption. This issue has been treated well by W3C, in particular with the standardization of the XML Encryption Syntax and Processing [6], which can be applied in the disc-player context to satisfy specific needs of application content protection and secrecy. XML Encryption can handle both XML and non-XML (e.g. binary) data, which makes it flexible to be used along with the interactive applications. A typical usage scenario foreseen in the above-mentioned systems is to encrypt markup applications residing in the disc along with the resources such as images and data. The player will decrypt the application and resources on execution of these markup applications. The content or referenced resources could be encrypted as well.

References [6] and [16] suggest that XML encryption can be done at various levels. The content could be encrypted and stored in parts or as a whole. This allows flexibility and better performance. A Player, for instance, can encrypt and store the high scores of a game in a local storage while keeping the general application markup unencrypted. When the game is being executed, the player needs to decrypt only the scores, which can be done in parallel to the execution of the markup.

Another advantage of XML encryption in ensuring confidentiality is that mechanisms such as Secure Sockets Layer (SSL)/Transport Layer Security (TLS) protocols only provide confidentiality while the information is in transit and not while it is stored at a server, but XML Encryption takes it one step further by maintaining the confidentiality of information, both while in transit as well as when stored. Notably, the secrecy is not dependent on the state or a particular session of the communicating parties.

The issue of Key Management could be dealt with using the XML Key Management Specification (XKMS) [33] from W3C. The XKMS helps manage the sharing of the public key realizing the possibility of signature verification and encrypting for recipients. The usage of XML based message formats for key management eliminates the need to support other specialized public key registration and management protocols for markup based interactive applications in the next generation optical discs.

In order to counter the Access control issue from Section 3.1, the XACML [19] Specification proposed by OASIS [18] provides access control mechanism for applications, based on assertions. This may allow content creators to add policies to request the disc player devices to provide certain rights to an application.

The mechanism defined by MHP [8] suggests the usage of XML based *"permission request"* files. In this case, the content provider can add the permission request file along with the markup as an attachment. This will be interpreted by the platform and will provide access rights to the application (e.g. rights to use return channel or rights to dial to a particular server). Based on the adopted policy, the platform can allow or reject the rights to the resources.

Having looked at the XML based security possibilities, we now broaden the discussion with an overview of comparison of XML based security mechanisms with other potential content download security mechanisms like OMA DRM (Open Mobile Alliance - Digital Rights Management) [34]. Reference [37] provides an interesting comparison between OMA DCF (DRM Content Format) extensions (see [35] [36]) and XML based security mechanisms on overhead and performance for data broadcast in mobile networks. The reference [37] suggests that XML based security incurs 2.5 to 5.1 times more overhead as compared to OMA DCF and performance wise the text based XML takes a back seat when compared to binary-based OMA DCF. Nevertheless, our scenario test runs using the developed prototype (see Section 8) convinced us that in the context of a consumer electronic device like optical disc player, this performance reduction while using XML based security would be within the allowable performance requirements. Additionally, the indicated overhead would also not be a significant issue, owing to the fact that the broadband Internet bandwidth (used by next generation disc players) is not as much of a concern when compared to the mobile over-the-air bandwidth, which the reference [37] refers to.

Additionally, the DVD (Digital Versatile Disc) Content Scrambling System (CSS) used on DVDs to encrypt media data thereby restricting the decoding to only licensed DVD players is less likely to be extended to downloaded application security scenarios in the next generation optical disc in lieu of differences in the nature of content data and usage scenarios. Particularly, the CSS is meant for the protection of digital content and lacks flexibility and scalability when extended to interactive applications. Moreover, CSS has been tampered.

In Section 5, we see various ways in which the XML Digital Signature is applied to interactive applications. In Section 6, we see how XML encryption and decryption is applied. Even though Key Management as a requirement was highlighted earlier, an example of XKMS application in the context of interactive application in optical discs has been left out of the discourse in this paper. Section 7 describes the order of integration of these two, along with additional mechanisms to provide order such that end-to-end security is ensured when applications are created and then later executed.

5 Applying XML Digital Signature in the End-to-End Usage

5.1 Global Scenario

Figure 3 examines the global scenario for usage of Digital Signature in the context of signing, transmission, and verification of Interactive Applications. In the previous sections, we introduced the notion of the player accessing the applications over the Internet in addition to accessing the applications on the pre-authored disc. Disc based applications are inherently trusted since they were authored into the disc by the content providers - provided the disc is authenticated [29]. The real security issue [12] lies with the interactive applications downloaded over the Internet and the Signing/Verification scenario identified in Figure 3 would facilitate in mitigation. Though the realization of the XML Digital Signature [5] in this section is addressed using examples from the over the Internet downloaded Blu-ray applications, the Digital Signature creation and verification can be extended to disc-resident disc-based Blu-ray applications too.

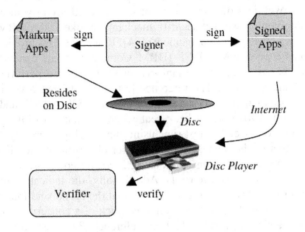

Fig. 3. Global Signing/Verification Scenario in Bluray

As seen in Figure 3, both at the content creators end and at the application authors' end, the applications can be digitally signed. When the player accesses any application from the Internet (e.g. Servers), it tries to authenticate the content by verifying the Digital Signature of the markup application. If the verification succeeds, the application is executed. In the case of signature verification failure, the application is barred from being executed. This implies that the player needs to have a Verifier component, which can carry out the signature (XML Signature) verification. Furthermore, the flexibility with this approach lies in the fact that this signing/verification mechanism can be applied in a variety of ways and levels.

5.2 Identified Signing/Verification Levels for Applications

To account for and prove the application of XML Digital Signature mechanism in next generation optical disc format, we look at the various sub-scenarios where the XML Signing and Verification can be achieved in the context of the interactive Applications as introduced in the "Content Hierarchy" section (see section 2). Even though these sub-scenarios can be extended with more detailed scenarios, here we only propose the general concept supported by examples here.

5.3 Signing/Verification at Interactive Cluster Level

We envision that the XML Digital Signature [5] can be applied at the level of Interactive Cluster (see Figure 2). Since the Interactive Cluster is Markup based, the XML Digital Signature can be used to sign/verify the Interactive Cluster in its entirety or can be used to sign/verify at Track (see Figure 2) Level. It is entirely up to the discretion of the Signer if (s)he wishes to sign the non-markup audio/video Content, which is nevertheless possible using XML Digital Signature. Since the main discourse is inclined towards Interactive Application authentication, a realization of selective Signing/Verification of application Track is hence commendable.

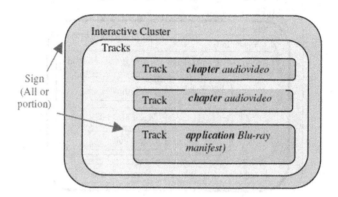

Fig. 4. Signing/Verification Scenarios in the Interactive Cluster Level

5.4 Signing/Verification at the Manifest Level

Taking the Signing and Verification one level deeper to the Manifest (see Figure 2) that forms part of the application Track, we notice that the control of authentication becomes much fine-grained or more granular. In this case, the choices available to the

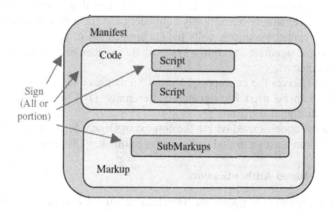

Fig. 5. Signing/Verification Scenario at the–Manifest Level

signer are quite large. (S)He can selectively sign only the Code or the Markup part (see Figure 2). Within the Code or Markup part itself, (s)he can choose to sign/verify only one of scripts or submarkups. The capability of the script to dynamically manipulate the Interactive Application makes it much more suited for authentication using XML Digital Signature [5]. Nevertheless, a maliciously tampered markup can be also detrimental to the Security of the Disc Player and the content.

From the above two example sub-scenarios we have seen that a number of Markup Items can qualify to be the target for XML Digital Signature. We refer to these as "Markup Targets".

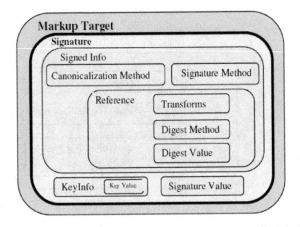

Fig. 6. Result of XML Signing on markup Targets

Figure 6 indicates the result of signing a Markup Target. The result of the signing process is the *Signature Markup* section that is demarcated in the figure by thick lines. This signature can be *enveloped* or *enveloping* [5] based on whether the markup target is parent or child to the "Signature". The signature can also be detached [5] if the target has no parent-child relationship to "Signature" element. The choice resides entirely with the content signer. The fact that XML based markups allows syntactic variations while remaining semantically equivalent and the nature of hash functions to be sensitive to syntax variations, calls for the application of *canonicalization* (XML-C14N)[32] to the signature to remove syntactic differences from semantically equivalent XML documents.

Reference [4] gives the concepts of Digital Signatures and the cryptographic algorithms which can be used for signatures. Reference [16] gives description of the markup tags for digital signature.

An additional concept used within the context of Digital Signature is the Certificate Handling [8], which uses a digital signature for public key [8] bindings.

5.5 Certificate Based Authentication

XML Digital Signature supports the insertion of digital certificates along with the signatures and provides syntax for the certificates present within the markups or referred to by the markups, which will be useful for the players to verify the authenticity of the keys. Reference [8] suggests a mechanism for the verification of certificates leading to a trusted root certificate within the player. It should be noted that the XML Digital Signature [5] could be used for such verification.

6 Applying XML Encryption to Markups

Having introduced the notion of XML based Encryption/ Decryption in the context of Interactive Applications in Section 4, we now take a look at how they can be applied in practice. As mentioned earlier, the XML Encryption could be used to encrypt both

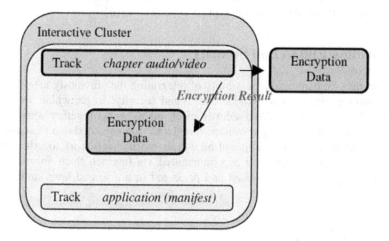

Fig. 7. Result of XML Encryption on Track Target

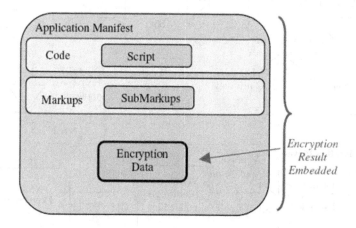

Fig. 8. Result of XML Encryption on Manifest Target

XML markup based or non-XML based content. This brings us two different scenarios for encryption of Interactive Applications, namely, the Encryption of the *Track Target* and the Encryption of *Manifest Target*.

Figure 7 illustrates the result of signing non-markup content, i.e. a chapter's audio/video track (see Figure 2) that is an Audio/Video Play list [23]. The result of encryption of non-markup content in this case is an "Encryption Data" [6], which is either created and embedded in the Interactive Cluster or jettisoned as a separate Markup.

However the scenario is different when markup content is encrypted. Figure 8 shows such a scenario where the manifest (see Figure 2) is encrypted.

In this case, the signing of manifest, an XML based markup, results in the Encryption Data being embedded in the manifest itself. For more details on XML Encryption and various elements within the Encryption Data refer to [5].

7 Providing End to End Security

In this section we explore the possibility of integrating the previously identified security mechanisms in order to provide end-to-end security. In particular, we consider how the above-mentioned XML security mechanisms works together when a typical application is created, packaged or transmitted and later executed in a CE optical disc player. Figure 9 shows an example of how these mechanisms work together when an application is created, packaged and transmitted via Internet. Such an order can be used when applications are created and packaged in a disc and later launched by a player.

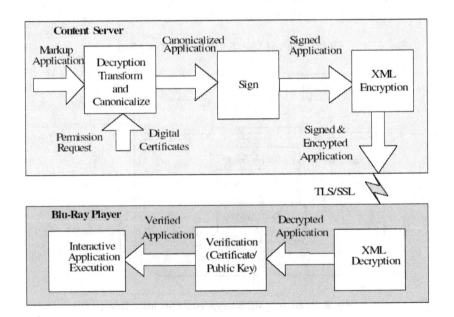

Fig. 9. Encryption and decryption process- end to end

To ensure the order between content encryption and signing, W3C specifies the Decryption Transform [21], which provides the signers with mechanisms specifying the order of signing and encryption. The resulting application contains sufficient information in the form of additional markup that enables the player to identify how the application needs to be decrypted and verified. The content creators also can add XML based permission request file, which requests permissions from the player to allow access to certain Player resources (e.g. access to graphics plane or writing to local storage). Furthermore, the XKMS [33] based Key Management could be used to convey key registrations and information requests to any "trusted source (trust server)" and to convey responses back from the server. Note that SSL/TLS mechanisms could be used for mutual authentication and secrecy between server and the player when applications are transmitted over the network.

8 Prototype

This section aims to substantiate the proposals mentioned in the previous sections with a prototype on a reference platform as a proof of concept. We chose Blu-ray as our optical disc format and aimed at prototyping the concepts mentioned above on a Blu-ray based optical disc platform.

For the choice of the markup target, we chose *Application Manifest* (see Figure 10), which represents the Interactive application. This choice is guided by the possibility to demonstrate the flexibility of the application of XML Digital Signature in a Blu-ray disc player.

8.1 Realizing the Reference Blu-Ray Interactive Application

The first and foremost need in the prototyping stage is to start with a reference Interactive Application with Blu-ray as a target system, along with appropriate choice of the markup target, the scripts and the sub-markups.

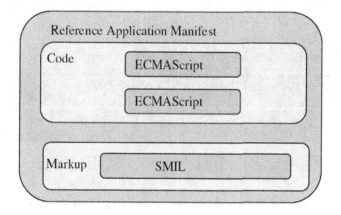

Fig. 10. Choices of Reference Blu-ray Markup Target, Script and SubMarkups

For the prototype we choose to represent the script with ECMAScript [10], a scripting programming language created to capture the common core language elements of both Javascript[11] and JScript[25]. For the timing and layout markup, we chose SMIL [9], a W3C [22] recommendation for describing multimedia presentations based on XML. It defines timing markup, layout markup, animations, visual transitions, and media embedding, among other things.

8.2 XML Security Library Implementations

At the time of prototyping available XML Security Libraries were from Apache Security Project [13] and IBM Alphaworks [14]. We selected the Apache XML Security libraries since it provides flexible licensing options for prototyping. At the time of the prototyping, two XML security implementations were available in Java and C++ from Apache. Each of these library flavors stood out as potentials for our cause. Our choice of Java was guided by the need of quick prototyping and stability of the available Java based Libraries over C++ based libraries. Apache XML security uses Java Cryptography Extension (JCE) and this was included in the prototype, along with the bundled Sun cryptography provider [31].

8.3 Reference Platform

We chose Linux based Blu-ray platform and created a prototype as discussed in this section.

Figure 11 shows the layered view of the software architecture.

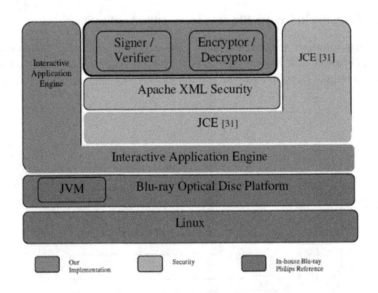

Fig. 11. Software Architecture for feasibility – Layered View

The Interactive Application Engine is the main component, which has access to the Interactive Cluster (see Figure 2) and is responsible for getting the application contents decrypted, if encrypted, and verified, if signed. In addition to the Verifier and Decryptor, a Signer and an Encryptor component were created to fulfill end-to-end requirements, which enabled the signing and encryption of Application Content.

The resulting prototype substantiated the pragmatic dimension of the proposal for using XML Security in the next generation optical discs. This prototype also demonstrated that XML based security and Interactive Application Engine (see Figure 11) can exist independent of the type the Disc format, be it Blu-ray disc [2], High Definition-DVD and enhanced DVD (eDVD) [31]. In addition, one of the main highlights of the proposal was the overall development time of the prototype, which took no more than 4 man weeks to complete. This demonstrates the simplicity and flexibility in the case of implementation of the proposal.

9 Conclusions and Future Work

We have seen that XML security offers a standard and interoperable mechanism that can be used by content providers to accommodate necessary security requirements for next generation optical discs. The content authors may use the flexibility of partially signing or encrypting the applications. For player platforms, this flexibility translates into better performance. The standard looks mature and implementations are available in Java and C++. The prototype enabled us to conclude the feasibility of proposal in an embedded platform, although we did not derive any performance constraints. We conclude that the usage of XML Security as a mechanism for markup based interactive applications can alleviate the security concerns pertaining to application security for content providers and CE manufacturers.

In lieu of future work, to expand the scope of XML Security mechanisms we envision that XRML [20], an XML based rights management language proposed by OASIS [18], to express digital rights for the usage of markup-based applications and resources, can be investigated for digital rights management in the next generation disc player context. Additionally, we intend to extend the current prototype with XML based Key Management [33].

Additionally, the current prototype could be extended to other underlying platforms, with respect to optical disc formats, Operating Systems and Hardware Platforms to account for the interoperability. Next, a scalable Interactive Application Engine library could be developed enabling ease of deployment. Finally, a performance model with comprehensive performance study measurements could be done for identifying and tuning the system resources needed for interpretation of the markup applications, and the associated XML based security.

References

1. Tim Bray et al., Extensible Markup Language (XML) 1.0 (Third Edition), World Wide Web Consortium (W3C) Recommendation. www.w3.org/TR/REC-xml/
2. Blu-ray Disc Association (BDA), Blu-ray Disc –Application Specification, BD-J Baseline Application Model Definition for BD-ROM – March 2005. www.bluraydisc.com

3. Blu-ray Disc Association (BDA), White Paper: Blu-ray Disc Format - General, August 2004. www.bluraydisc.com
4. Bruce Schneier, Applied Cryptography, Wiley, Second Edition, 1995, ISBN: 0471117099.
5. Mark Bartel et al., XMLDigSig - XML-Signature Syntax and Processing, World Wide Web Consortium (W3C) Recommendation 12 February 2002. www.w3.org/TR/2002/REC-xmldsig-core-20020212/
6. Takeshi Imamura et al., XML Encryption Syntax and Processing, World Wide Web Consortium (W3C) Recommendation 10 December 2002. www.w3.org/TR/2002/REC-xmlenc-core-20021210/
7. Uche Ogbuji, A survey of XML standards. www-106.ibm.com/developerworks/xml/library/x-stand1.html
8. European Telecommunications Standards Institute (ETSI), Digital Video Broadcasting (DVB), Multimedia Home Platform 1.2.1, ETSI TS 102 812 V1.2.1 (2003-06).
9. Jeff Ayars et al., Synchronized Multimedia Integration Language (SMIL 2.0), World Wide Web Consortium (W3C) Recommendation, 07 January 2005. www.w3.org/TR/2005/REC-SMIL2-20050107/
10. European Computing Manufacturing Association (ECMA), ECMAScript Language Specification, Standard ECMA-262 ISO/IEC 16262, 3rd Edition - December 1999.
11. Mozilla, JavaScript 2.0 Specifications. www.mozilla.org/js/language/js20/
12. G Gopakumar, A Gopalakrishnan, Threat Model based on STRIDE, OOTI Project Report 2005, TU/e.
13. Apache Security. xml.apache.org/security/
14. IBM Alphaworks, XML Security Suite. ww.alphaworks.ibm.com/tech/xmlsecuritysuite
15. Frank Swiderski et al., Threat Modeling, Microsoft Press 2004 ISBN: 0-7536-1991-3
16. Blake Dournaee, XML Security, RSA Press, McGraw-Hill/Osborne 2002, ISBN: 0-07-219399-9.
17. Balal Siddiqui, Exploring XML Security. www-106.ibm.com/developerworks/xml/library/x-encrypt/
18. Organization for the Advancement of Structured Information Standards (OASIS). www.oasis-open.org
19. Tim Moses et al., Extensible Access Control Markup Language Specification (XACML) version 2.0, Organization for the Advancement of Structured Information Standards (OASIS) Committee draft 04, 6 Dec 2004. docs.oasis-open.org/xacml/access_control-xacml-2_0-core-spec-cd-04.pdf
20. Simon Godik, Tim Moses et al., Xtensible Digital Rights Markup Language (XRML), OASIS Standard, 18 February 2003. www.oasis-open.org/committees/xacml/repository/
21. Decryption Transform for XML Signature, World Wide Web Consortium (W3C) Recommendation, 10 December 2002. www.w3c.org/TR/xmlenc-decrypt
22. World Wide Web Consortium (W3C). www.w3c.org
23. Blu-ray Disc Association (BDA), Audio Visual Basic Specifications version 0.89 July 2004. www.bluraydisc.com
24. ISO/IEC 13818-2 1996 Information technology, ISO/IEC 13818-2 1996 Information technology—Generic coding of moving pictures and associated audio information—Part 2: Video (MPEG-2 Video)
25. Microsoft Corporation, Jscript Language Reference 5.5, MSDN library.
26. Ola Andersson et al., Scalable Vector Graphics (SVG) 1.1 Specification, World Wide Web Consortium (W3C),Recommendation 14 January 2003. www.w3.org/TR/2003/REC-SVG11-20030114/

27. Steven Pemberton et al., XHTML1.0 The Extensible HyperText Markup Language (Second Edition), World Wide Web Consortium (W3C)Recommendation revised 1 August 2002. www.w3.org/TR/2002/REC-xhtml1-20020801

28. Sharon Adler et al., Extensible Stylesheet Language (XSL) Version 1.0, World Wide Web Consortium (W3C) Recommendation, 15 October 2001.

29. Intel et al., Advanced Access Content System (AACS), Technical Draft, July 14 2004 www.aacsla.com

30. DVD Forum, Enhanced DVD Specification version 0.9, DVD Forum news, Vol 19, October 2003, Office of the secretary, DVD Forum.

31. Sun Microsystems, JavaTM Cryptography Extension 1.2.2, API Specification & Reference. java.sun.com/products/jce/

32. John Boyer, Canonical XML Version 1.0, World Wide Web Consortium (W3C) Recommendation 15 March 2001. http://www.w3.org/TR/2001/REC-xml-c14n-20010315

33. Phillip Hallam-Baker et al., XKMS – XML Key Management Specification, World Wide Web Consortium (W3C) Recommendation 2 May 2005. http://www.w3.org/TR/2005/PR-xkms2-20050502/

34. OMA DRM 2.0, OMA-DRM-DRM-V2_0-20040716-C www.openmobilealliance.org

35. OMA DRM Content Format, OMA-DRM-DCF-v2_0-20040715-C, www.openmobilealliance.org.

36. Nokia, S3-040781 Extensions to OMA DRM V2.0 DCF for MBMS Download Protection,S3#35, Oct 2004, 3GPP.

37. Nokia, Overhead and Performance Comparison of OMA DRM V2.0 DCF and XML for MBMS Download Protection, 3GPP TSG SA WG3 Security S3#36,

Improvement of Hsu-Wu-He's Proxy Multi-signature Schemes

Yumin Yuan

Department of Managerial Science, Xiamen University of Technology,
Xiamen 361005, P.R. China
yuanymp@163.com

Abstract. In 2005, for reducing Yi et al.'s proxy multi-signature schemes in terms of computational complexity and communication cost, Hsu, Wu and He proposed new proxy multi-signature schemes. Unfortunately, with this paper, we will show that their schemes are insecure, because any malicious attacker can alone forge valid proxy multi-signatures for any message to impersonate an original signer (or a proxy signer) by choosing proper public key as long as he has obtained some users' public keys. We further improve their schemes to eliminate the security flaw of Hsu-Wu-He's schemes. Moreover, the improvements still maintain the advantages of their schemes while reducing the computational complexity.

1 Introduction

The concept of proxy signature was first proposed by Mambo, Usuda, and Okamoto in 1996 [1,2]. In such a scheme, an original signer is allowed to delegate his signing power to a designated person as his proxy signer. After that, the proxy signer is able to sign the message on behalf of the original signer. Consider the situation that two or more original signers might want to delegate their signing power to the same proxy signer. To achieving such purpose, the concept of the proxy multi-signature scheme was proposed by Yi et al. [3]. It allows an original group of signers to authorize a designated proxy signer under the agreement of all signers in the original group so that the designated proxy signer can generate proxy multi-signatures for all original signers. Proxy multi-signatures can play important roles in the following scenario: For a large building, there are some conflict among the constructors and the householders. All householders of the large building want to authorize a lawyer as their agent. So the lawyer is authorized to act on behalf of all householders.

According to whether valid multi-signatures are generated only by the proxy signer, proxy multi-signatures can be classified into two types. One is a proxy-unprotected multi-signature, in which besides the proxy signer, only the cooperation of all members in the original group can create valid proxy signatures. The other is a proxy-protected multi-signature, in which only the proxy signer can create valid proxy signatures.

In 2000, Yi et al. presented two proxy multi-signature schemes based on Mambo et al.'s [2] and Kim et al.'s schemes [4], respectively. However, Hsu, Wu and He pointed out that Yi et al.'s proxy multi-signatures have the weaknesses that

W. Jonker and M. Petković (Eds.): SDM 2005, LNCS 3674, pp. 234–240, 2005.

computational complexity and communication cost are too high [5]. To overcome these weaknesses, Hsu, Wu and He proposed two new proxy multi-signatures in [5]. One is a proxy-unprotected scheme and another is a proxy-protected scheme. Their new schemes have following three advantages compare with Yi et al.'s schemes: (1) the size of a proxy signature is constant and the same as that of an ordinary proxy signature, (2) it is no need to transmit public key certificates to verifiers for ensuring the authenticity of their public keys, (3) the authenticity of public keys of original signers (and the proxy signer) and the validity of the proxy signature can be simultaneously carried out in the proxy signature verification.

Unfortunately, in this paper, we demonstrate that both of new schemes are not resist a forge attack. That is, when a malicious attacker knows some public keys with the corresponding identities, he can forge valid proxy signatures for any message by extracting a proper public key. And then, we propose two improvements to prevent this attack.

The organization of this paper is described as follows. In next section, we will only review Hsu-Wu-He's proxy-unprotected scheme. Then, in Section 3, we propose an attack on their schemes. After that, in Section 4, we offer modified Hsu-Wu-He's schemes, and analyze the security of the proposed schemes. Finally, the conclusion will be given in Section 5.

2   Hsu-Wu-He's Proxy Multi-signature Scheme

Let p be a large prime number, g be a generator for $\mathbb{Z}_p^*$, and $h(\cdot)$ be a secure one-way hash function. The parameters (p, q, g) and the function $h(\cdot)$ are made public. CA owns his private key γ and public key $\beta = g^\gamma \bmod p$, respectively. Let A_1, $A_2, \ldots, A_n$ be n original signers, and A_0 be the proxy signer. Hsu-Wu-He's scheme consists of three stages: registration stage, proxy share generation stage, and proxy signature generation and verification stage. Here, we only review briefly Hsu-Wu-He's proxy-unprotected multi-signature scheme.

2.1   Registration

Each user A_i with the identity ID_i randomly chooses an integer $t_i \in \mathbb{Z}_{p-1}^*$, computes $v_i = g^{h(t_i \| ID_i)} \bmod p$ and sends (v_i, ID_i) to CA. CA chooses $z_i \in \mathbb{Z}_{p-1}^*$, computes

$$y_i = v_i h(ID_i)^{-1} g^{z_i} \bmod p \tag{1}$$

$$w_i = z_i + \gamma h(y_i \| ID_i) \bmod p - 1 \tag{2}$$

returns (y_i, w_i) to A_i, and publishes y_i as the public key for A_i. Upon receiving (y_i, w_i) from CA, A_i verifies the validity of (y_i, w_i) by checking whether the following equation holds:

$$\beta^{h(y_i\|ID_i)}h(ID_i)y_i = g^{w_i+h(t_i\|ID_i)} \bmod p \tag{3}$$

If it holds, then A_i computes his private key as

$$x_i = w_i + h(t_i \| ID_i) \bmod p-1 \tag{4}$$

2.2 Proxy Share Generation

Let $A_1, A_2, \ldots, A_n$ be the n original signers who jointly delegate their signing power to the proxy signer A_0. Each original signer A_i randomly chooses an integer $k_i \in \mathbb{Z}_{p-1}^*$, computes $K_i = g^{k_i} \bmod p$, and broadcasts K_i to other original signers. Upon getting all K_j's from A_j (for $j = 1, 2, \ldots, n$ and $j \neq i$), A_i computes $K = \prod_{i=1}^{n} K_i \bmod p$ and $\sigma_i = h(m_w \| K)x_i + k_i \bmod p-1$. Then, he sends (K_i, σ_i, m_w) to A_0 via a secure channel. After receiving (K_i, σ_i, m_w), the proxy signer A_0 verifies its validity by checking

$$g^{\sigma_i} = \left(\beta^{h(y_i\|ID_i)}h(ID_i)y_i\right)^{h(m_w\|K)} K_i \bmod p \tag{5}$$

If all (K_i, σ_i, m_w)'s are valid, A_0 computes his proxy signature key as

$$\sigma = \sum_{i=1}^{n} \sigma_i \bmod p-1 \tag{6}$$

where $K = \prod_{i=1}^{n} K_i \bmod p$.

2.3 Proxy Signature Generation and Verification

For signing m on behalf of the original signers $\{A_1, A_2, \ldots, A_n\}$, the proxy signer A_0 uses σ to generate a valid proxy signature $(Sig_\sigma(m), K, m_w)$. For verifying the signature, a verifier first computes the proxy public key for these original signers as

$$y_P = \left(\beta^{\sum_{i=1}^{n} h(y_i\|ID_i)} \prod_{i=1}^{n} h(ID_i)y_i\right)^{h(m_w\|K)} K \bmod p \tag{7}$$

then verifies the signature with the checking operation correspondent with the generation of the signature.

3 On the Security of Hsu-Wu-He's Schemes

In this section, we will show that with knowing some users' public keys, any malicious attacker can impersonate an original signer of an original group (or a proxy signer) to forge a valid proxy multi-signature for any message without the agreement of the other participants.

In the following, we first propose the attack on Hsu-Wu-He's proxy-unprotected scheme. Suppose that a malicious attacker A' with the identity ID' obtains the public keys $y_1, y_2, \ldots, y_n$ of users $A_1, A_2, \ldots, A_n$. A' can forge a proxy signature on the message m which looks as if is generated on behalf of original signers $A', A_1, A_2, \ldots, A_n$. For forging the signature, A' first randomly selects an integer $t \in \mathbb{Z}_{p-1}^*$, computes

$$v' = \left(\beta^{\sum_{i=1}^{n} h(y_i \| ID_i)} \prod_{i=1}^{n} h(ID_i) y_i \right)^{-1} g^{h(t \| ID')} \bmod p$$

Then, he sends (v', ID') to CA to extract his public key. Following the normal procedure, CA respectively computes y' and w' by Eqs.(1) and (2), returns (y', w') to A', and publishes y' as the public key of A'. After receiving (y', w') from CA, the attacker A' fabricates an appropriate warrant m_w', randomly selects a random number $k' \in \mathbb{Z}_{p-1}^*$, computes $K' = g^{k'} \bmod p$ and $\sigma' = h(m_w' \| K')x' + k'$ mod $p-1$, where $x' = w' + h(t \| ID') \bmod p-1$ is his private key. Then, A' uses σ' to create a proxy signature $(Sig_{\sigma'}(m), K', m_w')$ for m. Because

$$y_P = \left(\beta^{h(y' \| ID')} h(ID') y' \beta^{\sum_{i=1}^{n} h(y_i \| ID_i)} \prod_{i=1}^{n} h(ID_i) y_i \right)^{h(m_w \| K)} K$$

$$= \left(v' g^{w'} \beta^{\sum_{i=1}^{n} h(y_i \| ID_i)} \prod_{i=1}^{n} h(ID_i) y_i \right)^{h(m_w \| K)} g^{k'}$$

$$= \left(g^{w' + h(t \| ID')} \right)^{h(m_w' \| K')} g^{k'}$$

$$= g^{\sigma'} \bmod p$$

and $Sig_{\sigma'}(m)$ will pass the corresponding signature verification since it is the signature generated by using key σ'. Thus, a verifier will believes that $(Sig_{\sigma'}(m), K', m_w')$ is a valid proxy multi-signature on behalf of the original signers with the identities $\{ID', ID_1, ID_2, \ldots, ID_n\}$ for m.

As considering another Hsu-Wu-He's scheme, since the register stage in this scheme is the same as the one in the proxy-unprotected scheme and the proxy signature verification equation in this scheme is similar to that of the proxy-unprotected scheme. It is easily show that the above attack is also successful for the proxy-protected scheme by using similar approach. Note that in Hsu-Wu-He's proxy-protected scheme, y_0 and each y_i are used in symmetric ways in proxy public key

$$y_P = \left(\beta^{\sum_{i=0}^{n} h(y_i \| ID_i)} \prod_{i=0}^{n} h(ID_i) y_i \right)^{h(m_w \| K)} K \bmod p$$

Thus, any malicious attacker can act as either the original signer of the original group or the proxy signer to generate proxy multi-signatures for any messages. Therefore, both of Hsu-Wu-He's schemes are insecure. The security leak inherent in Hsu-Wu-He's schemes mainly results from that the structure of v_i is not restricted strictly by CA in the registration stage. A possible solution to remedy this weakness is to add an exponential on v_i.

4 Improvement of Hsu-Wu-He's Schemes

We modify Hsu-Wu-He's schemes as follows:

4.1 Improved Proxy-Unprotected Multi-signature Scheme

In registration phase, we replace Eq. (1) with Eq. (8)

$$y_i = v_i^{y_i} g^{z_i} \bmod p \tag{8}$$

Consequently, the corresponding verification equation Eq.(3) should be changed to:

$$\beta^{h(y_i \| ID_i)} y_i = g^{w_i + v_i h(t_i \| ID_i)} \bmod p \tag{9}$$

and the corresponding private key Eq.(4) should be changed to:

$$x_i = w_i + v_i h(t_i \| ID_i) \bmod p - 1 \tag{10}$$

In proxy share generation stage, the verification equation Eq.(5) of σ_i should be changed to:

$$g^{\sigma_i} = \left(\beta^{h(y_i \| ID_i)} y_i \right)^{h(m_w \| K)} K_i \bmod p \tag{11}$$

In proxy signature generation and verification stage, we replace the proxy public key Eq.(7) with Eq.(12)

$$y_p = \left(\beta^{\sum_{i=1}^{n} h(y_i \| ID_i)} \prod_{i=1}^{n} y_i \right)^{h(m_w \| K)} K \bmod p \tag{12}$$

4.2 Security Analysis

The security of the proposed improvement is similar to that of Hsu-Wu-He's scheme [5]. Here, we only discuss the pointed out weakness in section 3. Assume that with the knowledge of the public keys $y_2, y_3, \ldots, y_n$ of users $A_2, A_3, \ldots, A_n$, an attacker A_1 attempts to forge a proxy multi-signature for a message m on behalf of $A_1, A_2, \ldots, A_n$. He has to choose a and v_1 to pass

$$g^a = v_1^{y_1} \beta^{\sum_{i=2}^{n} h(y_i \| ID_i)} \prod_{i=2}^{n} y_i$$

If the v_1 is determined first, then A_1 has to solve the discrete logarithms to find a without knowing CA's private key. If a is determined first, he has to obtain v_1 by solving the equation

$$v_1^{y_1} = g^a (\beta^{\sum_{i=2}^n h(y_i \| ID_i)} \prod_{i=2}^n y_i)^{-1} \mod p$$

It is an extremely difficulty thing. Thus, no one can choose his v to create valid proxy multi-signatures. Hence, our attack cannot work on this new scheme.

4.3 Performance Evaluation

Compared with the original scheme, only one more exponentiation and one more multiplication are required just in the registration stage of the improved scheme, while the hash function $H(ID_i)$ is not required in all stages of the improved scheme. So the cost of computing hash function can be reduced, while Hsu-Wu-He's scheme requires n hashing operation in the proxy share generation and the proxy signature generation and verification, respectively. It is obvious that the improved scheme is more efficient than the original scheme in these stages. Furthermore, the improved scheme keeps the advantages of the original scheme.

4.4 Improved Proxy-Protected Multi-signature Scheme

Based on the above improved proxy-unprotected multi-signature scheme, it is easy to construct a proxy-protected multi-signature scheme only by replacing Eqs.(6) and (12) with Eqs.(13) and (14)

$$\sigma = \sigma_0 + \sum_{i=1}^n \sigma_i \mod p - 1 \tag{13}$$

$$y_p = \left(\beta^{h(y_i \| ID_0)} y_0 \beta^{\sum_{i=1}^n h(y_i \| ID_i)} \prod_{i=0}^n y_i \right)^{h(m_w \| K)} K \mod p \tag{14}$$

where (x_0, y_0) is the key pair of the proxy signer A_0 with identity ID_0, $\sigma_0 = h(m_w \| K)x_0 + k_0 \mod p - 1$ and $K_i = g^{k_i} \mod p$ are computed by A_0, and $K = \prod_{i=0}^n K_i \mod p$. The security analysis and performance evaluation of this scheme is almost the same as the previous one.

5 Conclusions

We have shown that Hsu-Wu-He's schemes are not secure enough by presenting a forgery attack on them. That is, any malicious attacker, under the knowledge of some users' public keys, can impersonate an original signer (or a proxy signer) to forge valid proxy signatures for arbitrary message. To eliminate the security leaks inherent Hsu-Wu-He's schemes, we proposed improvements. The improved schemes not only keep the advantages of Hsu-Wu-He's schemes but also could effectively avoid the attack proposed in this paper and are more efficient for generating and verifying proxy share and proxy signature in terms of computational complexity.

References

1. M. Mambo, K. Usuda, E. Okamoto, Proxy signatures for delegating signing operation, Proceedings of the Third ACM Conference on Computer and Communications Security, ACM Press, 1996, pp. 48–57.
2. M. Mambo, K. Usuda, E. Okamoto, Proxy signatures: delegation of the power to sign messages, IEICE Transactions on Fundamentals of Electronic Communications and Computer Science E79-A (9) (1996) 1338–1354.
3. L. Yi, G. Bai, G. Xiao, Proxy multi-signature scheme: a new type of proxy signature scheme, Electronics Letters 36 (6) (2000) 527–528.
4. S. Kim, S. Park, D. Won, Proxy signatures, revisited, ICICS'97, Lecture Notes in Computer Science, vol. 1334, Springer-Verlag, 1997, pp. 223– 232.
5. C.L. Hsu, T.S. Wu, W.H. He, New proxy multi-signature scheme, Applied Mathematics and Computation 162 (2005) 1201–1206.

Author Index

Azgın Hintoğlu, Ayça 155

Bettini, Claudio 185
Böttcher, Stefan 143
Brinkman, Richard 33

Chinaei, Amir H. 63

Damiani, E. 16
De Capitani di Vimercati, S. 16
Doumen, Jeroen 33
Dragovic, Boris 200

Eastman, Caroline M. 124

Farkas, Csilla 124
Foresti, S. 16

Gabillon, Alban 86
Gopalakrishnan, Ajeesh 217

Hacıgümüş, Hakan 1

Ionita, Cecilia M. 73

Jajodia, Sushil 16, 185
Jonker, Willem 33

Kemper, Alfons 47

Mauw, Sjouke 217
Mehrotra, Sharad 1
Moll, Erik 217

Nair, Gopakumar G. 217

Osborn, Sylvia L. 73

Paraboschi, S. 16
Policroniades, Calicrates 200
Power, David 170

Ramesh, Ganesh 104

Samarati, P. 16
Saygın, Yücel 155
Schoenmakers, Berry 33
Simpson, Andrew 170
Slaymaker, Mark 170
Steinmetz, Rita 143

Toland, Tyrone S. 124
Tompa, Frank Wm. 63

Wang, X. Sean 185
Wimmer, Martin 47

Yuan, Yumin 234

Lecture Notes in Computer Science

For information about Vols. 1–3562

please contact your bookseller or Springer

Vol. 3687: S. Singh, M. Singh, C. Apte, P. Perner (Eds.), Pattern Recognition and Image Analysis, Part II. XXV, 809 pages. 2005.

Vol. 3686: S. Singh, M. Singh, C. Apte, P. Perner (Eds.), Pattern Recognition and Data Mining, Part I. XXVI, 689 pages. 2005.

Vol. 3674: W. Jonker, M. Petković (Eds.), Secure Data Management. X, 241 pages. 2005.

Vol. 3672: C. Hankin, I. Siveroni (Eds.), Static Analysis. X, 369 pages. 2005.

Vol. 3671: S. Bressan, S. Ceri, E. Hunt, Z.G. Ives, Z. Bellahsène, M. Rys, R. Unland (Eds.), Database and XML Technologies. X, 239 pages. 2005.

Vol. 3664: C. Türker, M. Agosti, H.-J. Schek (Eds.), Peer-to-Peer, Grid, and Service-Orientation in Digital Library Architectures. X, 261 pages. 2005.

Vol. 3663: W. Kropatsch, R. Sablatnig, A. Hanbury (Eds.), Pattern Recognition. XIV, 512 pages. 2005.

Vol. 3662: C. Baral, G. Greco, N. Leone, G. Terracina (Eds.), Logic Programming and Nonmonotonic Reasoning. XIII, 454 pages. 2005. (Subseries LNAI).

Vol. 3660: M. Beigl, S. Intille, J. Rekimoto, H. Tokuda (Eds.), UbiComp 2005: Ubiquitous Computing. XVII, 394 pages. 2005.

Vol. 3659: J.R. Rao, B. Sunar (Eds.), Cryptographic Hardware and Embedded Systems – CHES 2005. XIV, 458 pages. 2005.

Vol. 3654: S. Jajodia, D. Wijesekera (Eds.), Data and Applications Security XIX. X, 353 pages. 2005.

Vol. 3653: M. Abadi, L.d. Alfaro (Eds.), CONCUR 2005 – Concurrency Theory. XIV, 578 pages. 2005.

Vol. 3649: W.M.P. van der Aalst, B. Benatallah, F. Casati, F. Curbera (Eds.), Business Process Management. XII, 472 pages. 2005.

Vol. 3648: J.C. Cunha, P.D. Medeiros (Eds.), Euro-Par 2005 Parallel Processing. XXXVI, 1299 pages. 2005.

Vol. 3645: D.-S. Huang, X.-P. Zhang, G.-B. Huang (Eds.), Advances in Intelligent Computing, Part II. XIII, 1010 pages. 2005.

Vol. 3644: D.-S. Huang, X.-P. Zhang, G.-B. Huang (Eds.), Advances in Intelligent Computing, Part I. XXVII, 1101 pages. 2005.

Vol. 3642: D. Ślezak, J. Yao, J.F. Peters, W. Ziarko, X. Hu (Eds.), Rough Sets, Data Mining, and Granular Computing, Part II. XXIV, 738 pages. 2005. (Subseries LNAI).

Vol. 3641: D. Ślezak, G. Wang, M.S. Szczuka, I. Düntsch, Y. Yao (Eds.), Rough Sets, Fuzzy Sets, Data Mining, and Granular Computing, Part I. XXIV, 742 pages. 2005. (Subseries LNAI).

Vol. 3639: P. Godefroid (Ed.), Model Checking Software. XI, 289 pages. 2005.

Vol. 3638: A. Butz, B. Fisher, A. Krüger, P. Olivier (Eds.), Smart Graphics. XI, 269 pages. 2005.

Vol. 3637: J. M. Moreno, J. Madrenas, J. Cosp (Eds.), Evolvable Systems: From Biology to Hardware. XI, 227 pages. 2005.

Vol. 3636: M.J. Blesa, C. Blum, A. Roli, M. Sampels (Eds.), Hybrid Metaheuristics. XII, 155 pages. 2005.

Vol. 3634: L. Ong (Ed.), Computer Science Logic. XI, 567 pages. 2005.

Vol. 3633: C. Bauzer Medeiros, M. Egenhofer, E. Bertino (Eds.), Advances in Spatial and Temporal Databases. XIII, 433 pages. 2005.

Vol. 3632: R. Nieuwenhuis (Ed.), Automated Deduction – CADE-20. XIII, 459 pages. 2005. (Subseries LNAI).

Vol. 3629: J.L. Fiadeiro, N. Harman, M. Roggenbach, J. Rutten (Eds.), Algebra and Coalgebra in Computer Science. XI, 457 pages. 2005.

Vol. 3628: T. Gschwind, U. Aßmann, O. Nierstrasz (Eds.), Software Composition. X, 199 pages. 2005.

Vol. 3627: C. Jacob, M.L. Pilat, P.J. Bentley, J. Timmis (Eds.), Artificial Immune Systems. XII, 500 pages. 2005.

Vol. 3626: B. Ganter, G. Stumme, R. Wille (Eds.), Formal Concept Analysis. X, 349 pages. 2005. (Subseries LNAI).

Vol. 3625: S. Kramer, B. Pfahringer (Eds.), Inductive Logic Programming. XIII, 427 pages. 2005. (Subseries LNAI).

Vol. 3624: C. Chekuri, K. Jansen, J.D.P. Rolim, L. Trevisan (Eds.), Approximation, Randomization and Combinatorial Optimization. XI, 495 pages. 2005.

Vol. 3623: M. Liśkiewicz, R. Reischuk (Eds.), Fundamentals of Computation Theory. XV, 576 pages. 2005.

Vol. 3621: V. Shoup (Ed.), Advances in Cryptology – CRYPTO 2005. XI, 568 pages. 2005.

Vol. 3620: H. Muñoz-Avila, F. Ricci (Eds.), Case-Based Reasoning Research and Development. XV, 654 pages. 2005. (Subseries LNAI).

Vol. 3619: X. Lu, W. Zhao (Eds.), Networking and Mobile Computing. XXIV, 1299 pages. 2005.

Vol. 3618: J. Jedrzejowicz, A. Szepietowski (Eds.), Mathematical Foundations of Computer Science 2005. XVI, 814 pages. 2005.

Vol. 3617: F. Roli, S. Vitulano (Eds.), Image Analysis and Processing – ICIAP 2005. XXIV, 1219 pages. 2005.

Vol. 3615: B. Ludäscher, L. Raschid (Eds.), Data Integration in the Life Sciences. XII, 344 pages. 2005. (Subseries LNBI).

Vol. 3614: L. Wang, Y. Jin (Eds.), Fuzzy Systems and Knowledge Discovery, Part II. XLI, 1314 pages. 2005. (Subseries LNAI).

Vol. 3613: L. Wang, Y. Jin (Eds.), Fuzzy Systems and Knowledge Discovery, Part I. XLI, 1334 pages. 2005. (Subseries LNAI).

Vol. 3612: L. Wang, K. Chen, Y. S. Ong (Eds.), Advances in Natural Computation, Part III. LXI, 1326 pages. 2005.

Vol. 3611: L. Wang, K. Chen, Y. S. Ong (Eds.), Advances in Natural Computation, Part II. LXI, 1292 pages. 2005.

Vol. 3610: L. Wang, K. Chen, Y. S. Ong (Eds.), Advances in Natural Computation, Part I. LXI, 1302 pages. 2005.

Vol. 3608: F. Dehne, A. López-Ortiz, J.-R. Sack (Eds.), Algorithms and Data Structures. XIV, 446 pages. 2005.

Vol. 3607: J.-D. Zucker, L. Saitta (Eds.), Abstraction, Reformulation and Approximation. XII, 376 pages. 2005. (Subseries LNAI).

Vol. 3606: V. Malyshkin (Ed.), Parallel Computing Technologies. XII, 470 pages. 2005.

Vol. 3604: R. Martin, H. Bez, M. Sabin (Eds.), Mathematics of Surfaces XI. IX, 473 pages. 2005.

Vol. 3603: J. Hurd, T. Melham (Eds.), Theorem Proving in Higher Order Logics. IX, 409 pages. 2005.

Vol. 3602: R. Eigenmann, Z. Li, S.P. Midkiff (Eds.), Languages and Compilers for High Performance Computing. IX, 486 pages. 2005.

Vol. 3599: U. Aßmann, M. Aksit, A. Rensink (Eds.), Model Driven Architecture. X, 235 pages. 2005.

Vol. 3598: H. Murakami, H. Nakashima, H. Tokuda, M. Yasumura, Ubiquitous Computing Systems. XIII, 275 pages. 2005.

Vol. 3597: S. Shimojo, S. Ichii, T.W. Ling, K.-H. Song (Eds.), Web and Communication Technologies and Internet-Related Social Issues - HSI 2005. XIX, 368 pages. 2005.

Vol. 3596: F. Dau, M.-L. Mugnier, G. Stumme (Eds.), Conceptual Structures: Common Semantics for Sharing Knowledge. XI, 467 pages. 2005. (Subseries LNAI).

Vol. 3595: L. Wang (Ed.), Computing and Combinatorics. XVI, 995 pages. 2005.

Vol. 3594: J.C. Setubal, S. Verjovski-Almeida (Eds.), Advances in Bioinformatics and Computational Biology. XIV, 258 pages. 2005. (Subseries LNBI).

Vol. 3593: V. Mařík, R. W. Brennan, M. Pěchouček (Eds.), Holonic and Multi-Agent Systems for Manufacturing. XI, 269 pages. 2005. (Subseries LNAI).

Vol. 3592: S. Katsikas, J. Lopez, G. Pernul (Eds.), Trust, Privacy and Security in Digital Business. XII, 332 pages. 2005.

Vol. 3591: M.A. Wimmer, R. Traunmüller, Å. Grönlund, K.V. Andersen (Eds.), Electronic Government. XIII, 317 pages. 2005.

Vol. 3590: K. Bauknecht, B. Pröll, H. Werthner (Eds.), E-Commerce and Web Technologies. XIV, 380 pages. 2005.

Vol. 3589: A M. Tjoa, J. Trujillo (Eds.), Data Warehousing and Knowledge Discovery. XVI, 538 pages. 2005.

Vol. 3588: K.V. Andersen, J. Debenham, R. Wagner (Eds.), Database and Expert Systems Applications. XX, 955 pages. 2005.

Vol. 3587: P. Perner, A. Imiya (Eds.), Machine Learning and Data Mining in Pattern Recognition. XVII, 695 pages. 2005. (Subseries LNAI).

Vol. 3586: A.P. Black (Ed.), ECOOP 2005 - Object-Oriented Programming. XVII, 631 pages. 2005.

Vol. 3584: X. Li, S. Wang, Z.Y. Dong (Eds.), Advanced Data Mining and Applications. XIX, 835 pages. 2005. (Subseries LNAI).

Vol. 3583: R.W. H. Lau, Q. Li, R. Cheung, W. Liu (Eds.), Advances in Web-Based Learning – ICWL 2005. XIV, 420 pages. 2005.

Vol. 3582: J. Fitzgerald, I.J. Hayes, A. Tarlecki (Eds.), FM 2005: Formal Methods. XIV, 558 pages. 2005.

Vol. 3581: S. Miksch, J. Hunter, E. Keravnou (Eds.), Artificial Intelligence in Medicine. XVII, 547 pages. 2005. (Subseries LNAI).

Vol. 3580: L. Caires, G.F. Italiano, L. Monteiro, C. Palamidessi, M. Yung (Eds.), Automata, Languages and Programming. XXV, 1477 pages. 2005.

Vol. 3579: D. Lowe, M. Gaedke (Eds.), Web Engineering. XXII, 633 pages. 2005.

Vol. 3578: M. Gallagher, J. Hogan, F. Maire (Eds.), Intelligent Data Engineering and Automated Learning - IDEAL 2005. XVI, 599 pages. 2005.

Vol. 3577: R. Falcone, S. Barber, J. Sabater-Mir, M.P. Singh (Eds.), Trusting Agents for Trusting Electronic Societies. VIII, 235 pages. 2005. (Subseries LNAI).

Vol. 3576: K. Etessami, S.K. Rajamani (Eds.), Computer Aided Verification. XV, 564 pages. 2005.

Vol. 3575: S. Wermter, G. Palm, M. Elshaw (Eds.), Biomimetic Neural Learning for Intelligent Robots. IX, 383 pages. 2005. (Subseries LNAI).

Vol. 3574: C. Boyd, J.M. González Nieto (Eds.), Information Security and Privacy. XIII, 586 pages. 2005.

Vol. 3573: S. Etalle (Ed.), Logic Based Program Synthesis and Transformation. VIII, 279 pages. 2005.

Vol. 3572: C. De Felice, A. Restivo (Eds.), Developments in Language Theory. XI, 409 pages. 2005.

Vol. 3571: L. Godo (Ed.), Symbolic and Quantitative Approaches to Reasoning with Uncertainty. XVI, 1028 pages. 2005. (Subseries LNAI).

Vol. 3570: A. S. Patrick, M. Yung (Eds.), Financial Cryptography and Data Security. XII, 376 pages. 2005.

Vol. 3569: F. Bacchus, T. Walsh (Eds.), Theory and Applications of Satisfiability Testing. XII, 492 pages. 2005.

Vol. 3568: W.-K. Leow, M.S. Lew, T.-S. Chua, W.-Y. Ma, L. Chaisorn, E.M. Bakker (Eds.), Image and Video Retrieval. XVII, 672 pages. 2005.

Vol. 3567: M. Jackson, D. Nelson, S. Stirk (Eds.), Database: Enterprise, Skills and Innovation. XII, 185 pages. 2005.

Vol. 3566: J.-P. Banâtre, P. Fradet, J.-L. Giavitto, O. Michel (Eds.), Unconventional Programming Paradigms. XI, 367 pages. 2005.

Vol. 3565: G.E. Christensen, M. Sonka (Eds.), Information Processing in Medical Imaging. XXI, 777 pages. 2005.

Vol. 3564: N. Eisinger, J. Małuszyński (Eds.), Reasoning Web. IX, 319 pages. 2005.